RELEASE
FROM
NERVOUS
TENSION

BY

David Harold Fink

M.D.

A FIRESIDE BOOK
PUBLISHED BY
SIMON AND SCHUSTER

FOR
MARIE BIDDLE FINK

Preface

SINCE *Release from Nervous Tension* was first published in 1943, much progress has been made in psychiatric theory and practice. Space does not permit a detailed account of the forward strides which have been taken, but I should like to state generally what has been done.

Theory of personality has been clarified by Gardner Murphy, Professor of Psychology at Columbia University. His scholarly book, *Personality,* is the most comprehensive and accurate exposition of the subject to date. The nature of emotional processes has been clarified by Dr. Nina Bull, author of *Attitude Theory of Emotion.*

There has been a growing tendency to interpret human behavior in the light of modern anthropology and social psychology. The Second World War, by turning our attention to distant parts of the world, did much to enlarge our horizons. To fight the Germans and the Japanese made it necessary for us to understand them; and to insure peace, it became necessary to achieve even greater understanding. Understanding the cultural forces which mold the attitudes of others makes it possible for us to understand ourselves better.

Furthermore, a better understanding of the biology of human behavior has led to even deeper understanding of human nature. Undoubtedly, the leader in this direction is Dr. Norman Cameron, Professor of Psychology and Psychiatry at the University of Wisconsin.

Thus Psychiatry now rests on a wider and firmer scientific

foundation than ever before, and its future looks even brighter.

Progress in therapy has been accelerated by the work of Carl M. Rogers of the Counseling Center, University of Chicago. He has done a tremendous job in changing the orientation of the therapist. Whereas the old time psychoanalyst attempted to force his theories upon the patient so that the patient would understand himself within the framework of the analyst's speculative concepts, Rogers reversed the process and demonstrated that this technique actually slows up progress in therapy. On the positive side, he demonstrated that success in therapy follows the successful attempt of the therapist to see the patient as the patient sees himself. As Robert Burns wrote, "Oh, wad some power the giftie gie us, To see ourselves as ithers see us."

This objectivity is indeed valuable; but even more valuable is the gift of being able to see others as they see themselves.

Dr. Ralph Linton, Professor of Anthropology at Harvard University, once said that the best collaboration between scientists is that which takes place within a single human skull. I have spent more than thirty years as a student of the various social and biological sciences in order to effect this collaboration.

In this revision I have clarified some of the points that were left somewhat obscure in the first edition, and I have corrected certain faults of misstatement. In general, I feel that this book leads the way to a more general appreciation of those aspects of psychiatry which have vitality and which will continue to live and grow.

Table of Contents

I   Even Dogs Get Neurotic   1

II   Meet the Interbrain   21

III   The Mind Tells the Body   46

IV   And the Body Talks Back   63

V   Self-Directed Relaxation: a Way Out   84

VI   Let Go—a Little More   97

VII   How Relaxation Works   112

VIII   Action Leads to Freedom   124

IX   Play Is Good Medicine   137

X   Words Are Triggers to Action   151

XI   Every Man His Own Analyst   175

XII   The First Ten Years Are the Hardest   194

XIII   Treat Yourself to a Fresh Start   214

XIV   Are You Allergic to Some People?   230

XV   Try On a New Attitude   251

XVI   Tranquility Without Tranquilizers   269

Foreword

MAN'S DARKEST CONTINENT is the human mind. In 1912, I decided to explore it.

Explorers, I am told, always read the discoveries of those who have gone before them. They do this as a part of their preparation. So I followed precedent in a way, and took the college courses and read the books. Almost before I knew it I found myself teaching Sociology at the University of Michigan.

This was a good beginning. When you teach, you learn. But to explore the mind, you have to meet people in more than the teaching situation. You have to mix with people. The dark continent of the human mind exists not in libraries but behind inscrutable human eyes. So I quit the University for social work. I taught physical education. I taught ungraded rooms of feeble-minded children. I taught in Teachers College. This, I felt, was not enough. I was still teaching and reading. I wasn't penetrating very far into the dark continent.

In my dissatisfaction, I asked: who has the basic information to interpret man's life? Who has the best opportunity to explore the human mind? The doctor. Of course. As soon as I asked the question, I enrolled myself in a medical college.

And I have never been sorry. The study and practice of medicine gave me my opportunity to know people, inside and out. Theoretical and practical knowledge met in sharp focus on human problems. I have helped many infants into the world. I have stood many times in the presence of death. I have had a part in the emotional struggles of thousands of people. In situations of fear and pain and despair and shame that were concealed from the rest of the world, I was there. And not as a passive spectator. I was there to help. I was there not only to explore (I did explore) but to find the way out of the jungle. I had to work out both methods of diagnosis and methods of healing.

I found that all desire is given both direction and urgency in social situations. In this book you will find no discussions of instincts, because there is no sense in discussing what does not exist. Human beings have no instincts. Their bodily activities are infinitely plastic. Social situations are the forces that give human activities their direction and drive.

When social situations are confusing man is confused. Then he wants to go in two directions at the same time. Perhaps he wants to quit his job to visit a dying mother, while he also wants to stay on the job to support his wife and children. He is in two family situations—his own and his father's—and each makes opposite demands upon him. Each tugs at his heart. This kind of conflict—so human, so understandable, so universal—gives rise to nervous tension. Social maladjustments produce personal maladjustments.

Nervous tensions do not exist within a vacuum. They do not exist exclusively within the nervous system. They exist within all the organs of the body. When there is an emotional tug of war within the individual, there is a pull of one organ against another. Nervous tension is physical. This is the reason that so many sicknesses are caused by emotional conflicts.

People do not recover spontaneously from emotional conflict. Internal conflict continues in the form of habits of organ behavior. So tensions have a way of accumulating over the years. And these tensions—maladjustments between the organs of the body—affect one's thoughts. The body tells the mind what to think. Some writers call this control of body over mind the subconscious. The subconscious mind consists of man's habits of organ behavior.

People try to relieve nervous tension by adopting some form of compromise behavior to render the unpleasant situation endurable. Often these compromises are invented in childhood, and, of course, they are childish. That wouldn't be so bad, if only they ended when the situation ceased to exist. But they don't. The child's compromise adjustment of today becomes his everyday habitual response, preventing adequate adjustments to adult situations.

I know a plumber who carries his childhood reactions around with him just as he carries his Stillson wrenches. He wonders why he cannot cope with life's problems. How would he cope with plumbing problems if he brought to them his toy tools that he had when he was eight years old?

These compromise habits of adjustment that do not adjust we call neurotic trends. They are not emotional tensions, but the result of attempting to adjust emotional tension. Doctors not versed in the sociology and psychology of nervousness have regarded these trends as the only condition to be treated. For man to function well, however, his underlying emotional tensions must be released.

This approach brings all modern science—sociology, psychology, and those sciences that we call medical—into your service. I should like to give credit to all who have created these sciences, and so have contributed to this book. This is impossible. To give proper credit only to the creators of modern medicine, I should have to write a history of medicine, thanking everyone from Vesalius, the father of anatomy, to Walter Alvarez, great physiologist and clinician; from Harvey, discoverer of the circulation of the blood, to H. Flanders Dunbar, great bibliographer whose *Emotions and Bodily Changes* will become an institution rather than a book. I have taken from them all and I thank them all.

This book contains many illustrative stories. Some of those who have read the manuscript have asked, "Are these cases really true?" The answer is "Yes and no." No, in the sense that they do not represent, in any recognizable form, the life stories of any of my patients or acquaintances. Their private lives belong exclusively to them, and what I know of them is no less theirs.

But the case histories are true. Yes, in the truest sense, for they are psychologically true. You may read about the doings of some Mr. Smith in the newspapers. Every word may be factual. Every fact may have been verified. Yet the real truth about Mr. Smith may not be in the story. The reporter in search of facts may have passed by the real truth about Mr. Smith. The chances are that even Mr. Smith does not know the real truth about himself. He does not recognize the forces within that make him do as he does. He does not know what keeps him from doing otherwise. Nor does the reporter. This unseen reality of Mr. Smith and his doing is psychological truth. This is the only kind of truth and reality that you will find in these case histories. This is the only kind of reality that you will find anywhere.

For this reason, you are more than likely to find yourself rather than your neighbors in these cases. Although the cases do not represent actual persons, they are servings from that mulligan stew which we call human experience. They are as true as my insight and interpretation permit. They serve their purpose if they help you to find yourself.

I wish to express my thanks for help in the preparation of this book to Miss Agnes Rumsey, whose editorial advice has been invaluable. Other persons who have read the manuscript while in preparation and who have helped greatly are Bee Freedman, Edelaine Gorney, E. Y. Harburg, Jo Pagano, and Elizabeth Perdix. I take this opportunity to thank them. And I confess indebtedness most of all to the thousands of persons who have permitted me to share their experiences and struggles, and who have thereby made this book possible.

D. H. F

CHAPTER ONE

Even Dogs Get Neurotic

1

THE PHONE WAKED ME, and I picked up the receiver. All that I could hear were explosions, as if blasting were going on. A man was coughing in paroxysmal attacks. Between paroxysms came a gasping, "Roses, those damn roses. Our maid put roses on the breakfast table. I can't get my breath. I'm choking to death."

"Take five drops of adrenalin by hypo."

"This asthma is killing me," he went on. "I took your adrenalin. It doesn't help. Something's got to be done. I'm coming to your office at eight-thirty this morning."

Then followed another paroxysm of coughing and strangling for air. An asthmatic attack is terrifying to see if you've never seen it before; it's distressing, no matter how many attacks you have witnessed. It's hard to listen to, even over the telephone.

Asthma is another name for spasm of the tubes that lead to the lungs. These tubes, or bronchi, are really hollow muscles. When poisoned by some substance to which the patient is allergic, the hollow muscular tubes clamp down after inhalation, making it impossible for the sufferer to expel the dead air from his chest. He coughs and wheezes until he is red in the face, and the veins on his forehead swell up prominently. He feels that he is suffocating, and he looks it.

I had never seen this particular patient in an actual attack.

1

He had refused skin tests; said that he had been tested, and that he was sensitive to roses. I took for granted that he ought to know. Some people are allergic to cats. Others are allergic to wheat flour. This man was allergic to roses.

I am sensitive to roses myself. I love them. Roses are the color of youth and love. A rose is the flower of romance. Ben Jonson sent his lady fair a rosy wreath, so that she could but breathe upon it, whereupon, according to Ben, it smelled not of itself but her. A superlative compliment, indeed; for who else could perfume the most fragrant of flowers? A rose is the symbol of love.

Yet, to my patient, roses meant suffocation.

He called my office at eight-thirty to break his appointment. He was feeling much better and said he would be in to see me at four in the afternoon.

At times during the day, I wondered why he had called me early in the morning. I felt that he was trying to tell me something, something that he did not understand, something for which he could find no words. And in the back of my mind I kept thinking that a rose is a symbol of love.

I decided to repeat the famous Korzybski experiment. When the patient came into the office at four that afternoon, the stage was all set. I had on my desk a huge bowl, heaped full of roses, white roses, yellow roses, red roses.

He gave one look at the roses. His jaw dropped, his forehead wrinkled, he gasped, and then went into a paroxysm of coughing. While I led him into a treatment room, he coughed and wheezed in a manner almost sickening to behold. I gave him a hypodermic injection, and finally his coughing stopped.

"How could you be so careless?" he gasped. "You know how sensitive I am to roses."

I stepped to my office, picked out a rose, tore it to pieces before his eyes. It was made of tissue paper. "Dennison's best,"

I observed casually. "And the hypo was sterile distilled water. No adrenalin. Water.

"You have asthma," I went on. "But it is not caused by roses; it is caused by neurosis. Now that we know the cause we can effect the cure."

2

One patient's asthma is the analogue of another person's fear of high places. Or fear of closed places. Or palpitation of the heart. Or fear of crowds. Or nausea and vomiting. Or attacks of faintness and weakness. Or pain between the shoulder blades, or in the small of the back. There is no limit to the number of physical symptoms that can be called forth by neurosis.

Pavlov, the Russian psychologist, wanted to study these things. But he couldn't experiment upon human beings very well, because if they have asthma or cramps in the abdomen, they do not like to contribute their persons to the cause of scientific progress. Under those circumstances, they are not in a philanthropic mood. And if they are perfectly well, they don't like to be made sick, even to gratify a doctor's curiosity.

So Pavlov used man's best friend, the dog, to assist him in his discoveries. Dogs have been used to help hunt lions and foxes and wild geese; Pavlov used them to track down the neurosis.

How can the flowers that bloom in the spring produce asthma? How can any harmless and irrelevant stimulus make the body behave as it was never intended to behave? This was Pavlov's problem.

Pavlov might have used roses as his experimental stimulus. He might have, but he didn't. Instead, he used a bell that can still be heard throughout the world of science. His discoveries about the behavior of dogs have helped doctors to understand your problems and your troubles. It is a long way from the psychological laboratories in Russia to the office of your doctor; but that is the distance the sound of Pavlov's bell has traveled.

You know that when meat is put in front of a hungry dog, his mouth waters. He sees and smells the meat, and the sensations of his sight and of his smell are telegraphed by his brain to glands in his cheeks. The brain tells these glands, "Secrete, secrete; food's coming," and the glands get busy. Through little pipes running from the salivary glands to the inside of the dog's mouth, saliva gushes; and the dog is slobbering.

Anyone would expect the dog's glands to salivate at the sight and smell of food. That's nature. But would some stimulus not in any way connected with food produce this automatic salivation? Pavlov asked the question and answered it by devising an ingenious experiment, simple but effective. He would bring meat to his dogs, and just before giving them the meat, he would ring a bell.

In a short time, whenever he rang the bell, the dogs' glands would pour out saliva. Meat or no meat, the bell alone stimulated those glands in the dogs' mouths. The dogs and their glands reacted to a mere bell—a signal not found in nature—exactly as they had reacted to the sight and smell of food.

Pavlov had discovered that glandular responses, an automatic function of the body not under the control of the will, could be trained to respond to an artificial stimulus. He called this response a conditioned reflex.

The hunger and food relatonship is a touch of nature that makes clear the kinship of all living things. When you are hungry, and you smell a tender, brown, juicy steak sizzling on the platter, your mouth waters. Tangy smells and promising sights excite your brain and your imagination. Your brain cells telegraph orders to your salivary glands to go to work. That's nature, again. That's the dog in you.

But when you sit in a restaurant and read the menu, you do not see or smell the food. Your brain is aware only of printed words, and still your mouth waters. That's your conditioned reflex. That's what reading and writing and civilization do to your salivary glands. To you, the traces of printer's ink on the menu card are as the ringing of the bell.

A patient salivated excessively whenever business was bad. He was constantly spitting. The wrong impulses were coming from his brain to his salivary glands. This represented the same process that Pavlov developed in his dogs, except that instead of a bell, an accountant's report would set off the condition reflex. He got that way in childhood, from learning to spit whenever he was angry, or crossed, or worried.

An architect whom I treated has occasion to examine structural details of churches from time to time. He could not enter a church without excessive salivation. Sometimes, when he went into a church, he felt nauseated and had to vomit. As a boy in Europe, where religious hatred was in good taste, he was taught to spit every time he passed a certain kind of church.

That's your conditioned reflex, again. An automatic glandular function of the body over which we have no voluntary control is stimulated by sounds and sights never found in nature. Stimulated by such artificial things as accountants' reports and religious hatreds.

A beautiful rose can become the trigger that releases the mechanism of the conditioned reflex. This is the story behind the asthmatic patient.

When he was in college, he fell in love with a girl, to whom, on certain mornings, he used to send a bouquet of lovely Cecile Brunner roses. "They were so pink, so small, so dainty," he told me. "So pure, if you know what I mean. I wanted her to know that that was the way I thought of her. I went without food to buy them."

He was poor, ambitious. He thought that they couldn't marry. She thought that he was trying to let her down slowly. The clandestine nature of their love made both feel guilty. Each projected this guilty feeling into distrust of the other, and this distrust led to jealousy, quarrels, fights. He left college and enrolled at another university. She became engaged to another man. He had a nervous breakdown.

Finally, he decided to forget her entirely, and did a pretty good job of it. In fact, he had forgotten her completely when he first came to see me. But his bronchial tubes had not forgotten. For at first, after the two had separated, he would gasp and become rigid whenever he saw a rose. Later, this habit became an unconscious reflex, something that he did without being aware of the cause. When it became very severe, he had asthma.

Suffocation meant many things to him. It was his way of kicking himself. It meant penance for the mistake he had made in yielding to his cowardice. He did not like to admit these things, even to himself. He liked to explain his troubles by saying "allergy." It sounds nicer than "hysterical bronchial neurosis." But you don't get well by dodging facts. There is no therapy in running from reality.

The conditioned reflex is at the root of all of your habit patterns, good or bad. It is this reflex that makes you go to work, punch the clock, lunch at noon, dine heavily at night, and wish that you hadn't by bedtime.

It is the conditioned reflex that ties up the behavior of your body with situations that are found only in civilization. When man lived in the jungle, his behavior was never conditioned by the need for clothing. Modesty is a conditioned reflex. He

was not conditioned by a desire to smoke the brand of cigarettes that are puffed by some publicity-minded jungle so-
cialite. Social emulation is a conditioned reflex. He did not
eat out his heart because the fellow at the next desk was getting a promotion. He did not get heartburn and indigestion
because he was afraid of losing his job. Primitive man was not
conditioned to any of these things; and primitive man did
not have the jitters.

Early in life we are conditioned in neurotic behavior.

Take the case of a patient who is afraid of high places.
When he was five years old, he was seated on the window sill
of a second floor, watching a parade. Some overly anxious
adult grabbed him by the waistband of his pants, pulled him
backward.

"You'll fall," he was told.

When he was still a little fellow, his parents would take him
for rides on the ferryboat. He loved to stand at the rail, watch
the waves swish by.

Again he was grabbed. "Don't go near the edge," he was
told. Then followed arguments, tears, scoldings.

This was the beginning of the conditioning of his reflexes—
involving the glands, heart, lungs—in situations where there
was danger of falling. Then, when he was about fourteen years
old, came the severe blow that he has never forgotten. With
a friend, he was climbing on a scaffolding of a building under
construction. His little friend fell and suffered a broken back
and paralysis of both legs.

Immediately, all of the old warnings came back to him.
There resulted such a fear of high places that today he cannot
go into a tall office building without his knees turning to jelly
and his innards doing a flip-flap.

He knows that it is silly to feel as he does, but he cannot
help it. His intestines, his glands, his heart—those parts of the

body that are under automatic control—respond to the situation in this unpleasant manner, and he is unable to control them. His whole body has been conditioned, just as the salivary glands of Pavlov's dogs were conditioned, and his body responds just as automatically.

It is natural for all of the functions of the body to adjust to critical situations. You could see this for yourself if you had an X-ray machine. You would feed a dog a meal containing bismuth, a substance that looks white under the X ray. Watching a dog under the X ray, you could see him swallow the bismuth meal, see his stomach and his intestines fill up. You could see the normal, slow, wormlike movements of his intestines as he digests the food.

Now bring a cat into the scene. The dog becomes tense, the hair of his neck bristles up, and all movement of his stomach and intestines comes to a stop. In anger or in any other emotion, such as fear or jealousy, the dog reacts with his entire body.

Just as the dog's salivary glands can be conditioned to respond to any stimulus, so can his stomach and intestines be conditioned. This goes for you, too.

A patient has a gastric ulcer. When he was a boy, the dinner bell was the gong that began the next round of a never-ending family fight. His stomach would go into spasms, his intestines into knots, just at mealtimes. His abdominal organs, not under control of the will, became conditioned to respond to fear at the very sight of food. At the time when his stomach and intestines should be gently relaxed, they now clamp down on whatever food he has swallowed, scraping and tearing at the soft lining of his stomach. A conditioned reflex of his stomach produced an ulcer that will not heal. Now an operation is necessary. This is what bad training or conditioning can do for a person.

3

Beneath every neurosis lies the conditioning of some automatic function of the body to behave in a manner never intended for it by nature. The salivary responses of a dog can be so conditioned as to respond at the sound of a bell. The fear responses, including spasm of the stomach, cowering, tension of muscles, can also be conditioned to respond at the sound of a bell.

What would happen if both reflexes, so opposite in their nature, were evoked at the same time? This experiment was made.

A dog was conditioned to react to a bell, a bell with a low musical note, just as he would react to food. Every time he heard the low musical note, food was brought and his tail would wag; he would jump about in happy anticipation, and his mouth would water. Soon he was conditioned to act this way whenever he heard the bell with the low musical note.

Next, his fear reflexes were conditioned to respond to a bell with a high musical note. An electric wire was attached to a storage battery, and every time the high note was sounded the dog received a slight shock. The dog, of course, was frightened. In a short time, he showed the same fear whenever the high note was sounded, even when no shock occurred. And when I say he showed fear, remember that I am talking about his muscle tensions, his cowering in a corner with his tail between his legs. Fear means the cramping of his intestines and the dryness of his mouth. His whole body, from the tip of his nose to the ultimate hairs on his tail, was conditioned to react to the high-pitched bell.

Then the bells were changed gradually. Every day, for the high-pitched bell, one a little lower in tone was substituted. Still the dog's behavior remained the same. He was no longer receiving electric shocks, of course, but he was fearing the bell with the high-pitched tone.

Now, while the tone of high pitch that set off the fear reaction was being changed daily for a tone of slightly lower pitch, the low-pitched bell that set off the salivation reaction was also being changed. Daily, for the low bell that promised good things to eat, were substituted other bells, each one of slightly higher pitch. Still, for a long time, the dog did not notice the difference. When the lower note was sounded, the dog's automatic bodily functions, such as salivation, relaxation of the intestines, secretion of gastric juices, and so forth, reacted exactly as they would to food itself.

The bell of lower pitch said, "Come and get it," and the dog would wag his tail, act happy. The bell of higher pitch said, "The goblins'll git you ef you don't watch out," and the dog would cower in a corner with his mouth dry, his tail between his legs.

Finally the day came when the sounds of the low- and high-pitched bells were so much alike that the dog could not distinguish between them. Two antagonistic conditioned reflexes were set off by an intermediate bell.

What did the dog do? Just what a human being would do under like circumstances. He developed a neurosis. He crept into a corner, trembled all over. He refused all food. He could not sleep. He was highly irritable, snapped at everyone. At times his heart would beat wildly. At other times he would slobber copiously. Sometimes his mouth would be cotton dry; but he refused all water. Conflicting conditioned reflexes had made the poor animal neurotic. It shouldn't happen to a dog, but it did.

It took six months of careful re-education to cure the dog of his neurosis. And, by the way, the next time that you are told that mental disorders are "imaginary," you can describe this experimental neurosis in dogs. Ask the "snap-out-of-it" adviser and the "just-go-home-and-forget-it" consultant whether he would know how to cure a dog's neurosis. If he can't cure a dog, why let him experiment on you? It shouldn't happen—not even to a man.

Experimental neuroses have been produced in dogs, sheep, and even pigs. The suffering of these animals has taught us much about the unhappy behavior of human beings, has taught us methods of relieving and preventing human suffering. Pavlov's bell can be heard in the practice of medicine in every country in the world. For sufferers from mental disease, Pavlov has sounded a veritable liberty bell.

The experimental neurosis produced in dogs by conditioning in conflicting responses is just what happens by accident to us humans. Our bodies are conditioned to react in a fear response to a certain stimulus; and then our bodies are conditioned to react in a love response to the very same stimulus. A father will slap his son for no good reason; and the next day will give him candy for the same reason. The child never knows where he stands. Father has become the stimulus that stands for a piece of candy and a sock on the jaw.

When we cannot distinguish between stimuli, we become confused. Conflict occurs within ourselves. There develops a tug of war between nerve cells in the brain. We feel that we must do two contradictory things at the same time. This conflict does not occur at a level of brain activity that is under our conscious control. The conflict involves our glands, our stomachs, intestines, blood vessels. All we know is that we feel nervous, that we have abdominal cramps, or that our feet are cold and clammy. If our digestion is affected, we take bicarbonate of soda and find fault with the cook.

Our bodies and our minds are taught thousands of behavior patterns, many of which are in complete conflict with each other. In almost every family, situations arise that produce friction, jealousy, and strain. Situations also arise which produce loyalty, security, affection, and love. The result is that children love, fear, and hate their parents at one and the same time, and are only vaguely aware of their conflicting emotions.

Freud stressed the attitude of a special kind of jealousy, calling it the Oedipus complex—so named after Sophocles' central fictional character in the drama, *Oedipus the King*. In this drama, it was prophesied that Oedipus would kill his father and marry his mother. To avert this catastrophe, Oedipus was abandoned by his parents immediately after his birth and left to die on a lonely hillside. The baby, however, was rescued by strangers and grew up without knowing who his real parents were. After he grew to manhood he set out to find his real parents. In a chance encounter, he unwittingly killed his father; later he married his father's widow, his own mother. When he discovered the truth, he blinded himself and left the country.

The point of this story has nothing whatever to do with jealousy. Sophocles was attempting to dramatize the notion that Man cannot beat Prophecy. According to Sophocles, predestination wins. Man proposes; God disposes.

Why this gruesome story of primitive mythology became the central theme of Freud's followers is difficult to understand. Oedipus was never jealous of his father, for he never saw him until he, himself, was a full-grown man. He didn't even know the identity of the man he fought and killed. And as a child he had never loved his mother. How could he when he did not know who his real mother was? He never saw her until she was a widow and he married her—not for love but to gain a throne.

When the superorthodox Freudian analysts tell you that

the central problem in therapy is to resolve the Oedipus complex, suggest to them that they read the play for themselves and apply a little commonsense thinking to their theoretical formulations. A theoretical foundation that is based upon ignorance and misinterpretation of Greek demonology is hardly a solid foundation for a medical specialty.

Greek mythology may be the mother of Freudian mythology, but scientific medicine indignantly denies paternity.

I admit that jealousy is an attitude which often gives rise to inner conflict. It is possible—indeed it often happens—that children are jealous of one or both of their parents. I have treated more than one case in which the son craved the fatherly love he did not receive and wanted to lick the old man at his own game. Here, indeed, was a conflict between emotional habit patterns which gave rise to feelings of guilt and of inferiority. This eternal conflict between fear, love, and hate has made literature, history, progress, and neurosis.

A doctor's son (ten years old) expressed the ancient conflict when he observed naïvely, "I'm going to be a better doctor than you because I'll know everything you can teach me and a lot more, besides." He's probably right; but if anyone doesn't realize that these conflicting habit patterns or complexes underline much of the antagonism and conflict between generations, he hasn't looked far beneath the surface of things.

Of late, psychiatrists have been playing down the father's place in the child's emotional life by putting into first position the mother's relationship with her children. The Oedipus complex is giving way in psychiatric literature to the Orestes complex (so named after a fictional character of Aeschylus). In this play, Orestes avenged the murder of his father, Agamemnon, by killing his mother, Clytemnestra.

The shift in emphasis from the so-called Oedipus complex to the new-found Orestes complex is due in part to those social and economic changes which have made the mother the more dynamic factor in the emotional climate of the modern home. In Freud's day, the one who wore the britches was boss. He had the last word in every detail involving the organization of the home. Today, many women wear slacks and many husbands are not adverse to putting on an apron while helping with the dishwashing and the care of the home. Mother's word carries a lot more weight today than it did in those Gay Nineties when the Freudians desperately pulled a fictional character out of antiquity to bolster a dubious scientific "law." So the fad for today is the Orestes complex.

Certainly, a child's emotional conflicts involving hostility, fear and love pertain at least as much to his relationship with his mother as with his father; so I am glad to see the narrow concept of the Oedipus complex giving way to broader and more flexible concepts of emotional conflict.

But like all other good things, this, too, is being overdone by those extremists who seem incapable of entertaining more than one idea at a time. I refer specifically to those woman-haters who blame "Mom" for everything which has produced conflict and neurosis in their own lives. It hurts me to think of the thousands of innocent mothers who will be burdened with feelings of guilt as a result of taking seriously such one-sided anti-feminist writings. Every time their mother's sons turn out badly, these women—blameless or not—will feel that they, indeed, are the lost sex.

Emotional conflict does produce anxiety and neurosis. Conflictual relationships with father or mother may underlie such neurosis. All this is common knowledge.

However, jealousy as the chief cause of anxiety has been sadly oversold. Social workers, teachers, ministers, doctors, and others who see neurosis in the making all recognize the importance of harmony between parents. Harmony in the home creates the atmosphere of serenity and security which the growing child needs; while parental bickering, quarreling, fault-finding and the like destroy the child's sense of security. In cold war or in hot, the child is caught in the crossfire. He may respond by becoming a problem child. Parents can prevent this by deliberately seeking ways and means for getting along together and by creating an easy-going, happy, friendly relationship with each other and with the rest of the world.

But parents are not the only significant persons in a child's life; nor is the family situation the only situation which matters to a child. There are grandfathers and grandmothers, aunts, uncles, brothers and sisters, school teachers, religious teachers, friends and neighbors, any of whom may induce irrational fears and undermine self-confidence and serenity. One, two or many of these may create emotional conflict and neurosis. Don't blame it all on Mom.

Let's look at this from the child's point of view. What persons are most important or significant in his life? After he reaches school age, the most important characters in his little drama are the boys and girls in his own age group; and as he gets older, these persons become increasingly important in his emotional life. Acceptance or rejection by his own age group makes all the difference in the world to his mental health; and whether he is accepted or rejected is a matter over which his parents frequently have no control. Once more, I say, don't blame it all on Mom.

Nor is emotional conflict always the product of unhappy personal contacts. The conflicting ideals or standards of a community can establish conflicting emotions within the individuals who make up the community. After all, social standards are personal standards which individual people hold in common; and when social standards of right and wrong are in conflict, the individual is bound to be confused.

The mind of man is many-faceted, like a diamond, reflecting various colors, each determined by the angle of approach. All of us belong to many groups or classes, each one of which has developed its own fair trade practices and standards, its own ideas of what is fair and what is foul. So we have many behavior patterns, each of which is appropriate for the specific group of situations in which we find ourselves.

Unfortunately, these standards differ so from each other that it is often difficult to reconcile one with another. It is all right for the baseball coach and for the fans to yell at a pitcher to rattle him or to distract his attention. The same coach would never do this to an opponent putting on the eighteenth green, and the gallery would frown down anyone who deliberately made an unnecessary sound. What is right behavior in baseball is not proper on a golf course. This consideration probably does not prevent the baseball coach who plays golf from sleeping nights. After all, baseball and golf are only games. But there are situations, many of them, in the experience of all of us, where conflict between our standards or ideals threatens the integrity of our very lives. These are the situations which produce the neurotic behavior of our times.

For example, the conflict between the ideals of patriotism and ideals of personal economic and social advancement explains some of the neuroses of our draft army. Here is Johnny Jones, brought up to believe in rugged individualism. He wants intensely to make something of himself, get ahead in the world, buy his own home, get married, and be well thought of in his own little world of relatives and friends. He's drafted and in the army. Perhaps he was getting somewhere in his trade or profession. Now what? If he could feel like a martyr in a concentration camp, there would not be the same mental conflict. But he knows that he isn't a martyr. He wants to do his duty to his country. Two conflicting emotional habit patterns are tearing many a Johnny Jones apart, producing war neuroses.

Our civilization is at once so complex, so diverse, and so closely knitted together that all of us suffer from conflict of habit patterns that cannot be reconciled. The gracious hostess in the living room may be somewhat less than gracious and considerate in the kitchen when the dining-room door is closed. A bullying, domineering husband may be quite a good fellow on the golf course or in the cocktail bar. The strait-laced moralist has been known to let down a bit when far from home at a convention. So he attends stag parties with the rest of the boys. All of us are quick-change artists with many uniforms and many flags, which we are able to doff and don, furl and unfurl, in a twinkling as we move from scene to scene. All of this, however, hardly makes for integrity and inner peace.

We have habit patterns for our life in the factory or store or office that are in conflict with the habit patterns for our life at home. At the store, Mother engages in her daily battle with the butcher, determined to get as little bone and gristle as possible, the best and the most for her money. At home, she takes the worst cut for herself, and the skimpiest helping, so that there will be enough for the children. But sometimes the habit pattern of greed that may be appropriate in her marketing is evoked in the home. Then there is family trouble. Or her husband may get bighearted and treat the customers the way he treats members of the family, until the sheriff puts a padlock on the door to end such nonsense. In such cases, habit patterns or standards of behavior are inconsistent and conflicting. People try to reconcile antagonistic habit patterns and get confused. Then come the long hours of the night, when they toss about in bed, coaxing the sleep that does not come. Conflict between habit patterns makes jitters.

4

It is hard to be aware of your emotional habit patterns, because they are tied up not so much with your mind as with the behavior of your muscles, heart, intestines, and glands. When inner conflict frustrates your habit patterns or when some external situation blocks your living a cherished way of life, you know only that you feel nervous, anxious and not your real self. Then there arises a sense of strain, of lack of fulfillment. Perhaps it is a job that is lost, or a farm that has gone with the wind. Perhaps you have been graduated from school and, come September, you miss the old school habits and associations. Perhaps you had a trade skill that has been replaced by an automatic machine.

There you stand, the gun loaded, sighted, ready to shoot, but the order to fire is never given.

This lopping off of an activity is a common thing in life. It occurs constantly in childhood. It occurs when people move from city to city and give up their old friends and associations. It occurs when they move from one job to another. It happens with divorce. It occurs when a girl marries.

Before marriage, one typical case had been an active, well-trained, happy private secretary. She read all of the ads, brushed her teeth for the smile of beauty; took cathartics for the smile of health; mouthwash for the smell of health; ate the vitamins that gave her pep and vivacity; recommended the right kind of decaffeinized coffee, and so she married the boss.

Then her troubles began. She hated housework. The boss, now her husband, said, "Hire a maid, a cook, a butler. For God's sake, quit whining. Enjoy the sunshine and fresh air. You haven't anything else to do." Nothing to do, and filled with habit patterns of action. Nothing to do, and burning up to do something, anything, except to plan another futile, empty day.

"Thinking up things to do is the hardest job I ever had," she told me. "Not knowing what to do next gives me the jitters."

A man of sixty-five was retired from his job on a nice pension. He had worked in one place for forty years. They gave him a farewell dinner and a gold watch. They told him how lucky he was to be able to take things easy. For the next six months he watched the seconds crawl by on his gold watch. Then he died, of nothing to do.

This tragedy of the elderly is familiar to everyone. Yet how little is done to help its countless victims! How to make old age dignified, creative, and comfortable constitutes a large social problem. Social security for the emeritus requires more than a pension check. Deprived, perhaps, of those dear to them and of familiar haunts and accustomed ways, they are strangers in a brisk new world. They need rescue from futility and boredom. We must establish a fifth freedom—freedom to serve in old age.

We are indebted to Pavlov for our knowledge that the supposedly automatic workings of our organs, our hearts, lungs, stomach, intestines, glands, are set in motion or restrained by artificial stimulation.

He showed that our bodies get all worked up over excitements as hollow as his bell. He showed that these physical responses are not under the control of the will. When you have been conditioned to blush at the drop of a garter, you can instruct the blood vessels of your face not to dilate, but they won't listen. They have been conditioned to respond, so when there's garter-dropping going on, your facial blood vessels will dilate, and you are going to feel embarrassed.

The experimental neurosis in dogs shows that conflicting conditioned reflexes produce severe neurotic behavior. Dogs, sheep, pigs, mice, or men, it makes no difference. Furnish the conflicting habit patterns, and up pop the jitters.

From these magnificent beginnings, we have made further progress. We are on our way to discovering how the conditioned reflex works. We have tracked down the reflex to its lair, have discovered that special part of the brain where nervousness lurks. The next step is to demonstrate the anatomy of nervousness, to help you win your war on nerves.

CHAPTER TWO

Meet the Interbrain

1

THE CONDITIONED REFLEX is just another name for emotional habits. I mention this because people in trouble do have emotions of which they are most unpleasantly aware; while conditioned reflexes, they think, are for dogs and psychological laboratories. Of course, you may continue to talk about conditioned reflexes; and I'll probably slip into professional jargon, too, when I forget. But I am interested in explaining the nervous ills of troubled people, in order to teach them how to take care of themselves, so I shall be content to use in the place of "conditioned reflexes" the homely expression "emotional habits."

When dogs slobber at the sight of food and go through all of the other motions that mean ecstatic expectancy, they are behaving emotionally. Pavlov proved that this emotional experience can be aroused not only by food but by some stimulus in no way connected with eating. His experiments have led the way to the proof that conflict between emotional habits gives us our nervous breakdowns. We have seen how this works out in the case of dogs. This is how emotional conflict worked out in the case of a certain woman, whom we will call Mrs. Jack Aranda.

Her strongest emotional habits were tied up in two great loves, the first for herself and the second for her daughter. Since childhood, the enjoyment of social esteem had been her greatest satisfaction in life. When her wealthy husband died, her claim to social distinction as the wife of a prominent man died with him. She was a has-been. She was just another rich widow with a little girl to bring up. She felt, rightly or wrongly, that her only chance to regain importance was through her daughter. So she gave the little girl every opportunity—dancing lessons, parties, the right neighborhood and the right friends, the right private school, riding lessons, tennis, golf, to fit her to marry the son-in-law who was to re-establish Mother's self-esteem. Of course, Mother didn't reason it out quite so cold-bloodedly. She simply hoped that her daughter would make a suitable marriage, "for the girl's own sake, you know." But subconsciously she was guided by her well-established behavior patterns of seeking social esteem through the achievement of some member of her family.

Well, in spite of all her advantages, the girl turned out to be a pretty decent sort. She went to college, learned to think for herself, and married—no, not a Filipino houseboy, but a petty officer in Uncle Sam's Navy.

Mrs. Aranda knew in her heart that the girl had made a wise choice. She also knew that her lifetime's effort, her cherished schemes and stratagems "for the girl," had been wasted.

"A petty officer," she wailed. "A *petty* officer!"

The conflict between the two emotional habits, her love for her daughter and her love for social position, was not petty. She suffered a complete nervous breakdown. For more than a year she had no emotional control, and she went through hells of suffering.

"I want my daughter to be happy," one part of her mind was saying. The other part of her mind was crying, "I want a son-in-law about whom I can brag."

"I love my daughter; she's all I have in the world," and "I hate my daughter; why did she let me down?"

These conflicts were not on a conscious level, of course.

Mrs. Aranda knew only that she was distracted, could not sleep, and was losing weight. Actually, she did not connect her emotional conflicts with her physical symptoms. She consulted a doctor because she thought she might have a cancer. People often think up such diagnoses for themselves under such circumstances.

Collision between opposing emotions is at the bottom of every neurosis. What is more, a great many people suffer to some extent from emotional conflicts over which they have no control. To that extent, they are that much more unhappy and ineffective than need be. Countless numbers of men and women, rich or poor, are living lives of unnecessary frustration and despair. Countless numbers have great possibilities of thinking and feeling and doing that they never express in thought or in action. Dissatisfied because of their unrealized capacities, they are living miserably on a level of thought and action that is far beneath their capacities.

The first step in acquiring emotional control depends upon understanding the nature of emotional habits. A lot of people talk as glibly about emotions as they do about television—understanding neither. This is satisfactory, as far as television goes, because most people will never be called upon to repair a television set. Emotional habit patterns, however, cannot be turned over to a specialist. The expert can advise, can tell you what to do about your emotional conflicts. To resolve them, each patient must minister to himself. It is essential, then, for you to understand just how your emotions work, if you want to know how to live and like it.

2

Fear is a typical emotion, easy to understand. When you are afraid, you think that you see some menace. You think that something is going to hurt you. It may be only paper roses. Pavlov's dogs were taught to fear a harmless sound as they would fear an electric shock. War refugees, safe in a far country, continue to duck while their blood curdles and their flesh crawls whenever they hear an airplane overhead. The cause of your fear may seem silly to your sister-in-law. But emotion is unreasoning, and if you have learned to see danger in any particular situation, you may be afraid every time you become aware of that situation.

Awareness of danger is not necessarily fear. Fear is unpleasant, but for many people the awareness of danger is exciting and exhilarating. For this reason Park Avenue people climb mountains and Coney Islanders ride roller-coasters. They like to feel that they are part of a dangerous situation. More imaginative minds get their kick out of their perceptions of ticklish situations in their daily routine of living. Always to feel safe is dull. The feeling of danger, whether evoked synthetically on a roller-coaster or excited by a flirtation with an attractive person or an unattractive grizzly bear, gives a flesh-tingling thrill.

Fear is a compound of physical and mental processes. To an awareness of danger, something more must be added. That something more is contributed by your physical reactions in preparation for running away. Danger, plus the muscle tensions that make the knees quake and the back shiver, is fear. Danger, plus the hotness of the eyeballs and the dryness of the mouth, is fear. Danger, plus a spasm of the bowls and of the bladder, is fear. These physical reactions of fear are under the direction of the nervous system, which also participates in the complex of fright behavior. Fear is activity, physical and mental, with rapid strategic retreat as its motive.

It is easy to think that fear is what you feel. But fear is more than that. Of course, when your knees knock and your hands shake and your forehead perspires, you feel these disagreeable sensations. You know only too well that sinking feeling in the pit of the stomach. All of your tense muscles and your churned-up insides are sending their messages to the brain, giving you the unpleasant emotional feeling that you associate with fear. But while these sensations are a part of the emotion of fear, they are not all of it or even most of it. Fear is what you do with your entirety—body and mind.

To understand yourself, it is important to distinguish between your *feeling* of fear and your *emotion* of fear. What you feel is only a part of your emotional process. If you were thinking of buying a house, you'd distinguish between its external appearance and the whole structure. The external appearance might be important, but it would be only a part of the whole. So with the feeling of fear. When you live through the emotion of fear, you feel only a part of what your body and mind have done in getting you ready for rapid retreat. What you feel is only one ingredient in your total emotion.

Let's get back to Mrs. Jack Aranda and her fear. Mrs. Aranda was afraid of what friends would say about her daughter's marriage. So every time that she met one of her friends, what happened? She wanted to run away. Her mouth became dry. Her eyeballs felt hot. Her knees trembled. The muscles of her legs felt weak, as if they had turned to jelly. Her heart raced, pounded. She could feel it palpitate beneath her Bergdorf Goodman gown. She would perspire, and her hands and feet felt cold as she ducked around corners to avoid people. Her breath would become short, and she would find herself panting. Her stomach, intestines, even her bladder would go into spasms. And although she could not be aware of it, her glands of internal secretion were doing their share to keep up with the rest of her body. The adrenals were pouring their secretion into the blood stream, and the adrenalin was having its effect in driving her liver to supply unneeded nourishment to her wearied muscles.

Fifty years ago, William James said that you do not run because you fear; you fear because you run. He was on the right track, for sensation follows organic reactions. To Mrs. Jack Aranda, friends had come to mean fear, and fear is a thing that you do with your entire body. Mrs. Aranda ran.

So what is this emotion that we call fear? It is not a thing but a process, something that we do in five stages. *First:* We are conditioned both to perceive and fly from whatever we have learned to fear. (One man's danger, of course, is another man's workaday life. The structural-steel worker who leans against the wind while riveting on high scaffoldings might turn green with fear in a small boat on a choppy sea. The sailor who scampers up the ropes on a mast might tremble at the very thought of catching red-hot rivets while keeping his balance on a narrow steel beam.) *Second:* When a situation arises that we recognize as dangerous, we respond with our muscles by preparing for flight or escape. We tense up as a sprinter does while waiting for the signal, "Go." *Third:* Here is where feeling comes in because, as a result of muscular attitudes preparatory to flight, there follow certain nervous and bodily changes. Recognition of a fear-inducing situation and the motor attitude of getting ready to run away lead to visceral and other changes, and we feel frightened. *Fourth:* Some of your bodily responses stir up disagreeable sensations and feelings which you want to be rid of and which create, *Fifth:* a secondary motive to find relief in safety. If for any reason you cannot run away and appropriate action is frustrated, your emotion of fear may build up into paralyzing terror.

You end your fear when you stop the process in any one of these five activities. You were afraid of burglars when you heard unusual noises in the living room. Shaking from head to foot, you peeked in. Only a window shade blowing in the wind. What a relief: an end to an awareness of danger—and of fear. You killed fear in its first stage.

You are afraid of climbing a mountain. The very thought of the narrow footpath on the edge of the canyon makes you shiver. After you do it a few times, you may no longer desire to escape from the situation. You learn to enjoy the danger. You take pleasure in your unsuspected gift for mountain climbing, and fear vanishes.

You are afraid of the future. You learn how to relax, and indirectly you relax the organs that had been giving you cramps. We will explain this later on. With no organic response, there can be no more fear.

And with no organic response to danger, no disagreeable sensations can arise to create the feeling that people call fear. Brain surgeons can end habitual fear by cutting the connections between the nerve centers of organic reactions and the centers of awareness. This is drastic and often impracticable, but it shows clearly that fear is eliminated by stopping the fear process in any one of its stages. When you stop doing any single thing that makes up the fear process, you do not have the secondary motive of seeking relief, which has served to increase the desire for escape.

Further along you will be given detailed instructions for controlling not only fear, but all of your emotional conflicts. For this is the pattern of all emotions. Muscular and visceral participation in our so-called mental processes is usually neglected in seeking the causes of unhappiness, so I have deliberately emphasized them, because their importance in treatment is fundamental.

For years classical psychologists have distinguished three general emotions: fear, love and anger. Of course, there are many different kinds and degrees of fear, love and anger; but regardless of kind and degree, every emotion can be classified under one of these three major divisions.

You will note that the psychological classification names emotions by their feeling components. We feel fear; we feel love; we feel anger.

The late Dr. Karen Horney improved upon this way of thinking when she gave emotions a more dynamic interpretation. She thought of emotions as feelings, of course, but also as tendencies to respond to situations.

She thought of fear as the tendency to withdraw, to run away, to protect one's self by moving away. Love was equated with the tendency to go toward the love object (persons or things or even ideas) with trust and affection. Anger or hostility is the tendency to go against whatever appears harmful or hateful. In social situations, this may be expressed by reasonable self-assertion, by standing up for one's rights and resenting encroachment upon whatever we cherish. You may see it in some as unreasonable hostility, in others as righteous indignation. Whatever form it takes, this is what classical psychologists call anger.

Our feelings comprise an important part of our emotional behavior. There is no reason why we should not name our emotions after the feelings they evoke, so long as we understand that our feelings represent only a part of the total emotional pattern. So I do not reject the terminology of the classical psychologist. Furthermore, there is no denying that emotions always involve a predisposition to respond in some specific manner; therefore, it is perfectly proper to think of emotions as tendencies. However, the tendency to respond emotionally is only a part of the total emotional pattern. It is the beginning of the emotional pattern but not the whole of it.

I like to think of fear, love, and anger, not simply as feelings, not merely as tendencies, but as dynamic processes. Every emotion, like a stage play, has a behavior pattern, a beginning, a middle, and an end.

Emotions begin as predispositions or tendencies; they are experienced as feelings; and normally they end with spontaneous, satisfactory expression in effective action, together with a feeling of relief.

Fear, love, and anger are not merely feelings, and they are more than tendencies. They are things we do.

Fear, love, and anger all are normal. Indeed, the man who cannot feel and express all of these emotions spontaneously and freely is a sick man. Whether an emotion is good or bad depends upon whether it is appropriate. We are often told how never to be afraid, but I should not like to be chauffered by the man who takes this advice literally. As Bonaro W. Overstreet has pointed out in her book, *Understanding Fear*, there are many dangerous situations, social and physical, which normally should evoke the response we call fear.

The same is true of anger. The man who cannot respond with anger, who does not hate what is hateful, is a moral imbecile. To kill in self-defense is not merely legal, it's laudable, for such self-assertion discourages murder. Sometimes it is wise and good to turn the other cheek, but there are occasions when it is wise and good to bring not peace but the sword.

Nervous breakdown often has its beginning in the denial of the existence of some emotion. My job is to try to make my patients aware of their conflicting emotions; and I try to teach my patients how to end their inner conflicts and anxieties by controlling their emotions.

I said that each of these three emotions take many forms and are felt in varying degrees of intensity. Let us consider fear—that group of emotions which we use to protect ourselves from danger. We can conveniently call this group of emotions the *avoidant* emotions.

We either learn or are conditioned to avoid and fear many things. Recognition or even memory of what inspires fear, together with those muscular and visceral reactions to ready us to avoid danger, produce fear emotions too many for enumeration. There is no limit to the number of avoidant emotions which might be named. Each has its special feeling tone. Dread, terror, dismay, panic, awe, fright and alarm are only a few which follow an awareness of whatever we consider dangerous. And not only fear, but all emotions, consist of combinations of organic responses, including the brain, as soon we shall see.

Love represents the going-toward emotions or, as we psychologists say, the *adient* emotions. Here, again, conditioning predisposes us to perceive certain things or persons or ideas as desirable; and conditioning predisposes us to respond to those things or persons or ideas with appropriate muscular attitudes. Here, again, a combination of intellectual evaluation, muscular tensions, and visceral responses gives rise to feelings of desire. (These feelings may range all the way from a tepid preference to a red-hot excitement.) Here, again, frustration increases the intensity of response which may become well near insupportable.

Anger represents the third group of emotions, the *opposant* emotions. We are conditioned to swat the disease-carrying fly and kill the harmless (or useful) snake and otherwise to recognize real and imaginary enemies. Our muscles are conditioned to tense up in readiness for such opposant actions. Thus predisposed to anger, our muscles do tense up when we recognize anger-provoking situations; our intestines participate in the free-for-all battle, and we feel like fighting. Frustration of this emotion intensifies it, sometimes to the point where we feel

beside ourselves. That's the reason why those with little tolerance for frustration are quick with their tongues or fists and
feel good after a fight.

When a single situation or person triggers two or three
of these emotional responses simultaneously, you experience
conflict. You want to make a friendly advance; at the same
time you feel hostile and perhaps, fearful. You are in the position of Pavlov's dogs who just didn't know what to do when
they heard the bell ring. Their conflicting responses upset
them and made them neurotic.

The reason must be obvious. In each of their emotional
responses their bodies participated. First, there was muscular
participation; the dogs were ready to act. Then their stomachs,
salivary glands, hearts, and other organs participated in the
emotional response. Now, ordinarily the completion of a single emotional response would have left the dogs satisfied and
at ease. Completion of an emotional response makes one feel
good. But with conflict preventing the completion of any one
emotional response, these unhappy animals were left in a
state of physiological and psychological imbalance. That is
what anxiety is: a state of continuous imbalance which is
caused by inner conflict between emotional responses.

This state of anxiety leads to various neurotic manifestations, makes people tired and unable to make decisions. Some
people attempt to deal with their anxiety by becoming over-
particular. Other people withdraw from all activity. There is
really no limit to the kinds of unrewarding behavior which
troubled people enact in order to allay their anxiety. In the
following chapters you will learn various techniques which
you can apply to control your own anxiety. Dissipating your
anxiety means controlling your emotions.

I do not think of love, hate, and fear as being good or bad
in themselves. Each represents a different type of emotional

response. These emotions are good or bad depending only whether their expression is socially acceptable. The important thing is to recognize your emotions and to control them so that your emotional conflicts may more easily be resolved and your anxieties dissipated.

Think of each of your organs as capable of making a certain sound when aroused or when slowed down. Your muscles, heart, breathing apparatus, your sweat glands, your stomach, your intestines, your tear glands, each might be considered to have its characteristic note. If several of these were to react together so as to produce a sound combination or chord, this would be the equivalent of an emotional response. Some combinations of reactions would be pleasant, even to the point of ecstasy. Other combinations would be unbearably disagreeable. Combinations of organ behavior are limitless in number. These, ecstatic or unbearable, constitute your emotional range.

The emotional habits of humans are even more sensitive to training than are the emotional habits of dogs. Think of all the things that can set your body to swinging in the fear rhythm. Not only do we fear things and situations that are really dangerous, but in our leisure moments we deliberately invent spooks with which to frighten ourselves. Most of our fears have nothing to do with physical danger. They involve situations affecting our adjustments to a confusing world of confused people. In our man-made economy, we fear that the gasman will cut off our cooking fire; we fear, too, that we will be roasted in the hell-fires of a man-made demonology. We spend much of our lives running around like people trapped in a theater fire. Even without a nervous breakdown, we are constantly under homemade nervous tension.

Consider the large number of situations that can make us angry. Or jealous. Or excite the emotions of love. The dog

leads a placid and even life, but we bipeds are intensely emotional, even when we are well adjusted to our surroundings.
Our hearts and stomachs and glands are in continual emotional uproar. Small wonder the human animal suffers more
sickness than any other species on this planet. Our nerves upset our bodies.

3

The function of the nervous system is two-fold: to keep us
in contact with the world around us and to integrate our life
activities. Integrate means to unify, to keep us all of a piece,
to co-ordinate effort. The nervous system is our chief communication and co-ordinating center.

The nerves which co-ordinate our senses and which control our muscles are located chiefly in the forebrain, the cere-
bellum and the spinal cord. These structures make up the
central nervous system. You would not be too far wrong to
think of the central nervous system as the center of intellectual
activity and motor control. Should a hemorrhage destroy large
parts of the forebrain, the power of abstract thinking and
motor control would likely be impaired.

Nerves also control and co-ordinate the activities of our
internal organs and glands. These nerves make up the autonomic nervous system—so-called because they function inde-
pendently of our attention and direction. Most of these nerves
are centered in one part of the nervous system, and it is this
central control which normally keeps our hearts, lungs, and
stomachs and blood vessels—all our organs and glands—working in harmony with each other. Since all feeling arises in this
part of the nervous system, it is of greatest importance to our
emotional processes. This nervous center of the autonomic
nervous system is called the interbrain.

Get acquainted with that word, interbrain. You are going

to hear a lot about it in the next few years. You will hear it referred to under a number of different names, so I'll tell you a few of them to keep you from becoming confused. You may hear it called the thalamus and hypothalamus, because these are two of its most important structures. Gentlemen who like to high-hat the world with their nodding acquaintance with Greek will call it the diencephalon. But I like the name interbrain, partly because it is English and partly because interbrain tells you what it is. It is the brain that lies between the modern, highly civilized forebrain and the more ancient lower nerve centers of the body.

So let me introduce you to your master of ceremonies, the interbrain. Here is the fountainhead of your feelings. Love, hate, and fear, with their various kinds of organic behavior, all take their start from this group of nerves. Even sex is located in this part of your nervous system. Some investigators operated upon the interbrain of guinea pigs, and thereafter even these affectionate little animals took no more than a Platonic interest in each other. Which may explain why nervousness and impotence so often go together. The mating moon gets back but a dull reflection from a ruffled interbrain.

Mrs. Aranda's nervous indigestion came from interbrain misbehavior. So did her mucous colitis. And spastic constipation. Dr. Harvey Cushing states that emotional storms coming out of the interbrain can cause ulcers of the stomach. Here is where you get that palpitation of the heart. Asthma that is a bronchial neurosis begins here. And isn't this logical, when you consider that this is the part of your nervous system that controls your organic behavior and so is the seat of your feelings.

The interbrain sits just above the base of the skull. Stick your fingers in your ears, and you will be pointing right at it. Each half of your interbrain is about the size of your thumb.

It is small, but it is important, because it sits in the driver's seat.

Below the interbrain is the spinal cord, a huge cable of nerves which distribute impulses to nearly all of the muscles and glands of the body, and which carries upward sensations of pain, touch, temperature, and muscle tension. All of these sensations are relayed to the interbrain. It has to know everything that is going on.

Above the interbrain is the forebrain, sometimes called the cerebrum. The forebrain, which is the most recently evolved part of the nervous system, occupies most of the space within your skull. This is the part of your nervous system that analyzes, thinks, decides. It lets you know just what is going on in the world. It is with your forebrain that you read your newspaper. Your forebrain interprets the general situation and sends its findings to the interbrain for action and feeling. The interbrain reports the situation back to the forebrain in terms of elation or depression. When you feel calm or happy or sad or depressed, or when you have the jitters or nervous indigestion, you know it because your interbrain has told your forebrain just how it feels.

What does the interbrain do? What is it good for?

The purpose of the interbrain is to co-ordinate all of the activities of the body. It keeps forebrain and bowels and stomach and eyes and ears and muscles and heart and lungs and thyroid gland all working together as a team. It keeps your various organs from saying to each other, "You go your way and I'll go mine." It makes the body and mind work together as a unit.

In the case of Pavlov's dogs, for example, the stomach telegraphs the interbrain that a little food would be acceptable. Interbrain receives the report, relays it to the forebrain. Dogs become aware of hunger, start to search for food. Along comes

Dr. Pavlov with nice ground round steak. Dog sees meat, smells meat. News gets to forebrain, which interprets situation optimistically, and from the sight and sound centers of the forebrain, bulletins go to the interbrain, "Soup's on." The interbrain starts giving orders to the entire body. To the salivary glands a telegram, "Start secreting saliva." To the stomach, "Start secreting hydrochloric acid. Start your digestive rhythms." To the legs and other muscles of the body, "Pep up, start dancing around; the depression is over."

When the bell is sounded along with the bringing of the dinner, the auditory center of the dog's forebrain will swing into action. This center will reinforce the messages from the sight and smell centers, will report good news to the interbrain. Later on, the auditory center will continue to be overly optimistic and report progress at the sound of a bell, even when no food is brought. The interbrain will receive these false reports and will cause the dog's organs to go through the same routine that followed the bringing of real meat.

The conditioning of reflexes in dogs and the training of emotional habits in humans means only the process of teaching the forebrain, the part of the nervous system that thinks, to send messages to the interbrain, that part of the nervous system that co-ordinates all physical activity and feels for you. Now, when you go to a restaurant, read the menu, and give your order, your entire body will be pleasantly prepared to do right by your dinner. There is co-ordination between your forebrain that reads and your interbrain that regulates your body.

The interbrain is a busy little mechanism. It regulates not only your digestive organs, but also your heart, your breathing apparatus, and your glands of external and of internal secretion. When the forebrain reports danger, the interbrain makes your heart beat faster. It makes you breathe more quickly, in order to supply your muscles with an extra order of oxygen. It makes your adrenal glands pour out adrenalin, a powerful chemical, into the blood stream, to stimulate your liver and your muscles into activity. It regulates your blood pressure. It keeps your temperature normal, by regulating the amount of blood that flows through the cooler areas of your skin. It even keeps in delicate balance the various chemical substances in your blood—a matter absolutely necessary to your continued existence.

You know how well and how automatically your body works when in health. A well man ordinarily doesn't know that he has kidneys or adrenal glands or a heart or lungs. He never gives them a thought. But behind their automatic functioning, the interbrain is in control. It manages the works, regulates the functioning of man, the animal. It knows more than you do, for within the interbrain resides what Dr. Walter B. Cannon calls the wisdom of the body.

The interbrain has been on the job for a long time. Long before man existed, our prehuman ancestors had an interbrain to think for the body. The fine, big forebrain, that takes up most of the space within your skull and which gets all the credit for your keen intelligence, was an evolutionary afterthought. Because of this newly evolved forebrain, man differs from other animals in his greater thinking ability. Not that apes do not have a forebrain. They do, and they are able to think in some dim, hazy fashion. Their forebrains are small as compared with yours and mine—that's the only difference. But their interbrains and our interbrains are just about the same in size. That's why Judy O'Grady and the Colonel's lady and the lady ape are three sisters under their interbrains.

The interbrain has kept the race alive in more ways than one. When the saber-toothed tiger crouched in the underbrush, and our ancient ancestor saw him there, ready to attack, it was the interbrain that gave spring to the muscles, speed to the legs, breath to the body, and force to the heart-beat that enabled our remote great-grandfather to outdo himself and the tiger.

Today, almost anything can throw the same interbrain mechanisms into gear, start up that fear response. A blue uniform was all that Mrs. Aranda had to see to make her feel blue. Paper roses could make an interbrain turn handsprings, send frantic messages to a man's breathing apparatus. I knew a famous football coach who had to trot to the boys' room every fifteen minutes every Saturday morning. The very thought of the scarlet-and-gray sweaters of Ohio State University would put his interbrain in such a state that it made his bladder clamp down in one spasm after another.

It isn't the fault of the interbrain that you shiver and shake when no man pursueth. It throws you into a fear reaction only when your forebrain gives the signal. And when your organs are going through the motions of a fear reaction, you're going to feel the emotion of fear. Will power, whatever that is, has nothing to do with it. Your nerves, physical things having length, breadth, thickness, weight, are kicking up a row; and nature has placed the nerves of your interbrain just out of the reach of conscious control.

4

Let's get back to Mrs. Aranda. She loved her daughter and wanted the best for her. When the girl married, Mrs. Aranda felt that she had lost the one person in whom she had invested most of her emotional resources. It's no laughing matter to lose a loved one. It's not something that can be brushed off with a "So what?"

Furthermore, Mrs. Aranda's ego was involved. She was a

snob; she admitted it. But this admission did not lessen the hurt to her pride. Had her daughter married a man whom she could have enjoyed as a son-in-law, she would not have felt that her life's work had been defeated.

Nor is this all. Mrs. Aranda hated the daughter for going against her will. This is understandable; parents have punished children for much less. Furthermore, Mrs. Aranda feared meeting her daughter and son-in-law, lest the meeting lead to acrimony and recrimination. She also feared meeting her own friends, because she felt disgraced.

So here is love, anger, and fear in a three way free-for-all conflict. Unaided, she saw no way of resolving the conflict by compromise. She didn't even recognize her troubles as emotional conflict. She just felt sick and confused.

Her interbrain was unable to take it. It went to pieces, broke down and refused to play.

Doctors called her condition psychoneurosis.

Yes, when the interbrain gets confused messages from the forebrain, so that the same situation sets off the behavior of conflicting emotional reactions, the old interbrain loses its power of producing perfect automatic co-ordination between all parts of the body. Signals go to organs to do the things that hinder rather than help. The stomach cramps when it should relax. The heart races or palpitates just when it should beat slowly and regularly. One organ of the body works against another. Instead of community effort, it's civil war. Instead of man against environment, it's man against himself.

So Mrs. Jack Aranda, sufferer from interbrain misbehavior, goes to her doctor. She may have some localized ache or pain. Anyhow, she feels rotten. She can't sleep a wink. She can't eat a thing. She takes no pleasure in anything. She is losing weight. She has no interest in life. She feels tired all the time. She cannot concentrate. She is irritable, hates herself for being such a crab. And naturally hates hating herself. Because she does not understand what it's all about, she is terrified.

If she is told that her troubles are "all imagination," she is hurt rather than helped. It is not imagination; her troubles are as real as her nervous system, some of the cells of which are diseased. But telling her that there is nothing wrong only confuses the sufferer, gives her one more cause for despair.

5

We are conditioned from early childhood to respond to various situations in certain definite directions. It's, "Don't touch that; it'll hurt you." Or, "Nice doggie, he won't hurt you; pet the doggie, darling." Or, "Stand up for yourself; if he hits you, you hit him back." This early conditioning teaches us to see certain things and to ignore others; to respond to situations in a definite way; and to feel certain emotions in certain situations. Seeing is selective. We see what we have learned to look for and we do not see what we have learned to ignore. This goes also for our responses and our feelings. Thus we are predisposed to emotion.

But why do our emotions raise us to the heights of ecstasy or sink us into the depths of despair?

Until recently science had no explanation, but today, thanks to the newer knowledge of nerves given us by researchers in the anatomy and physiology of the nervous system, we now have the answer.

When Mrs. Aranda perceived a situation which she felt was threatening and beyond her control, her muscles became tense. Nervous impulses traveled from her muscles to a central communication system, the interbrain. From her interbrain many messages were sent out, each to a different organ of her body. One message went to her forebrain and she experienced the feeling of fear. Another went to her salivary glands; her mouth went cotton-dry. Another message went to her stomach and intestines, which went into spasm and cramped. Separate messages were sent to her endocrine glands —her pituitary, thyroid, and adrenal glands; these organs shot their powerful chemical secretions into her blood stream. In short, every part of her body was alerted by the interbrain for emergency action, and all her body processes were stimulated and speeded up for defense in the emergency.

When a person gets a shot of adrenalin from his own adrenal glands, and when the other emergency reactions occur, his muscles become even more tense. This increase in tension is reported to the interbrain which sends out more urgent messages. These increase the intensity of physiological response and of feeling.

This building-up process within you constitutes the essence of the emotional process. Each response in one part of the body stimulates the other parts of the body to respond in higher and higher peaks of activity. Thus every excitement breeds another at every level of activity, from the hair on your arms to the gray cells within your skull, until finally a balance is reached where this building-up process can go no farther.

Naturally, when these events take place within your body you feel more nervous and excited. The psychological experience grows faster and faster in step with the events which occur within the nervous system and the rest of the body. In practical terms, one feels worse and worse, or better and better until he reaches his limit for feeling.

What I have just described is known as the feed-back process, or the reverberating effect.

This feed-back process, this reverberating effect, is an emergency response to stress and in popular language is an emotional state. But it isn't a state, because an emotion is a process, an acute disturbance which involves many interrelated bodily changes and which is experienced as intensified, agitated feeling.

As we have seen, your emotional responses to stressful situations can become a habit. We have a tendency to remember our strong emotions. Perhaps this is because an emergency reaction to stress tends to persist long after the conditions which gave rise to it have disappeared. One blow can set the pendulum to swinging for quite a while.

So memory has a good deal to do with your emotional reactions. Some trivial thing may cause you to remember the time when you felt deeply humiliated or violently angry. A memory can trigger the entire emotional process in such a way that it repeats itself for no apparent reason. Thus, habitual motor tensions tend to persist to sensitize us to situations which set off an emotional response. What is worse, these habitual muscle tensions multiply each other. For one set of tensions will activate another set until you are all tied up in knots. This answers the question, "Why am I tense now when I used to be relaxed?" The answer is that your muscle tensions have increased and have multiplied each other until they have reached the point where they have become unmanageable.

A single emotion, even when habitual and violent, does not necessarily lead to anxiety and neurosis. You have seen people who rave and rant one moment and who are cool and collected five minutes later. Such persons might be unpleasant at times, but this would not necessarily make life difficult for them. Only their family and friends would suffer.

But when a person has two or three conflicting emotions (such as love, hate, and fear) set in motion by a single situation or thought, that person is in trouble. Then he is literally mixed up, mixed up physiologically as well as psychologically. He feels confused, uncertain and anxious. His internal warfare paralyzes decision and action while it energizes self-doubt. Self-esteem is destroyed. So the neurotic mind, torn by civil war between its conflicting emotions, finds no inner peace, no feeling of self-trust. It is restless, distractable, given to futile, wasteful day dreams, uncontrolled feelings, and even explosions of violent action.

Add to these troubles the neurotic's concern over his frightening physical pains and discomforts; multiply this with his feelings of guilt for his hostility; and, top it all with his feelings of shame for being neurotic, and you have an outline picture of what the neurotic thinks about on his off days. There is no way of describing what the neurotic thinks about on his off days except to say that it is a preview of Hell.

6

In a clinic, some time ago, I was examining a patient. He was an inarticulate, terrified sufferer who said only that his nerves were "all shot." Another doctor watched my examination, then contributed, "The trouble with him is too much imagination. All he needs is a swift kick in the pants."

I felt like giving the doctor a kick in the pants because of *his* lack of imagination. I felt like it, but didn't. Instead, I wrote this book.

The first and most important thing to know about nervousness is that it is a physical disease. It is not a disease of the imagination. You can no more imagine yourself into mental health than you can imagine yourself into a cure for a broken leg. To get well, if you are nervous, you must treat physical things, the nerves in your interbrain. If I had to make a choice between a broken leg and a severe neurosis, I'd say, "Make mine the broken leg. It can't hurt so much."

I'd know that in six weeks the leg would be out of the cast; in eight weeks I'd be well. And during those few weeks there would be little suffering, much sympathy, and generous offers of help. The man with the jitters endures tortures of suffering and gets nothing but blame and resentment. He loses his friends because his nerves are sick.

Poisons consisting of the body's waste products will cause the nerves of the interbrain to misbehave. When a person becomes overtired, and not enough time has passed for him to get rid of the waste substances formed within his body, he may suffer from interbrain symptoms. He has a mild nervous breakdown. The nerve cells of the interbrain are poisoned. With a couple of days of rest, the fatigue poisons are eliminated, and all is well again.

A physical shock can shake up the nerve cells of the interbrain, producing what doctors call a traumatic neurosis. Anyone who has ever been in a bad automobile accident will know what I mean. Hunger will do the same thing to an interbrain. If there is not enough sugar in the blood, the interbrain will not work right. The interbrain likes to be fed, too. It is not an epicure, but it must have its food.

But generally the cause of the interbrain misbehavior is conflict between emotional habit patterns. And what does this conflict do to the nerve cells? For one thing, it spoils their timing of incoming and outgoing impulses. Timing is the essence of co-ordination. When the interbrain isn't working right, the normal rhythm of the body is working like a car with the timing gear and distributor out of whack.

Another form of interbrain misbehavior results from the fact that some of its groups of cells discharge too much energy, while other groups discharge too little. Imagine how your car would work if one cylinder had a mixture of gas as strong as T.N.T., while the next cylinder was given dishwater.

We have seen, too, that sometimes the cells of the interbrain having opposite functions may discharge their energy simultaneously. Then the same organ gets a "stop" and "go" signal at the same time. Thus the signals neutralize each other, producing a kind of interbrain deadlock. This tug of war going on in the interbrain will stop anyone in his tracks, make it impossible for him to act or think decisively. None of this misbehavior of the interbrain is directly under voluntary control. People become aware of their stomachs when stomachs do not act properly and of the intestines that cramp, but they cannot say, "Look here, Mr. Stomach," because Mr. Stomach takes orders, not from the forebrain, but from the interbrain.

To a greater or less extent, all of us have suffered from interbrain misbehavior. But many of us have brought the interbrain back to normal functioning. Interbrain trouble is definitely reversible. That is what so many doctors mean when they say that this trouble is "functional" rather than "organic."

This change produces no permanent damage, as is evidenced by the large number of people who have won their war on nerves. Half the battle is to understand what it is all about. The other half is to do something positive about it.

CHAPTER THREE

The Mind Tells the Body

I

YOU NOW KNOW that conflict between emotional habit patterns leads to interbrain misbehavior, gives you the jitters. Your entire organism which should be working as a unit becomes disorganized. You sweat when you are not warm, and you have goose pimples when you are not cold. Glands of internal secretion cease to function properly. The delicate balance of the chemistry of your blood is disturbed, which in turn further disorganizes the proper functioning of your mind and body. Your stomach, your intestines, your bladder, lungs, and heart cease to work properly. Your blood pressure may become abnormally low or may shoot up like a rocket. Even the muscles of your arms and legs and back and neck are tense when they should be relaxed. All this, because your conflicting emotions have thrown a monkey wrench into the mechanism of your interbrain. The nerve cells of this organ have ceased to regulate the activities of your body so that the various parts of it keep in step with each other, and, as you say, your nerves are all shot.

It has long been established that emotional conflicts produce bodily disease. The late Dr. H. Flanders Dunbar, of Presbyterian Hospital in New York City, has demonstrated that unpleasant emotions produce changes in the body tissues, changes that we call physical disease. In some cases ulcer of the stomach is a result of interbrain disturbance. Heart disease may be another. These conditions—there are many others

46

—when caused by emotional upset are called psychogenic. The mind is father to the disease.

Here is a typical case. A woman had been going the round of medical offices for three years, chasing the cure for mucous colitis. She had alternating diarrhea and constipation, abdominal colic, with mucus and sometimes blood in her stools. She had been told to rest in bed, to go to Florida, not to walk across a room, to take up golf. She had tried every kind of diet. Her colon had been irrigated with gallons of water. Some enterprising person had given her sour-milk enemas; nevertheless, she was not relieved. The ulcers inside her rectum had been painted with antiseptics, but the intracolonic art did not heal her.

Putting her happiness ahead of her colon, I encouraged her to tell me her life story. The emotional head-on collisions that were making her sick appeared at once. Three years ago, she said, she had had an affair with some man and she was afraid that her husband would find out. The man lived in another city where she had been visiting. She had not seen him since. Her husband did not know the man, and there was small likelihood of their meeting. Three years, I observed, is a long time to worry.

Actually, she wanted to tell her husband in order to get even with him. He was a stern, cold proposition, while she was of the clinging-vine type that requires warmth and affection. Subconsciously, she blamed her husband for her indiscretion. She wanted him to suffer for it as she had suffered for want of love. But she was afraid even to think of telling him. So she walked in dread lest she let the truth out.

After I had met her husband, I advised her to tell him the whole truth. It hurt his feelings sufficiently to make him take notice of her—something he had forgotten to do for years—and I surmise that his pain gave my patient the bittersweet satisfaction of squaring old scores of neglect. At any rate, there was a scene, a reconciliation, and the mucous colitis of three years' duration ceased at once. The ulcers of the mucous membranes of the bowels healed up within days.

Mucous colitis is generally recognized as a mind-fathered, or psychogenic, disorder. But it is only one of the diseases of the gastrointestinal tract that is brought on by interbrain misbehavior.

The gastrointestinal tract is essentially a long, hollow muscular tube, extending from mouth to anus. It includes the gullet (esophagus), the stomach, the small intestines, and the bowels. This tube is lined with mucous membrane, like the inside of your mouth, but the walls are made of muscle fibers, as are your cheeks.

Every part of the gastrointestinal tract responds to emotion. The salivary glands stop their secretion. The glands of the stomach stop their production of hydrochloric acid. The muscle walls go into spasm. All of this has been proved by X-ray and chemical studies upon dogs and cats. Fear ties up their digestive machinery.

Suppose that every time you sat down to eat, you were subjected to violent fear. Your salivary glands, like those of the dog and cat, would stop their secretion. You would not know it, but the glands of your stomach would stop their secretion of hydrochloric acid. The muscle walls of your gastrointestinal tract would go into spasm, close up like a fist. After a while, spasm and lack of secretion would become habitual, occur when there was no special occasion for fright. You would have nervous indigestion or mucous colitis, brought on by a mental state.

If this habitual squeezing of the stomach wall should scrape off its tender mucous membrane, leaving it exposed to the corroding gastric juices, this might produce a gastric ulcer. Drs.

Stewart Wolf and Harold G. Wolff had the unique opportunity of seeing this happen. Working in their laboratory was a small, wiry man with a hole in the abdominal wall leading directly into his stomach. He was fifty-six years old, married, and the father of one child. When he was nine years old he had swallowed scalding-hot clam chowder. As a result of this his throat was burned and he became unable to swallow. Surgeons had to make a permanent opening through his abdomen. Thereafter he put his food directly into his stomach through a funnel. He chewed the food first, of course, in order to start the digestive processes, so he didn't lose out on the fun of eating. It sounds horrible, but he has been getting along this way for forty-seven years, which tells us something of the adaptability of the human organism.

The two doctors often looked directly into his stomach through the hole in his abdomen. There were times when the patient's life situations led to contentment, joy, frustration, anxiety, hostility, and other emotional processes. These were carefully recorded, together with observations of the mechanical and chemical behavior of the stomach. The two doctors (one a captain in the U. S. Medical Corps) observed the formation of stomach ulcers as a result of emotional conflict. They conclude, "It appears likely, then, that the chain of events which begins with anxiety and conflict and their associated overactivity of the stomach and ends with hemorrhage or perforation is that which is involved in the natural history of peptic ulcer in human beings."

This report appeared in the *Journal of the American Medical Association* of November 7, 1942. One week later Drs. Samuel Morrison and Maurice Morrison reported two hundred and eight cases of duodenal ulcer associated with a total personality pattern that included hypersensitivity and hyperirritability. Current medical literature amply substantiates their findings.

Dr. Vonderahe, of the University of Cincinnati, made the important discovery that in addition to psychogenic causes, hemorrhages of the interbrain produce ulcers of the stomach. This is one more finger pointing at the location in the brain where nervous disease or misbehavior can produce distant results. You draw the conclusion that treatment should consist not merely in prescribing diet and alkalies but should include treatment of the underlying cause, a diseased interbrain.

From ideas to interbrain to stomach, downward the course of nervous stimulation makes its way. This applies to much of the nausea of pregnancy. Pioneer women do not have time for "morning sickness." But when a modern woman has reason to believe that she is pregnant, she confides in a friend, who asks, "Do you feel nauseated in the morning?"

A patient complained that she had not menstruated for three months. "It must be glandular," she said. "I know that I'm not pregnant. When I'm pregnant, I can't keep a thing on my stomach."

I examined her. The cervix was like a sponge; the uterus was as large as a big grapefruit. She had been pregnant for more than three months. "You'll feel your baby kicking in about a month," I told her.

"Quick," she cried, "get me a basin," and up bounced her dinner.

2

Dr. William Faulkner of San Francisco arranged things so that he could directly observe the spasms of the esophagus under conditions of emotional upset. He introduced a small tube fitted with a tiny light and lenses—an esophagoscope—down his patients' throats, so that he could see the inside of their

gullets. Then by verbal suggestion, he called forth an assort-
ment of destructive emotions, such as grief, anxiety, apprehension, and fear. The entire length of the patient's esophagus
would go into spasm, clamping down on the esophagoscope.
When suggestions eliciting such emotions as enthusiasm, contentment, and happiness were presented, the spasm relaxed,
and the inside diameter of the esophagus widened immediately.

Faulkner used the same technique to examine the windpipe, the hollow muscular tubes leading from the throat to
the lungs. These tubes went into spasm or relaxed as the result
of emotional suggestion. Doesn't this remind you of the man
who was "allergic" to roses?

Like the esophagus, the tubes leading from the windpipe to
the lungs are also muscular. They are your bronchi. How often
have you seen children gasp in fear or amazement? As a matter of fact, just such a gasp constitutes your salutation to life.
Draw in a deep quick breath and hold it (produce a spasm of
the bronchi). If this reaction were to become a regular, unconscious habit, you would have asthma. I know that spasm of the
bronchi has been "explained" by the unexplained word,
allergy. Some people acquire an habitual physical response to
certain substances—or situations—which causes their organs
to behave abnormally. These substances—or situations—become their poisons, which produce bronchial spasm. The victim cannot relax his lungs to exhale normally. I have seen
many cases of asthma, including the gentleman who was sensitive to roses, where the allergy was social. Treated unsuccess-
fully for the allergic asthma of pollens and other substances,
these cases cleared up in a few months under psychotherapy.

However, habitual spasm of the bronchi, continued over a
period of time, can produce serious changes in the lungs. The
air chambers are stretched; the tissue between the air cham-

bers becomes scarred and thickened. The lungs become susceptible to infection. A disease of the interbrain can permanently damage the lungs.

3

Emotional tensions can strain your muscles to produce symptoms such as backache. I discovered this in my early days of medical practice, when I was called to treat a patient for pain at the base of the skull. X rays showed no arthritis. He did not have diabetes. His tonsils were blameless. His dentist assured me that his teeth were perfect. Still, he had his pain, so I gave him diathermy treatments for a tentative diagnosis of muscle strain.

While he was taking his treatments, we became better acquainted. He had a good job, was married, and his wife's brother was living at his house. Something about the way he wrinkled his nose led me to ask, "What's the matter with your brother-in-law?"

"I feel like a heel for talking about him," my patient said. "He's a goodhearted guy. He's been wonderful to my wife, but I can't call my soul my own when he's around. He tells me how much to spend on groceries, how to bring up my boy—how to arrange the furniture. Gee, I feel like a boarder in my own home. He's helped us out a lot, and I shouldn't be talking this way about him. I feel sorry for him, in a way, too. Still and all, to me he's just a pain in the neck."

A pain in the neck! That undiagnosed pain at the base of the skull! I called up his wife, and when she came to my office, I told her that if she wanted a healthy husband, she would get another home for her brother.

On his next visit, my patient looked like a new man. "That last treatment sure fixed me up," he said, "That pain in the neck is gone." Certainly—to a new boardinghouse.

Since then, I have paid closer attention to the words my patients use in describing their symptoms. Not all heartaches are angina pectoris: some may be caused by a wayward son. Cold feet may be symptomatic of some disease of the arteries: they may be an expression of habitual fear. When a young typist told me that "everything makes me sick to my stomach," I found that she had no gastric ulcer, no gall-bladder disease, but disgust for her mother, who had not (according to my patient) been faithful to the girl's father. And while there are many causes of head pain, a ledger with red ink is often the headache of which the businessman complains.

Yes, emotional strains produce physical symptoms, some of which develop into permanent tissue change difficult to cure. Let us get back to muscle soreness as a symptom of interbrain disturbance. How can fear or hate produce a backache? And how can nervous strain lead to permanent changes in the muscle tissues?

You know that emotion is behavior, something that you do with your entire body. Tensing your muscles is a part of emotional behavior. Muscle tension is really the common denominator of emotion. Dr. Edmund Jacobson, of the University of Chicago, says that you cannot feel an emotion when your muscles are completely relaxed, and he is one hundred per cent right.

When a muscle contracts, it shortens. This automatically shortens the connective-tissue membrane that covers the muscle like an elastic stocking. This connective tissue (it's what makes meat tough) is called fascia. Examine it the next time you carve a roast. It's interesting, if not tasty. When fascia is excessively thick and short, the condition of the patient is called muscle-bound. Habitual muscle tension eventually produces permanent fascial shortening and thickening.

Fascia has some stretch to it, but not much. Stretch the

fascia of the muscles of your back suddenly, and it tears, giving you lumbago, or low back pain. A surprisingly large amount of low back pain results from fascial shortening. Investigating such cases, I have found that a goodly percentage comes from postural defects associated with the habitual expression of emotional attitudes.

The actor's art demonstrates how each fear or sorrow has its own group of muscle tensions or postures. The body gradually takes on the shape of one's habitual emotional tensions. Then fascia that gives muscles their external support becomes the stiff frame that limits motion. Thickened, shortened fascia can produce painful and disabling low back pain.

When the fascia is gradually stretched by medically directed exercises carefully selected and graded individually for each patient, and when the emotional attitudes and postures are corrected, such backaches usually disappear.

Of course, all low back pain is not the result of fascial shortening. Lumbago may be caused by a number of conditions, including flat feet, arthritis, or an abscessed tooth. On the other hand, as Dr. Frank Ober of Boston has shown, fascial shortening can give rise not only to low back pain, but also to sciatic neuralgia, by putting tension on the nerve where it emerges between the stiffened fascia and muscle. In this case, the overgrown shortened fascia acts like scar tissue, squeezing the sciatic nerve. Ingeniously devised, Dr. Ober's exercises often stretch the fascia, freeing the nerve from pressure. When this fails, his simple operation lengthens the fascia, ending nerve pain at once.

Pain between the shoulders and along the ribs often results from muscle tensions and shortening of the fascia. These muscle tensions often occur during sleep, the very time when a person should be most relaxed. Emotional habit patterns under partial control during waking life are given full rein during sleep. Then muscles go into a kind of spasm, so that instead of waking up rested, the sufferer from interbrain troubles wakes tired and muscle-sore. A hot bath and a good massage may give temporary relief; but cure comes from dissipation of the emotional behavior patterns that make the muscles habitually tense.

Wry neck, or torticollis, is a peculiar condition in which a patient's head is rotated so that he looks only to one side and cannot turn his head to face forward. This condition may be caused by irritation of the eleventh cranial nerve. It also may be psychogenic. The following case demonstrates the way in which emotional tensions create more organic pathology.

My wry-neck patient had been a bookkeeper. He got the idea that his employer suspected him of stealing. He became ill, had to quit his job, and wry neck developed. He said the condition began while he was on the job. He kept looking over his right shoulder, could not turn his head straight.

Under treatment he developed enough insight to realize that his wry neck was an attitude of fear. He looked over his right shoulder continuously to see whether he was being watched. But why should he fear detection, or even suspicion? Because he wanted to steal but didn't dare. He was one of the wicked who flee when no man pursueth. Here was his collision of behavior patterns, the conflict between honesty and dishonesty, the desire to steal and fear of detection. Out of it came the thought that he was being watched. He wanted to be watched, to protect himself against his own errant impulses. His wish fathered the thought, and brought wry neck as the policeman.

But after he had developed insight and after his desire to steal had been cured by psychotherapy, the wry neck continued. The muscles that rotate the head had shortened. The guy ropes were uneven. To stretch them back to normal was another job. Psychogenic disease had become structuralized—as it had been symbolized—in his shortened neck muscles.

4

In the free-for-all battle between conflicting emotions, the body, innocent bystander, gets it in the neck, in the small of the back, between the shoulder blades, and even in the heart. At Cedars of Lebanon Hospital in Los Angeles, I heard a great cardiologist say that high blood pressure is a disease of civilization. The mechanism involved is simple. Everyone has seen the face of a friend go white with fear or with excitement. What has happened? Simply this. The blood vessels in the face are muscular tubes. With fear, these muscles contract, squeezing the inside diameter of these tubes down to almost nothing. The result—no blood in the skin of the face. If the same process takes place in an organ containing many blood vessels, the flow of blood from the heart is impeded; it has to pump faster and harder to force the blood through these vessels suddenly grown smaller. The result is heightened blood pressure.

I have seen blood pressure rise fifty points just from excitement. I have taken blood pressures before and after relaxation, and have demonstrated a fall from 160 to 120 points after twenty minutes of controlled rest.

The tissues, the cells of muscles and glands, are nourished by food brought to them by the blood. Blood is the body's transportation system, whereby chemical substances are brought to cells that need them, and whereby waste products of these cells are carried away to those parts of the body where they can be eliminated. Every organ in the body has its own blood supply, including the heart.

When the blood vessels of the heart go into spasm, a pain results that we call angina pectoris. This heart pain is very common in nervous conditions. Such expressions as "heart-ache" attest to the frequency of this trouble.

If the disease stopped with the pain, this might not be so serious. Unfortunately, this does not appear to be the case. From spasm of the vessels which can be cured to irreversible heart disease is only a matter of time. It is no coincidence that so many surgeons who work day after day under conditions of intolerable strain should die of heart disease. Their profession is literally heart-breaking, and coronary sclerosis (hardening of the arteries of the heart) seems to be their occupational disease.

Yet this need not be so. Many surgeons pass through one tense situation after another with no special wear and tear on the heart. These men have learned to control their emotions, to operate with brain and hands, and not with their blood vessels and intestines. They put into their work all of their hearts—except the heart muscles.

Spasm of the blood vessels, as a result of emotional stress, can produce strange results. One of these is called Reynaud's disease, in which a finger or a hand or a foot becomes white, cold, and numb. In some cases, the condition is so severe that all blood stops flowing through the arteries; the tissues get no nutrition; and as a result they starve to death in a condition called dry gangrene.

In similar cases, the skin may become so thickened that the patient is unable to bend his fingers or close his hand. This is called scleraderma. There are many other skin conditions that are nervous in origin, but I mention only two that are caused by a neurotic spasm of the blood vessels.

5

We used to think that sickness caused unhappiness. Now we are finding that unhappiness is the cause of sickness—even those diseases associated with specific germs. Dr. Arlie V. Bock, in a study of 1667 Harvard students who were treated for colds or for grippe, stated that ". . . the role played by the tension of living must be recognized more generally in our assault on the problem." Every specialist in diseases of the nose has recognized nasal neurosis, a condition in which the eyes water and the mucous membranes of the nose secrete fluid, become swollen and inflamed, as a result of emotional upset. This sets the stage for an invasion by germs that would be repelled by healthy tissues.

A ten-year-old girl, an only child, had been treated in a clinic for weeks for inflammation of the eyes. When I examined these eyes, there were only a few red veins on that transparent film that is called the conjunctiva. Then I examined her throat. Her tonsils were greatly enlarged, infected, and her adenoids almost prevented her breathing through her nose. I suggested that she have her tonsils and adenoids removed. She started to cry. Almost instantly, the veins in her eyes became so red that hardly any of the white part could be seen. "Look," her mother cried. "That's the trouble I was talking about." Her conjunctivitis was a vascular neurosis, a condition brought on by fear. If it becomes chronic, she will have scar tissue in the conjunctiva, a condition that eye doctors call a pterygium, that can be helped only by surgery. This is just another instance to show how a vascular neurosis may lead to the formation of scar tissue—how nervousness may perpetuate itself in changed body tissues.

A sick mind does not let the body do its work properly. It causes changes which can become permanent and serious. Neglect of attention to emotional factors as a cause of disease will result in failure to prevent them in time.

The symptoms of interbrain misbehavior are symptoms of bodily disfunction. They are the same symptoms as those produced by germs and accidental injuries. A pain between the shoulder blades may be caused by tuberculosis or by pleurisy, a knife stab or an uneasy conscience. Weakness, loss of appetite, excessive fatigability, loss of weight, and low blood pressure are symptoms of interbrain misbehavior. But these symptoms are not inconsistent with the disease that we call diabetes, nor with tuberculosis of the adrenal glands (Addison's disease), nor with cancer. Often abdominal symptoms have led to "exploratory" operations with the resultant removal of an inoffensive appendix or ovary.

This is the time to give a very important warning. Because nervous troubles give rise to exactly the same aches and pains and discomforts that are caused by other diseases, no patient should consult anyone except a medically trained doctor, experienced in diagnosis. The patient may think that he is "just nervous," go to a consulting psychologist for treatment, and all the while be suffering from a toxic goiter or diabetes.

A psychiatrist is first of all a medically trained doctor. He is presumably, a competent diagnostician. In addition, he has special training in psychology and the other mental sciences. But his knowledge and his experience are not limited to just these branches of biology. He understands the architecture of the body in minutest detail, and the way it works in health and in disease. A psychiatrist always makes sure that his patient is not suffering from some disease of the stomach or heart or lungs before he thinks of treating the mental troubles. Sometimes he helps his patient's mental condition by improving first the general health of his patient.

A young woman suffering from a nervous breakdown was so run-down physically that mental therapy could not be considered. She was given rest, diet was prescribed, and insulin was administered to improve her appetite. Under this regimen she put on weight, felt stronger, and her entire mental attitude changed in the course of only a few weeks. Building up her body was the foundation for treating her sick interbrain. The approach to health may be along many different converging routes. Its direction should be left only to one trained along general medical lines, and not to a "psychologist" who lacks the necessary knowledge. If a psychologist wants to practice medicine, and there is room in medicine for many such, let him first study medicine or work under medical direction. Playing doctor is a dangerous pastime.

6

Among doctors there is a growing tendency to realize and to accept the part that mental sciences play in the treatment of disease. The old bromide that some diseases are "organic" while others are "functional" is fast dissolving. There is no dividing line between the mental and physical. The body, acting as a unit in any situation, is an organism; any disease or condition affecting that organism is organic. Because the physical changes and the chemical changes in the body that affect a person's thinking cannot always be demonstrated under a microscope or within a test tube does not prove their absence. Perhaps the microscope is not sufficiently powerful, nor the chemical test sufficiently delicate.

Modern doctors take the same scientific interest in the personalities of their patients that they take in blood counts and urinalyses. When the scientific doctor can find no cause for aching muscles, he will not prescribe aspirin. Many intelligent patients do not want to disguise their symptoms by taking aspirin. They want a straight answer to their questions. They want to know the cause of their aching muscles, and they want treatment of the cause. It is granted that physiology of the nervous system is a new field in medicine, and it is granted that there are many unanswered questions in this science. But the one thing that once prevented doctors from using available knowledge was their attitude—an unscientific attitude, and a hangover from primitive demonology—that the mind is somehow separate from the body. Today, few doctors talk about "diseased imagination" when they should be thinking in terms of a disordered brain.

The function of the nervous system is adjustment. Through our nerves we acquire awareness of our environment, and through our nerves we adjust to our environment. We see fire and we back away. We see food and move to the table. We can call this activity external adjustment. But our nerves do more than this. Through the functioning of the nervous system, the activities within the body are co-ordinated. When we exercise strenuously, heart rate and rate of breathing are speeded up, adjusted to the tissues' increased need for oxygen. We call this activity internal adjustment. In health, external and internal adjustment work together, and the activities of the body and mind are integrated. The healthy man is at peace with himself and with his environment.

The interbrain regulates internal adjustment. It regulates the stability of the delicate chemical balances within the blood; the force and rhythm of the heartbeat; the flow of blood through the arteries; the emptying of the stomach; the secretions of the glands of the body. Misbehavior of nerves in the interbrain gums up internal adjustment, interferes with external adjustment, and creates physical disorders among the other organs of the body. Much physical disease has its basis in the way the nerve cells of the interbrain work, when they work the wrong way. Mental troubles make you sick, literally. That is because mental trouble, in itself, is a physical disease, brought on by collision between opposing types of organ behavior, or, as we said previously, by collision between conflicting emotions.

The brain is an organ, an organ of adjustment. Its functioning affects the function and structure of all of the rest of the body. When it works well, your other organs get better than an even break. When it ceases to function properly, the rest of the body is out of luck. To enjoy good health, you must first get right with your interbrain.

CHAPTER FOUR

And the Body Talks Back

1

IF NERVOUSNESS IS a physical disease located in the interbrain, why do we call it a mental disease? Why is the sufferer told it is "just imagination," to go home and forget it? To call a condition "functional" is much easier than effecting a cure but, from the patient's point of view, somewhat less than satisfactory.

Old Grandpa Oakroot did not use his legs for twelve weeks. The wasting away of his muscles was functional. His jovial doctor told him so. "Nothing wrong with your muscles that a little exercise won't cure," he had said. "It's purely functional." But he didn't call Grandpa's trouble "just imagination." How could his muscles function with his broken leg in a plaster cast?

But if instead of a broken leg his heart had been broken, and if the interbrain had caused an hysterical paralysis resulting in atrophy; if, in other words, his leg had been imprisoned within the pale cast of an obsessive thought, who would have given him a pipe and a bottle of old brandy on Father's Day? "I have no patience with him," Aunt Amanda would have said. "You can't tell me that it's not all in the mind."

Now Aunt Amanda is nobody's fool, as she often admits. She has been around, she has kept her eyes open. "It's all in the mind" is her answer for all unhappiness. She never learned that when the little gray cells are not working right, thoughts

63

and ideas come out all askew. She and millions of other Aunt Amandas don't consider the little gray cells functioning behind those thoughts and feelings. We know that without those little gray cells there could be no thoughts and feelings. All she knows is that when people are nervous, they don't think right. It is our present job to find out just how and why a disordered interbrain produces disordered thinking.

It is most important for us to do this. So far, the nervous sufferer has been able to find some relief in the assurance that his symptoms, shared by many others, are not caused by local disease in those parts of the body where they are felt. It's a relief for him to know that that difficulty of swallowing and of getting one's breath are caused only by muscle spasm resulting from interbrain misbehavior. That relief, alone, is a step toward cure. The victim can discount his present suffering against hope for the future. He is freed of one more unknown terror taken out of the realm of fearsome darkness.

It is time now for him to relieve his mind of dread of frightening mental symptoms. It is time now for him to learn that his depressions, his obsessive ideas and morbid compulsions, his terrifying fears, are only the reactions of his body when it does not work properly and starts talking back.

For here, again, the aquisition of knowledge about oneself is the beginning of treatment and of cure. We use "important" again to underline the idea that we must know when to discount our morbid thoughts and feelings against the knowledge that they are produced by organs that are misbehaving, playing badly conceived practical tricks on us. When we are aware of this fact, and understand the process, we can bear our own thoughts, however unhappy, with the same resignation that we stand up under temporary physical pain, consoling ourselves with the truth, "This, too, shall pass."

And here is the place to solicit the help of Aunt Amanda.

Her reaction to the nervous sufferer can be of great assistance in a more rapid cure. She must learn to recognize that hysterical paralysis and all other mental disease are physical in origin. She must learn to control her own intolerant behavior with reference to the annoying physical and mental behavior of the trying but sorely tried sufferer.

I know that it is no joke to have to live with a neurotic. When a man comes home after a hard day's work to find that his wife has not lifted a hand to clean the house or to prepare the meals, he can hardly be blamed for growling. And when she explains that she has been unable to move because she is worried about what the neighbors think of her, it is natural for him to retort, *"Aw,* that's all in your mind. If you'd quit thinking about yourself so much and do something worth while, you wouldn't have such screwy ideas." Natural, but not helpful. If he wants to help his wife to get well, his first job is to attempt to understand the condition that he wants cured.

That the body talks to the mind, puts thoughts in our heads, is not altogether a new and revolutionary idea. What every woman knows includes this item, that a full stomach makes a man more amiable; and this item, too—that a pair of silk stockings helps springtime to turn a young man's fancy. We all know that an empty stomach has but little conscience. Muscles, when tense and quivering, will not be silenced. We may not always know from what part of the body we are hearing when the words pour forth; but we are safe in saying that at least seven eighths of our thinking consists of rationalization of organ needs and desires. The mind does the dancing while the body pulls the strings.

Keep this fact in mind the next time you feel that you are going to lose your temper, and you will keep your mouth shut and your fists in your pockets. When your anger has cooled, you will be able to pride yourself upon your self-control, upon your triumph of reason over brute impulse. Never forget that anger is an emotion, a way of physical activity. When you surrender to emotion, you are permitting the organs of your body to dictate to only a portion of your brain, while holding the rest of your brain a gagged prisoner. When emotion rules, the body controls the mind. When the entire brain works as a unit, mind controls matter and reason prevails. So does comfort.

2

Emotion is hypnotic. Emotion prevents one from thinking clearly, from seeing sharply, from hearing acutely. It makes one blind, deaf, and dumb. It paralyzes activity that is just under your hand, keeps you from doing what you really want to do, and makes you do things that you would not do, if you were in full possession of all of your faculties. How emotion can cut one off from even physical sensation is demonstrated by a football player who went through half a game with broken ribs, entirely unaware of the pain. Under emotional stress he enjoyed what amounts to hypnotic anesthesia that blocked his awareness of severe physical suffering.

Consider a typical teen-ager, madly in love with some girl friend. He says that he is just crazy about her. His friends nod glumly, and mutter, "That's right. You're hipped." They know that it is useless to reason with Harold. They know that Harold's entire organism, physical, mental, emotional, craves certain satisfactions. They realize that Harold's intense emotion is really a selfish preoccupation with his own self, hypnotizing him into unreasoning ideas about the girl and himself that have no basis in reality.

Should they tell him that the girl of his dreams is a lazy, self-centered, inefficient fathead? That she permits her mother to

clean up her room and wash her soiled clothes? That she cannot spend five dollars without wasting three? That she cannot
hold friends? Or a job? Or an intelligent conversation? No
use, no use. Harold's emotion has so hypnotized him that he
is blind to any fact that interferes with the satisfaction of his
emotions. He is anesthetic to sound, sight, or idea that does
not fit in with his preoccupation. He's hipped.

If love is blind, rage is entirely out of contact with environment. Even our courts, and I say "even" because the law
is conservative in taking cognizance of such matters, even the
courts recognize "temporary insanity" as a defense against
prosecution of crimes committed under certain circumstances
that might make a fellow very angry. Oddly enough, the
courts make no allowances when interbrain diseases affect behavior in such a way as to produce an irresistible compulsion
to steal (kleptomania). Perhaps when the victim is caught in
flagrante delicto, the law looks at homicide through the fingers
and uses "temporary insanity" as an easy out.

But this is beside the point. The point is that even simple,
uncomplicated emotion limits the field of perception, warps
the judgment, and stimulates one pattern of action while inhibiting or blocking all other reactions. Emotions hypnotize.

The payoff is double when conflicting emotional habit patterns finally bring about a breakdown of interbrain function.
You see this most clearly in cases of hysteria. The lips and
mouth of one of my patients are numb. You can stick a pin in
her lips; she feels no pain. The nerve endings that give rise to
a feeling of pain are stimulated; the impulse goes up the
spinal cord to the interbrain; but between the interbrain
and the forebrain there is a blockage that prevents her becoming aware of the pin prick. This case is the analogue of
the one of the football player who was not aware of his broken
ribs. It is the analogue of the hypnotic subject who reacts

posthypnotically to the suggestion that he will be anesthetic to pain.

Another hysterical patient feels pain when the nerves carrying painful impulses are *not* stimulated. She suffers from a burning sensation in her right foot. I give her a hypodermic injection, and for a time she experiences relief. The injection is sterile water. Was the pain "imaginary"? Not to her. Although it arose from stimulation of nerve cells in her brain and not from stimulation of nerve endings in her foot, the pain was real. To cure her, one must treat the nerve cells in the brain so that they will not give rise to the feeling of pain in the toe. One must treat the interbrain, put an end to the conflicting emotional habit patterns that underlie her condition.

A third patient has a paralysis of the hand. An orthopedic surgeon is called in. He hopefully X-rays the neck, sadly admits that there is no cervical rib to operate. He finally suggests that a neurologist be called in consultation. After a very careful checkup, the neurologist reports that the great nerve trunks from the neck to the finger tips appear to be normal. Still the patient cannot open her hand. A psychiatrist puts her into a hypnotic sleep, says, "Open your hand." Her hand opens wide, like a flower.

Was she faking her paralysis? Does a canary fake a paralysis when a snake waves its head back and forth until the poor bird is stiff with fear? Have you ever been scared stiff so that you were unable to move a muscle? Were you faking a paralysis?

Interbrain misbehavior can send impulses to the motor centers of your brain in such a way as to cause the nerve cells of the motor centers to block or inhibit all muscular movement. That is the meaning of hysterical paralysis. This same interbrain can also send impulses to the motor centers causing them to make muscles twitch or even jerk. We call such twitchings and jerkings a nervous tic or a choreaform movement.

Add these four cases together, and you can sum them up in a single sentence. Nervousness can stimulate or inhibit the awareness of sensation, can stimulate or paralyze muscular activities.

It can make you forget your name and anything connected with your identification. Or it can make you forget the name of the banker to whom you owe money. It can make you stammer or stutter. It can paralyze your creative activities. Worse than anything else, it can control your thinking. Interbrain misbehavior is hypnotic.

A designer of railway equipment suffered from an anxiety neurosis. To avoid going to work, he took his wife on a short trip to show her a car that he had designed. As the train pulled out of the station, all of his symptoms bubbled up within him. The slick, streamlined design for travel—his brain child—suddenly became his sign for travail. All of his nausea, shortness of breath, chilliness, and pain under the left ribs suddenly flooded down on him.

He wished that he had never started on the trip. He wondered whether the conductor would stop the train if he explained that he felt sick. He was sick, he reasoned; they ought to let him get off whenever he felt like getting off. Leaving that train became an obsession. He felt that he would have to jump off if he couldn't get out in any other way. He became terrified at the thought that he might have to jump from the moving train. He knew that his forehead was beaded with sweat; he felt that other passengers were staring at him. Because he realized that he could not control his thinking, he was sure that he was going crazy.

Your body dictates to your mind, and this dictation is essentially an hypnotic process. We see this work out in all forms of obsessions and in all forms of inhibitions. We see, for instance, people who cannot get a certain tune out of their heads. We see people who have to work out some problem in arithmetic before they can go to sleep. We see people who cannot stay in a room where the windows are closed. Or open. There are millions of ways in which the sick interbrain dictates to the forebrain. And because you have to use your head in order to straighten out your life, it is essential for you to learn what hypnotism really is.

3

The spontaneous, partial hypnotism induced by interbrain misbehavior resembles in many respects the more spectacular artificial hypnotism involving hypnotist and subject. Artificial hypnotism is a state that is much like natural sleep. Like sleep, this state is induced by suggestion. So before considering artificial hypnotism, let us think about its cousin, natural sleep.

At night when you go to bed, your suggestion of sleep comes from the room itself; from the bed and its covers; from your habits of undressing, preparing for bed, and from all of your previously acquired habit patterns related to going to sleep. Fatigue, of course, when not excessive, predisposes toward sleep. The waste products of fatigue are suggestions carried by the blood to stimulate the sleep centers in the brain. In addition to these ordinary suggestions, some people give themselves special suggestions, such as a peculiar arrrangement of pillows or some individualized posture, in order to induce sleep. Some people recite prayers or verses. One of my patients used to recite the multiplication table. Conditions conducive to sleep include a reasonable degree of comfort, absence of exciting and stimulating suggestions, and various suggestions putting one in the frame of mind for sleep. Monotony and expectation of sleep are the usual soporifics.

In artificial hypnotism, the conditions are about the same. The subject is placed in a comfortable position. Except for a light which the hypnotist shines in the subject's eyes, all stimuli are excluded. The light tires the subject's eyes, and helps to exclude other sensations. Meanwhile, the hypnotist suggests sleep by saying, "Going to sleep, going to sleep. Eyelids getting heavy, going to sleep." And if the subject is willing, he goes to sleep.

While asleep, the hypnotist may make a suggestion to be carried out at some future time when the subject is awake. This is called a posthypnotic suggestion. He may say, for example, "When the clock strikes four, you will take an umbrella, go to the store for cigarettes." After the subject wakes up, he may glance at the clock and, sharply on the stroke of four, pick up an umbrella, start for the store for cigarettes. If asked why he takes an umbrella, he may smile sheepishly and explain, "One never knows when it is going to rain." He can't tell you the real reason for taking the umbrella because he cannot remember the suggestion. The intention to take it exists, but below the level of his conscious memory. So he invents a good reason to explain his compulsion.

Suppose the subject were an alcoholic, and the hypnotist had suggested that upon awaking, he would no longer desire to drink. Would this cure the alcoholic of his habit? I am sorry to report that it would not. Suggestion is effective only when no contrary suggestion is present. As sure as morning comes, the old craving reasserts itself. The stomach churns while the nerves quiver. This acts as a powerful suggestion, and out of the conflict between the verbal and physical suggestions, the old bottle scores another victory. "I'm not really going to drink," the alcoholic says. "I'll just have one or two to quiet my nerves."

Artificial hypnotism is a state of abnormal inhibition of ordinary suggestions. This state makes the suggestions given by the hypnotist more effective because they are not contradicted. So if the hynotist tells the subject that his arm is paralyzed, the subject will not be able to move that arm. He may say that the subject can feel no pain in the lips, and the lips will become anesthetic to pin pricks. Temporary absence of the ability of the entire brain to control and to organize behavior produces the abnormal suggestibility of hypnotism.

Here is one way of understanding how hypnotism works. Think of the forebrain as a checkerboard. The green squares will represent nerve cells whose impulses stimulate muscles to contract. The red squares will represent nerve cells whose impulses prevent or inhibit the contraction of muscles. Red says "stop" and green says "go." We will call the red squares the inhibitory nerve centers, and the green squares the nerve centers of stimulation. The inhibitory nerve centers actively block sensation, muscular activity, and thought. The stimulatory nerve centers, when activated, cause muscle contractions, or give rise to awareness of sensations.

An hypnotic state is reached when one center of inhibition after another is activated, until nearly all centers of stimulation are blocked out. Impulse spreads from one center of inhibition to another, until practically the entire forebrain is covered as by a net. Inhibitory impulses also spread downward, preventing sensations from reaching the forebrain. In this way, suggestions that might activate the centers of stimulation are shut out. A part of the mind is put out of commission. As the subject of hypnotism would say, he is not himself; he is not all there. This, for the time being, is true.

Temporary absence of the ability of the entire brain to con-

trol and to organize behavior produces the abnormal thinking of nervous disease. Indeed, this partial loss of function of
the brain explains the silly and irrational things that we do
under the grip of any strong emotion. Misdirected organ activity, emotion, paralyzes a portion of our brain cells, im-
mobilizes them, holds them inactive prisoners, preventing
the entire brain from working as an organ of adjustment. In
emotional states, we are in a trance: an hypnotic trance.

When conflicting emotional habit patterns throw the interbrain into an uproar, the state is no longer temporary. Then
thinking is controlled by various organs fighting among themselves in a state of anarchic civil war. Emotional conflict puts
one into a state of chronic partial hypnosis, where he is no
longer in control of his thoughts.

4

The physiology of sleep is much like the hypnotic mechanism, for sleep, like the hypnotic trance, is induced by activa-
tion of the nerve centers of inhibition. These centers are activated partly by monotony, which does not excite the centers
of stimulation. In sleep, as in hypnotism, impulses spread over
the forebrain from one center of inhibition to another, and
downward to the sleep centers in the interbrain, and sleep
results.

When little Willie Periwinkle sits in church on a warm
Sunday morning, the heat, the forced inactivity, and the droning of a monotonous voice vocalizing incomprehensible words
activate one inhibitory center after another in little Willie's
forebrain. These impulses spread across his brain, until the
droning voice becomes as a distant beating of the surf. The
various colors of church decorations and what the well-dressed
churchwoman is wearing become a confused mixture of pastel
shades without shape or meaning. Even the hardwood bench

on which little Willie was squirming becomes softer as his muscles relax. From inhibition center to inhibition center the impulses spread, until little Willie sleeps the sleep of the just bored.

The depth of sleep depends upon the amount of inhibitory impulse to the interbrain. For here is located the sleep center. Certain disease processes can stir up this center to produce pathological sleep. Animal experimenters have devised delicate electrical instruments to activate the sleep center, putting their experimental animals to sleep very quickly. Probably this is the center attacked by hypnotic drugs of the barbital series. At any rate, when sleep comes, further impulses go out from the interbrain to the heart, causing it to beat more slowly; to the lungs, causing one to breathe more quietly. Thus, fewer stimulations come from the viscera to interfere with sleep, which progressively becomes deeper.

Dr. Paul Schilder, in his book on hypnosis, states that there is no doubt that the facts of hypnosis can be explained only with the aid of the psychology of sleep. This explanation has been offered by Dr. P. De Rabinovich in essentially the way that it has been presented here. The nerves that cause sleep are the ones that produce the hypnotic state, artificial or spontaneous. Sleep, hypnotism, and emotional blocking of thought are all evidences of busy little inhibitory nerve cells.

5

It was twinkly-eyed Ivan Petrovich Pavlov, of the bald head, Santa Claus beard and mustache, who pointed out the relationships between nervous states and hypnotism. In so doing, he took psychiatry out of the hazy realm of speculation, to bring this specialty under the roof of scientific anatomy and physiology. For this, all doctors and millions of sufferers from nervous diseases owe him an undying debt of gratitude. He showed that mental symptoms are not "imaginary," but are caused by sick nerves. Now when we treat mental diseases, we know what part of the nervous system is not working properly, and we know what to do in order to restore these nerves to a normal condition. *Pavlov demonstrated that to cure sick nerves, the patient must be dehypnotized.*

A young woman who had been supporting her mother found herself getting more and more nervous until she at last was unable to go to work. People, she said, were talking about her. They pointed at her when she walked down the street. Other girls in her office were whispering that she was carrying on an affair with the good-looking bookkeeper. "It wouldn't be so bad if it were true," she told me. "But I never even went out with him: not to so much as a movie."

It was useless to point out that no one took the bleakest interest in her goings and comings, her getting up and her lying down. When told that other people are too immersed in their own problems to bother with her affairs, she smiled knowingly. "They know," she would repeat cryptically. "They know."

For fear of meeting these whispering people, she contracted her range of interests and activities, until finally she remained in bed twenty-four hours a day. She lost all interest in life. Although previously she had been more than fastidious about her person, she now refused to bathe or comb her hair. "Why should I bother?" she would ask. "I don't want to see anybody. Go away. Let me be.'

Her mother and other relatives supplied the facts which, when pieced together, showed the collision between her emotional habit patterns. She had been brought up in the belief that the fear of sex is the beginning of morality. No one, she believed, would ever marry a girl who had departed from sexual abstinence. Nevertheless, she had had an affair with a young man who forgot to legalize the proceedings. When this broke up, her mind was in a turmoil. Still later, she met the bookkeeper where she was working, and played around with the idea of going out with him. If she did go on a date, should she tell him about her previous experience? If she didn't tell him and married him, what would he do if he should find out? Her conflicting emotions over the entire situation (and remember that emotion is the way the entire body behaves) went into a free-for-all, knock-down and drag-out battle.

Despite that the situation was entirely conjectural, the interbrain went into a tailspin. It sent abnormal messages to all parts of her body and to her forebrain. In the forebrain were the centers of inhibition and the centers of stimulation, both being bombarded with contradictory impulses. The stimulatory center said, "Take the bull by the horns, tell him." The inhibitory centers cried, "Lie low. Hide." From stimulation centers, "I wish I could marry him." From the inhibition centers, "It's no use. So what? Nothing's any use."

From the wish for honesty and the wish for concealment finally comes the rationalization, "Everybody knows. There isn't anything for me to do but hide out, take my medicine."

So impulses spread from one center of inhibition to another, partially hypnotizing her into mental paralysis, and shutting out all suggestions that would allow her to deal with her problems realistically. The suggestions that had produced this partial hypnosis had come not from her environment but from her disordered interbrain and from her emotionally churned-up viscera. The lower centers of organic adjustment had taken control of the higher. The body was dictating to the mind.

How did it all turn out? Sanitarium, metrazol shock therapy, a return to a semblance of rationality, psychotherapy, and cure. She was dehypnotized. Let's turn to the next case.

Her parents left fourteen-year-old Gertrude sitting in my waiting room with a magazine while they explained to me how she was driving them frantic. Her disobedience was carried to a limit beyond what they considered the borders of sanity.

They had a hard time making her get up in the morning. Once up, she would dawdle over her dressing, while she listened to the radio or monkeyed with articles on her dresser or her writing desk. She had no friends. When guests visited, she became surly and would not speak to them. Often she would run out of the house to avoid them. You couldn't get her to answer the telephone or to help around the house. When she talked—here her father imitated, "I . . . uh . . . was thinking . . . uh . . . I . . . uh . . . was going to say . . . uh . . . that . . . uh . . . I don't want to eat right now."

The girl's account of her life was fantastic in its lack of realism. All of the kids at school were dopes. None of them ever wanted to do anything. She never co-operated in doing anything around the house because if she did, people would expect her to continue to do the housework regularly, and considering her allowance of a dollar a week, her work would be paid for at a rate of ten cents an hour; so it wasn't worth while to help her father with the garden or mother with the dishes. She could make more money doing housework for neighbors. Did she do housework for neighbors? No; she had to come home from school to study. Did she study when she got home? No; she was generally too tired.

Behind this picture of egotistical, resistive, spiteful negativism, there developed an interesting story. Her father worked for a company that had transferred him from place to place about once in three years. In her fourteen years, this girl had lived in five different cities. Each move meant the necessity for making new and painful adjustments to another school system, another group of friends, another neighborhood. Each move meant the breaking up of old ties, of satisfactory adjustments, to start all over again. No one likes to have all of one's activities blow up in one's face; least of all, a child with a limited technique of adjustment. After a while, even the most optimistic is likely to ask, "What's the use of starting all over again?"

Add to these discouragements a nagging mother, who demanded from her daughter a perfection that worrisome mamma would have difficulty in demonstrating in her own life. She had a habit of quizzing, scolding, kidding, and otherwise putting people on the defensive; getting the jump on the other fellow, she called it. It probably never occurred to her that getting the jump on her daughter was depriving the girl of a fair start. The most common cause of negativism in childhood is the aggressive competition of some bullying or otherwise offensive adult who feels no shame or compunction in pitting uneven strength and skill against the naïve and unresourceful techniques of a little child's defense.

So here was a girl whose most important life experiences consisted of failure after failure, disappointment after disappointment. Since she lacked habits and memories of face-flushing successes, her mother's attitude further developed her sense of inferiority. In her brain, one nerve center of inhibition after another was activated. These inhibitory impulses spread across the brain, weaving a net to trap every normal stimulatory impulse before it could get started. So she talked as if she had a cogwheel in her throat. Her walk somehow suggested that in the waistband of her skirt was an invisible hook attached to a ton of brick. All her ideas about herself and her world were dictated by the disordered behavior of her brain.

She was tied down by a partial self-hypnosis that deprived her of free and complete self-control.

In this stammering, confused, and frightened problem child, habit patterns of bodily behavior involving every part of her organism were putting up a steady bombardment of impulses against her interbrain. These impulses were activating the nerve centers of inhibition in her forebrain, causing a secondary limitation of freedom of thought and of action.

Her cure depended upon dehypnotization. But what is not so clearly understood is that this same process goes on to some extent all of the time in everyone. The fact is, the greatest volume of our thinking and doing is the result of suggestions that arise out of our habit patterns and of which we are for the most part completely unaware.

6

Did you ever think of how dynamic are your habit patterns? Of how they demand expression? How they are constantly sending a stream of suggestions to your brain, egging you on into some activities, restraining you from other activities, controlling your thinking? You don't think habits amount to much? Then consider the trivial and unimportant pattern of your smoking habits. Trivial and unimportant? Yes, in the general scheme of things in your life. But not to the man pawing over the ash tray to discover a sizable butt. There are times when a man will walk not one mile, but five, if necessary, to get a cigarette. I have seen the same mileage attached to a cup of coffee. The common impression is that habits, involuntary impulses, play a small part in the mental life of a mature, rational being. The uninformed stress the voluntary aspect of behavior. But among those who know psychology best, it is habits, two to one.

The older schools of psychology based their laws upon the method of introspection; their subjects looked into their souls and wrote. Naturally, some valid psychological material that dealt with voluntary thought and behavior was obtained in this way. But they overlooked the much more important facts of involuntary drives to activity, because our involuntary drives lie deep below the level of consciousness, hidden from the peering eyes of self-analysis. We have not the gift of seeing ourselves as others see us; nor has any mortal had the gift of seeing his brother as he really is. The subconscious mind, made up of the organization of habit patterns, is not open to easy inspection.

Sigmund Freud emphasized the importance of the subconscious in relation to nervous and mental troubles. What a hornets' nest of criticism fell upon his honest head! All of the nice professors, who in his day wore gray striped pants and shiny black cutaway coats and silk hats, but who nevertheless considered themselves to be highly rational human beings, screamed like frightened apes as they read his words.

The nice professors liked to think that all of their choices, all of their peculiar ways of life, were based upon Logic and Pure Reason. Animals, they thought and taught, were controlled by Instinct. Wicked people, they preached—and here the scattering of coeds would pull their dresses over their knees and blush—were dominated by their lower natures. But a rational man lived the life of sweetness and light, guided by Reason, Intelligence, and Will. Class dismissed.

The attitude of the nice professors may have been a rationalization, a kind of whistling in the dark, to pep up their moral courage, sapped by guerrilla attacks from the subconscious. Just so, you will find that the potential alcoholic is often the most ardent prohibitionist. He makes speeches directed chiefly at himself in the presence of an audience.

At college I knew a very moral young man who wrote letters to the dean of women, complaining that the coeds were constantly tempting him, trying to seduce him. He wrote letters to the papers, protesting against women wearing short dresses. He was a one-man purity league, who talked, read, thought about nothing except sex. He considered himself a very fine fellow, indeed, who spurned all use of four-letter words. But he fooled only himself and a few like-minded brothers-in-misery.

Criminals project their subconscious personalities into every prosecution reported in the newspapers. They want the defendant to beat the rap, not because they have an interest in the accused, but because subconsciously they have identified themselves with the man in the dock. Some of us habitually identify ourselves with the underdog. This underdog may be a volunteer on a radio quiz program who happens to be out of a job. Immediately, we hope that he will win the sixty-four-dollar prize. Why are we so concerned? Is this bias a sort of weakness of intellect, kindness of heart, or a rather tough worm of frustration inside the subconscious mind?

Remember the subject of artificial hypnotism who was given the posthypnotic suggestion to take an umbrella and go to the store for cigarettes? Remember how he explained the umbrella, "You never know when it is going to rain"? This manifestation of hypnotism—rationalization—is a large part of the thinking of all of us. It covers a lot of territory that was once labeled "conscious thinking." It includes those pleasant reveries that we call daydreams. Once you know the content of a person's daydreams, you begin to understand the most important part of his subconscious trends.

A Caspar Milquetoast dreams of catching the football on his own ten-yard line and running the length of the field for a touchdown while thousands cheer. Very funny. Not so funny is the thought of the never-ending sufferings of Caspar, when, as a spindling, thin-shanked, vitamin-starved boy, his classmates nicknamed him "Bird-legs."

We can sum up the whole thing by saying that conditioned reflexes or emotional habit patterns send wave after wave of suggestions to the interbrain and to the centers of inhibition and stimulation in the forebrain. Nerve impulses spread from one center of inhibition to another, producing a condition of partial hypnosis. This condition limits the activities of some nerve centers of stimulation, and puts other uninhibited nerve centers on hair-trigger edge, abnormally ready to receive and distribute impulses. The result is loss of physical and mental balance, self-control. It is the fact of partial self-hypnosis that makes nervousness a mental disease.

While members of the family resent the irritability and inconsistency of the patient who makes all sorts of unreasonable demands upon their thought and patience, the sufferer is confused, all muddled up. The tragic victim of his own emotional conflicts is terrified by the physical sensations produced by his nerves, and shrivels in despair when told that they are imaginary. His own attempts to understand himself are tripped up by his own hypnotic rationalizations. For these reasons, he needs an explanation of his troubles and a chart to follow that will bring him through the maze into which he has wandered.

Dr. Walter C. Alvarez, of the Mayo Clinic, says that one of his hardest jobs is to convince the patient with nervous indigestion that his stomach trouble is caused by storms that come out of the interbrain. Why is this a hard job? Because the patient is self-hypnotized by his nervous behavior and so is not open to reason. Emotions block thinking. Hot blood is more convincing than cold facts.

I do not ask my patients to believe anything. I give them the explanation and the chart. "Follow the chart," I tell them, "and in three months reread the explanation. When your nervous indigestion has subsided, when you no longer have the jitters, when you are dehypnotized, you can better judge the reasonableness of the explanation. To get well, to break this vicious circle of nervous and physical mental misbehavior, you must be dehypnotized."

The chart for dehypnotization is found in the next few chapters. You will need no compass to follow its course—only a will to reach your destination.

CHAPTER FIVE

Self-Directed
Relaxation: a Way Out

LET'S REVIEW our problem. We have a vicious circle. Emotional conflicts upset the proper functioning of the body, including the nervous system. The nervous system ceases to function properly, interferes with thinking that might set the nervous sufferer back upon the right road. Beset by a swarm of self-appointed amateur advisers, and torn by indecision, the victim of interbrain misbehavior does not know where to start in his quest to become normal.

In readjusting our lives so that we may live more abundantly, more freely, with greater energy and vigor, there is always this question of the first step. We must begin by learning the technique and habit patterns of muscular relaxation. This is always the first step to health. I cannot overemphasize its importance.

By following directions carefully, a reasonably intelligent adult can teach himself to relax in about ten weeks. The learner should provide himself with a quiet, darkened room with a bed, four small pillows,* and warm, light blankets. He should undress or loosen his clothing so that there are no constrictions to hamper his breathing. Then he should get into bed and arrange the pillows. (*See cut on opposite page.*)

* Publisher's Note: Any pillows will do, but if you would like information about suitable pillows especially designed to implement Dr. Fink's system of self-directed relaxation, write to Simon and Schuster, Inc., 630 Fifth Avenue, N. Y. 20, N. Y.

A good method of arranging the head pillow is to grasp both lower corners of the pillow and pull them over the shoulders. Thus the pillow is pulled under the neck, and the head rolls back toward the head of the bed. It is absolutely essential that the head and neck be perfectly comfortable before proceeding further. Any cramping of the neck will cause failure before you get started.

The next step is to place the second pillow under the knees, so that the knees are bent upward and outward at a slight angle. This takes the tension off the large muscles back of the thigh. If this is not done, these muscles will be under tension, whether you will it or not. The pillow support prevents too great a strain upon the knee joint (hyperextension of the leg, it is called, if you care, which, properly relaxed, you won't).

The knees should be bent, the legs spread so that the weight of the legs will be felt on the outside of the calf of the legs. Of course, the legs should not be crossed, as this only puts the burden of supporting one leg on the other, instead of on the bed, where the weight belongs.

The two other pillows are placed upon either side of the chest. Lay your arms upon them so that your elbows are about eight inches from your body. Then bend the elbows so that your wrists are close to your body. If these two arm pillows have been arranged properly, your hands will hang over the ends of the pillows, resting lightly upon them.

If you have followed these directions carefully, you are now in a position most conducive to learning to relax, and you are ready to begin. *Having achieved this position of minimum strain, do not change it at all while practicing.*

You start by beginning with the muscles you use for chewing. Let your jaw relax. This is just the opposite of biting hard, holding the teeth together. I have had people tell me that they were trying to relax, while clenching their jaws like bulldogs to prove their determination to do so. Let go of that grip upon nothing. Let your jaw sag.

Let your tongue relax so that it does not cleave to the roof of your mouth. I have seen patients whose tongues were sore and painful because they never let them relax. The proper position for your tongue is forward and downward with the tip of your tongue behind your lower teeth. But keep your lips lightly together. If you breathe with your mouth open, the mouth becomes dry and the discomfort and the necessity for moistening the lips is distracting. Some people put a little cold cream on their lips, but usually this is unnecessary.

Now close the eyes. Not hard. Just enough to let the eyelids come together. You do not squeeze the lids together. You let the eyelids drop together.

So there you are, lying on your back in bed, a pillow under your head and neck, but not under your shoulders; a pillow under your knees; your legs apart so that the weight of your legs falls on the outside of the calves of the legs; pillows under both arms, elbows eight or nine inches from the body; wrists almost touching the body, and the hands supported by the ends of the arm pillows. Your jaw is relaxed; your tongue is relaxed with the tip downward and forward behind your lower teeth; your lips just touch each other, and your eyelids are closed, but not tightly.

The first time or two, you might have someone check your position against these directions, because every detail, while simple, is important.

Now talk to your arms. Yes, talk. Not out loud, but to yourself. Every time you breathe out or exhale, say to your arms, "Let go. Let go."

As you become more relaxed, the number of breaths taken each minute will become fewer; periods of exhalation will become longer. You will have more time to talk to your arms. Since you are going to achieve the greatest possible degree of relaxation, you will say to your arms, "Let go. Let go more. Let go more—more, more."

Why talk to your arms? Can't you learn to relax without verbal command? The answer is that talking to the muscles greatly shortens the learning time, greatly increases the degree of relaxation that will be attained. The reason is obvious, once you think of it. You already have established verbal habit patterns for the control of your muscles. Now you are using skills you have already acquired in order to acquire further skill in relaxation.

I must admit that I came upon this bit of technique by a round-about route. I had noticed that patients who had suffered an injury to the brain involving the speech centers became clumsy, even when there was no injury to other parts of the brain. It occurred to me that there must be a close connection between muscular skill and verbalization.

Then I remembered how I used to verbalize my operations when I was learning to do surgery. "Make the incision, tie off bleeders, cut the fat, tie off bleeders, cut the fascia, separate the muscle fibers with blunt dissection, pick up the peritoneum," and so on. For every operation that I performed in the surgery, I practiced a hundred in my own study, verbalizing every step.

The skills of children learning muscular techniques are taught through the verbalizations of their elders. So they learn to talk, to walk, to swim, to write. Later, they teach themselves through their own verbalizations. Muscular control is a conditioned reflex, in which the word is an important factor in the situations.

Vocabulary is one measure of the progress of techniques of various civilizations. You can't be artistic without an artistic vocabulary; you can't be scientific without a scientific vocabulary. "In the beginning was the word." A vocabulary of relaxation teaches you to relax.

So as you lie on your bed, you say to your arms, "Let go, Let go, more, more, more," every time you exhale.

At first, you may find this difficult. Remember that you are not doing anything you have not done before; you are only doing it differently, more intelligently, and better. And for a reason! The result will be a new experience—an experience of diminishing muscular tension, of renewed muscular strength, a sensation of increased bodily tone and vitality.

Patients usually begin a course in learning to relax by saying that they know how to relax. Their eyelids twitch; their foreheads wrinkle; they stand or sit in strained positions, totally unaware of their muscle tensions; but they are sure that they know how to relax. One patient told me that he played poker all night for relaxation. Actually, he played poker to prevent his thinking about other things, in an unavailing flight from reality. He didn't know the meaning of real relaxation. He had never experienced it. Diversion is not relaxation. Recreation is not relaxation. Only relaxation is.

After a few lessons, these same patients invariably tell me that they had never realized they had been so tense. In learning to relax, they experienced a new sensation. Describing this sensation to one who has never experienced it is like trying to describe colors to a person born blind. When you see a blue sky, you experience the color; but if you have never been able to see, all of the verbal descriptions of all the imagist poets cannot tell you what you have been missing. A relaxed body is a physical sensation, entirely different from anything you have ever experienced. You will recognize your mislaid ability to relax when you recover it, and you'll like it.

Some patients tell me that after their first few lessons they experience a tingling in the hands. Is this because they are enjoying a better blood supply because of relaxation of the blood vessels? I do not know. I do know that some highly resistant cases of long-standing eczema of unknown origin have cleared up following training in relaxation. At any rate, the tingling soon passes away, and after a few more practice periods, it never recurs; so for practical purposes, you may disregard it as unimportant.

Practice letting the arms relax as often as you can. Set yourself a minimum practice time of two one-half-hour periods a day. Some of my patients lie down after each meal. Two of them have daybeds in their offices upon which they lie down in the middle of the morning and late in the afternoon.

Don't tell yourself that you have no time to relax. Prime Minister Winston Churchill reports in his autobiography that he always took time out to relax, especially when he had on his mind the feeding and housing of 40,000,000 people, the direction of a huge Army and Navy airforce, and the planning of the foreign policy of an empire. President Woodrow Wilson used to give himself a relaxation break for fifteen minutes in the middle of every morning. Thomas Edison relaxed more often during the day and accordingly diminished his hours of sleep at night. Only high-pressure executives with low-pressure jobs are too busy to relax. If the person wants to find time to relax, he can—and I repeat: if he wants to.

Frequency and regularity of practice is the secret of success.

Practicing relaxation the same time every day is helpful, but this is not absolutely necessary. Eventually one should learn to let go of unnecessary muscle tensions all of the time.

After you have practiced relaxing your arms for about two weeks, you will begin to notice results. You will notice first that the type of muscular relaxation in your arms is different from anything previously experienced. You will notice also that your entire body rests better when your arms are relaxed. You have relieved them of the compulsion to keep doing. Later on, you will relieve your legs of the need to keep going. Now you are ready to learn to relax the muscles you use in breathing.

If you will put the tips of your thumbs and the tips of your fingers together, so that the tip of the right thumb is against the tip of the left thumb, and the tip of the right index finger is against the tip of the left index finger, and so on, you will have a rough representation of the bony cage that makes up the architecture of your chest. When you look at your fingers, think of your ribs.

Do this now; the book will wait.

Now, with the finger tips still touching, spread your fingers apart, so that the index fingers move up, the little fingers move down. That is what your ribs do when you draw in a breath. You notice how much more space you have in your hands when you spread your fingers apart. Just so, you have more space in your chest cavity when you spread your ribs apart, as you do when you inhale.

Now close the fingers together. This decreases the capacity inside of your hands. So your ribs fall together when chest muscles relax, to decrease the capacity inside of your chest.

It takes muscular effort to inhale. Muscles pull the ribs apart. When these muscles relax, the ribs fall together, and exhalation occurs. It is as though your chest were a bellows or

an accordion, sucking in air when pulled open, and letting
the air out when allowed to shut of its own weight.

Understanding this should enable you to see why you were
told to let your arms relax during exhalation. You were co-
ordinating the relaxation of your arms with the natural relaxation of the muscles of your chest.

And now you are ready for the second lesson.

Lie down as you did when you let your arms relax.

Spend about five minutes getting your arms relaxed. When
you feel that they are heavy, your hands warm; when you experience that pleasant glow of relaxation—by now you will
know what I mean—talk to the muscles of the chest.

Every time that you inhale, say to your chest (not out loud
of course but to yourself) "Chest," and when you exhale say,
"Let go. Let go. Let go. More—more—more."

Now observe three things, easy to remember and easy
to apply.

1. Pay no attention to the way you inhale. Let your chest
take in as much or as little air as it wants.

2. You can always let more air out of your chest than you
think you can, and as you continue to practice, continue to
lengthen the period of exhalation. As you exhale at first you
will say, "Let go, let go. More—more—more." But as you become more adept you will say, "Let go. Let go. Let go. More—
more—more—more—more—more."

3. At the end of exhalation do not be in a race to inhale.
Rest for just an instant.

There are several good reasons for these rules. The first
one is that nervous people pant, and their panting prevents
their relaxing. You control your overworked emotions by
doing just the opposite, that is, by lengthening your period
of relaxation.

Furthermore, you restore the normal carbon dioxide-oxygen ratio in the blood when you breathe in a relaxed manner.

One of my patients went to a famous clinic for a check-up. He was told that nothing was wrong with him except that the carbon dioxide-oxygen ratio in his blood was disturbed. The doctor suggested that he carry a large brown paper bag with him to stick his head in so that he could rebreathe the carbon dioxide that he exhaled. My patient felt rather aggrieved at this advice. "This procedure will certainly restore the normal carbon dioxide-oxygen ratio," I pointed out. "Yes," replied my patient, "but I can't go around town with my head in a brown paper bag. I think I'll practice your technique of relaxation. It is less trouble and more dignified."

Practice relaxing your chest for about a week and when you get the hang of it, use the same technique in practicing on your arms. That is, when you relax your arms you think, "Arms," as you inhale, and you think, "Let go. Let go. More—more—more—more—more," as you exhale.

Many people inhale and exhale from between sixteen to twenty times a minute. But during practice in relaxation they have so prolonged the period of exhalation that the entire respiratory cycle takes about ten seconds so that they breathe about six times a minute. It takes about three weeks of practice to reach this goal.

At the end of three weeks' practice in relaxation, you should have no trouble at all in falling asleep at night. And your sleep should be restful, really doing you good.

You have now been practicing to relax for three weeks. Perhaps you started to practice in a skeptical frame of mind. You were not convinced, but you had nothing to lose but your tensions, so you were willing to give the thing a whirl. By this time your skepticism is ended. You know from actual experience just what intelligent practice in relaxation can do for you.

This is the place where most people get off. Most people are easily satisfied with their own achievements. Perhaps they may have had a dinner in one of San Francisco's finest restaurants, where food is prepared by world-famous chefs, only to come home to find fault with their hapless cook. They may see a picture of a home built by Frank Lloyd Wright and they are no longer satisfied with the architecture of their own homes. They pay a small sum to see a moving picture that required months of planning, and which was acted by the most skillful performers; but if one scene has been directed with less than genius, they criticize and complain. Yes, people demand perfection when asking others for services or goods. They may be ultraconscientious in their dealings with others. But when it comes to giving themselves services or goods, they are quite content with just getting by.

Most people can get by, if they know how to relax their arms and the muscles of the chest. This is where those easily satisfied with their own achievements usually desert themselves.

But if you desire exuberant good health, greater energy than you have ever known, you will not be satisfied. You will want to go on. So let us begin our fourth week by progressing to the muscles of the legs.

Relax in your practice periods in the usual way. Spend five minutes getting your arms relaxed. Spend the second five minutes getting your chest relaxed. Remember always to talk to your muscle tensions, telling them as you exhale to let go, more, more, more.

After ten minutes devoted to relaxing your arms and chest, start talking to the muscles of your legs. Spend ten minutes on this exercise.

At the end of the fourth week you will be able to relax your arms, your chest, and your legs. You're doing fine.

Entering the fifth week of practice, you will begin each period by spending five minutes each upon your arms, your chest, and your legs. When these parts are relaxed, you can spend the next fifteen minutes in learning to relax the muscles of your back. "Let go; let go."

Always remember to verbalize your relaxation. Talk to your muscles as you inhale, and order them to relax as you exhale.

In the sixth week, start as usual with review of the relaxation of arms, chest, legs, and back, in that order. During this week learn to relax the muscles at the back of the neck.

In the seventh week, try to learn to relax the muscles that control facial expression. If you were to gaze upon a statue of Venus or of Minerva, you would feel the calm and power of facial repose. The Age of Pericles knew all about relaxation of the facial muscles.

In the eighth week, relax the muscles of the scalp, and watch that nervous headache disappear.

In the ninth week, learn to relax the muscles that control the movements of the eyeballs. There are six muscles attached to each eye. These are the muscles that turn the eye from side to side, up and down. In learning to relax these muscles, I tell my patients to let go of their eyes, so that they fall from their sockets. The eyes won't fall, although many people hold their eyes so fixedly that one might suppose it to be a precaution against their eyes falling out. Just let go of them. Nothing will happen, except that you will lose that feeling of eyestrain.

In the tenth week, learn to relax the muscles of speech. One way to do this is to get as relaxed as possible, by first relaxing other parts of the body, and then to speak as softly, as calmly, as quietly as possible. Use words suggesting calm, peace, pleasant ease. You might even use these very words—calm, peace, pleasant ease. This applies especially to teachers. A high-pitched, shrill, neurotic voice means a class of nervous students. A rasping file sends unpleasant tension down anyone's back; but a human voice that sounds like a tutor tooting a cracked flute is worse.

SELF-DIRECTED RELAXATION

INHALE and direct your attention to	EXHALE say to yourself (not out loud)	
Arms	Let go,—more—more—more	1st and 2nd week
Chest	Let go,—more—more—more	3rd week
Back	Let go,—more—more—more	4th week
Legs	Let go,—more—more—more	5th week
Neck	Let go,—more—more—more	6th week
Face	Let go,—more—more—more	7th week
Scalp	Let go,—more—more—more	8th week
Eyeballs	Let go,—more—more—more	9th week
Speech muscles	Let go,—more—more—more	10th week

Now that you have completed ten weeks of practice, begin all over again. The second ten weeks is a postgraduate course. Most people who have learned to relax realize they have acquired a precious skill that they are determined to keep for the rest of their lives. They had better, for they have acquired a paid-up health-insurance policy.

This technique has been aptly named *self-direction in relaxation* by Dr. Dorothy H. Yates, Professor of Psychology in San Jose State College.

Many people have asked me whether self-direction in relaxation is the only way to learn to relax. The answer is no. Dr. Edmund Jacobson uses a method of negative practice. The patient is told to tense his muscles more than usual and then to let go. You will find this technique useful at times. Dr. Josephine Rathbone of Teachers College, Columbia University, has worked out an ingenious method for teaching relaxation in connection with physical education. For group teaching her methods are very effective and I recommend them to all teachers of physical education.

I worked out my methods in the clinical situation and in my experience self-direction in relaxation seems to be the most effective way of teaching tense people to relax.

Summary

Ten weeks is not a long time to learn to acquire a new skill. You could not expect to learn to swim well or to play a good game of golf in that time. So do not be in too great a hurry. Spend the first two weeks learning to relax the arms. The third week give to the arms and muscles of the chest. The back comes in for attention during your fourth week. The fifth and sixth weeks are devoted to the muscles of the legs and back of neck. In the seventh week you learn to relax the muscles of the face. In repose, your face will lose its hard lines, acquire a new beauty. You learn to relax the muscles of the scalp during the eighth week. The ninth week is given to the muscles of the eyeballs, and the tenth to the muscles of voice production Thus, in ten weeks, you have re-educated most of the muscles of your body and, incidentally, you have re-educated your emotional behavior patterns. For no one can experience an unpleasant or harsh emotion when he is completely relaxed.

CHAPTER SIX

Let Go—A Little More

1

AFTER TEN WEEKS of practice in the technique of relaxation, you will become sensitive to muscle tensions that you had never known. They were there. They were oppressing you, holding you down, interfering with your thought and action. They had been preventing you from being as intelligent, as decent, and as kind as you naturally are—but they were unseen bonds.

"I never realized that I had been so tense" is a thing all students of relaxation say at one time or another.

Re-education of the muscle sense, learning to recognize and evaluate your muscle tensions, is one of the most important results of learning how to relax. So after ten weeks of systematic practice, you will know how to recognize some of your localized muscle tensions, and to let go of them as they occur. Here again, intelligent practice will hasten your period of learning and will enable you greatly to diminish any residual tension.

You can learn to relax while you sleep. In fact, while sleeping you can get in your most continuous and your most effective practice. Those who resent having to spend any of their waking hours upon their health can take pleasure from the thought that by relaxing during sleep, they are utilizing their sleeping hours to their greatest advantage. By directing yourself wisely, you can permanently eliminate emotional conflict, dehypnotize yourself from paralyzing inhibitions, and improve your general health—while you sleep.

97

You are never completely unconscious while asleep. Some of the nerve centers of stimulation within your forebrain are constantly receiving impulses from your environment. These nerve centers are not inhibited from adjusting your body to your environment. During sleep you are constantly making minor adjustments of your body and of your covers. When you are cold, you snuggle deeper under the blankets. When you become too warm you throw them off.

Studies have been made of the number of times persons turn over or move around while asleep. Restless people may average eight or ten squirmings and twistings an hour. These adjustments are so habitual that when the sleeper wakes up, he does not remember having moved at all—not having aroused himself to the level of conscious perception. Your sleep is not a thing apart from your waking life. The farmer's wife wakes at the slightest sound of her infant's cry; she would not wake up if a thunderstorm shook the house. The farmer will wake at the slightest patter of raindrops on the roof and jump from bed to check over the stock; but he sleeps soundly even though their infant children yell until they are blue in the face. I knew one mother who could get out of bed at two in the morning, warm an infant's feeding, feed the child, change his diaper, and go back to bed without waking up at all.

The boy who can hardly be aroused on school days wakes up at the crack of dawn on the Fourth of July. While asleep, he has been keeping track of the time. These facts may be commonplace, but they have an importance for you.

They mean that your mental attitude while falling asleep is going to decide the quality of sleep you will enjoy. It is characteristic of neurotics to say that they wake up more tired than they were when they went to bed. Of course they are tired. Their muscles have been working all night, one muscle group against its opposite group. The muscles that flex the arms have been working against the muscles that extend the arms. No wonder, then, when they wake, that they feel muscle-weary and exhausted.

You can lose your habitual muscle tensions while you sleep. That is why, as you feel yourself dozing off, you should give your muscles their last-minute directions. Say over and over, every night, "Going to sleep completely relaxed the whole night through." And you will. Your going-to-sleep attitude will persist all through the night. You will wake up renewed and refreshed. You will have enjoyed that sleep that "knits up the raveled sleeve of care."

I do not ask any of my patients to believe this, any more than I would ask them to believe that cascara is a cathartic. I ask them only to try it, and to judge the results by their own intimate experience.

As soon as you get the hang of saying, "Going to sleep completely relaxed the whole night through," you can learn to coordinate this formula with your breathing. Say it in four breaths. On inhalation, you say "Going to," and on exhalation you say "sleep." On the second breath you say "completely" as you inhale and "relaxed" as you exhale. In your third breath, say "the whole" while inhaling, and "night" as you exhale. In your fourth breath, you say "through" on inhalation and simply relax during exhalation. "Going to sleep —completely relaxed—the whole night—through," in four breaths, appears from experiment to be the most effective method. The timing is that of a very slow waltz.

The therapeutic effects of relaxed sleep are too great for computation. Simply lying in bed, apparently quiet, is not necessarily restful. But relaxed sleeping is good for persons suffering from tuberculosis, from peptic ulcer, from heart disease, and especially good for patients suffering from nervous disorders.

You can learn to sleep well if you follow the directions that have been given. And using the same technique, you can train yourself to sleep under any conditions. A quick-tempered doctor would call a patient a pampered fool if she complained that she could not sleep except with shades over her eyes to keep out light and plugs in her ears to keep out sound. He can tell her that during the blitz in London, 8,000,000 people slept crowded buttock to buttock and thigh to thigh on the platforms of subways and on the floor in cold cellars, during the air raids.

Perhaps you don't need special conditions for restful sleep. But thank God for your private room and your warm bed. And if you worry because you hear your neighbor's rooster crowing, and want the bird's head chopped off, please remember that it's your head, not the rooster's, that needs attention. You could sleep in a boiler factory if you trained yourself to do so, and be none the worse for it, unless you worked there. Remember the formula. Relax as soon as you go to bed. As you feel yourself dozing off, say over and over, "Going to sleep —completely relaxed—the whole night through." You will, too.

2

Giving yourself last-minute directions before going to sleep is called "controlled sleep." Indian boys of certain tribes used to practice it at puberty when they were expected to take an adult name. The boy would sleep in a secluded spot and dream of some animal. In the morning he would name the animal that had visited him in his sleep, and so he would get his name from the visiting animal. His expectancy of dreaming of some animal produced the dream. Selection must be made, too. It would hardly do, under the circumstances, to dream of a mouse or a polecat.

Many people enjoy certain of their dreams and deliberately repeat them night after night, simply by saying before falling asleep, "Tonight I'll dream about what I dreamed last night." This is controlled sleep, and is explained by the fact that one is partially conscious, even while asleep.

Mystics practice this same technique in order to communicate with what they call "The Invisibles." They relax completely and go into a sleep more or less deep, expecting to hear voices. They do hear voices. The voices they hear are those conjured up in their own imaginations. That is why the "voices" never tell them anything they do not already know. So in his sleep, a mystic may dream of being visited by President Lincoln. I notice, however, that the Lincoln of his dreams never dictates any second Gettysburg Address. He does pretty well, if he just gets through the first. The mystic may sincerely believe that he saw Lincoln, but the words and visions came from the mystic's own memories.

In like manner a mathematician may solve a difficult problem in his sleep. He thinks about his problem before going to sleep. While he sleeps, nerve impulses that had been blocked in his waking life pass through, giving him the right answer. This same process is sometimes called inspiration.

You can use this method of controlled sleep for good purposes other than the practice of relaxation. You will remember that emotional behavior results in partial self-hypnosis. As one patient put it, "I can't make myself do anything. I can't even feel normally. It is as though my mind were embedded in concrete." Using controlled sleep, you can make yourself do what you know you ought to do easily. Controlled sleep can give you waking self-control.

A patient who had begun to learn to relax was told to do

some work in which she was interested. Her life had been a
series of disappointments and failures, of partial starts and
turning around again to begin all over. To say that her failures had been caused by her neurotic trends does not erase the
fact that the failures were poisonous memories. Now she was
asked to make another start.

"I just can't do it," she cried. "I can't want to want to. I
can't care about anything. All that I want is to die."

Fair enough. But why didn't she die? Because she wanted
to live. When she said that she wanted to die, she was not an
integrated personality. She was talking through her no-thor-
oughfare, inhibitory cells in her forebrain. But how to quiet
those busy cells, extinguish their red lights, so that the go-
ahead cells could get to work?

"You know how to relax," she was told. "Do it tonight. Lie
down in bed and relax as you were shown. Then, just as you
feel yourself dozing off, say over and over again, 'Tomorrow
I'll write the beginning of my story. Tomorrow I'll write the
beginning of my story.' "

She called me up the following day. "I started that story,"
she said.

You owe no one as much as you owe yourself. You owe to
yourself the action that opens for you the doors to the goodness, the variety, and the excitement of effort and success, of
battle and of victory. Making payment on this debt to yourself is the exact opposite of selfishness. You can best pay your
debt to society, that has made you what you are, by being just
yourself with all your might and as a matter of course.

You fulfill the promise that lies latent within you by keeping your promises to yourself. This seems so simple and reasonable. Why is it so difficult? The catch lies in the activity
of the "don't-do-it" cells in your forebrain. They have been
goaded into abnormal busyness. Your problem is to get

around these nerve cells and to make them leave you alone.

You can use this technique of controlled sleep to get started back into normal living. You simply decide what it is that you would like to do. Don't challenge yourself with too much play or too much work. Bite off only what you can chew easily. It tastes better that way—any epicure can tell you that.

Then apply the method used by the authoress. As you doze off at night, repeat over and over again your intention. When you wake, it won't be an intention. It will be a compulsion. The road to heaven is paved with good compulsions.

Another patient wanted to break the habit of smoking. At night he said over and over, "Tomorrow cigarettes will nauseate me."

The following morning he had forgotten all about it. Forgotten? Well, his interbrain and stomach hadn't forgotten. As he puffed his before-breakfast, wake-me-up cigarette, he felt nauseated. His head started to spin. In another minute he was vomiting, and then he remembered his suggestion of the night before.

The smoking habit, like all other habits, is a form of self-hypnosis. Conscious suggestion while completely relaxed de-hypnotizes, and breaks the habit.

An office manager was morbidly suspicious. Everywhere he scented a plot. If two clerks left the room together to go to the washroom, he wondered what they were talking about. About him probably. He couldn't concentrate upon anything until they returned, and then he had to question them separately to compare their stories. When the stories checked, he suspected that they had agreed upon a tale to circumvent his inquiry. He wasn't doing himself any good, and he knew it.

He learned to relax. Never mind the cause of his neurotic trend. That isn't part of this story, because he couldn't confess it until it no longer had a hold on him.

Every night, as he fell asleep relaxed, he repeated over and over, "I have nothing to hide. I have nothing to fear. No one is against me."

After he had cured himself of his compulsion to suspect everyone, he was able to laugh at it and to talk about it without distress. Self-analysis followed disappearance of his unhappy suspicious habits and completed his cure.

In these cases, controlled sleep not only helped to break up habits of emotional tension through relaxation in sleep; it helped to free the brain from secondary habits of self-hypnosis. This proved to be valuable in treatment, because their new freedom enabled these people to find joy and fulfillment in their workaday adjustments to life situations. They increased the number of situations in which they were happy and they gave themselves more opportunity for enjoying the beauty and gaiety of living.

Remember to use controlled sleep—last-minute directions to do tomorrow what you wish you had done today. In being happy, the accent is on doing. By using controlled sleep, you will be able to make yourself do the things that you know will make you happy. You knock out nervousness before it gets a chance to hurt you.

When you are returning to ways of creative living, you are breaking another wheel in the machine of self-destructive emotional behavior. Your daily adjustments become more and more satisfactory. Causes of fear, jealousy, and hatred diminish. The vicious circle of nervousness, maladjustment, and more nervousness is out. You're getting out of the rough going and back into the fairways.

3

Let us return to other ways of practicing relaxation. You remember that when you relax, you are breaking one of the five wheels in the machine of emotional behavior. You may see your danger—Wheel No. 1—and—Wheel No. 2—desire escape. Wheel No. 3 consists of your organic responses and muscle tensions. But if you are relaxed, you will not be afraid. You will use your head and not your intestines to cope with the situation. So practice relaxation whenever and wherever you can. Do it consciously, and you'll get results.

You can practice relaxation while you sit. Many hours of our lives are spent in a sitting position. Most of us sit at least four hours a day; some of us spend ten hours a day in a chair. So it is important for us to learn how to relax while sitting.

To find the proper position, sit as far back as possible in a straight chair. The seat should not be more than seventeen inches from the floor. Fifteen inches is better. This naturally varies with the length of your shinbones.

When furniture manufacturers begin to design chairs and tables for restful living, they will consult anatomists and physiologists for design for sitting. As it is, they make replicas of what were smart for Louis XVI. And look what happened to him.

Get yourself the best, small, straight chair available, and sit in it as far back as possible. Now take off your shoes and, if your socks or stockings are tight, remove them also. *Incidentally, here's an important tip: take off your shoes whenever and wherever you can do so.* Substitute slippers or loafers if necessary for warmth, but get those shoes off your feet. You'll feel better.

Put both feet flat on the floor, about fourteen inches apart. Let your arms hang loosely at your sides. Then sit as straight as possible, arching your back so that the lumbar curve—the curve at the small of your back—is as far as possible from the back of the chair.

Now, holding your back stiff, slowly sway forward and backward from the hips, until you find that position which feels most comfortable. This will be the position where the center of gravity from the waist up is in balance, has the most support, is in greatest equilibrium.

Now you are ready to practice relaxation while sitting down.

Let your chin drop. Bend your neck until your chin rests upon your chest. Now talk to your arms. Every time you exhale, say, "Let go. Let go, more, more, more." You are to sit as though you had weights on your fingers, pulling them to the floor.

While talking to your arms, you will notice that your shoulders sag with every exhalation. This will let you know that your position is correct. You will also notice that your back is no longer stiff. The lumbar curve is less accentuated, and the curve of your back at the level of your ribs has become rounder. This is as it should be.

After having talked to your arms for about two minutes (thirty exhalations), talk to your legs in the same way. Give your weight to the chair. Imagine that you are sitting on a spring scale and that, for doing this, you are being paid by the pound. You want to weigh as much as possible. Let your weight push the seat of the chair.

The sitting position is ideal for learning to relax the muscles of the chest. So many people have a feeling of soreness around the ribs, just a little under the armpits. This is caused by tension of the muscles between the ribs, the intercostal muscles. You can relax these muscles by talking to them while in a sitting position. Some of my patients put a pillow or a rubber sponge upon a table in front of them, and let their foreheads rest on these while they practice relaxing the muscles of the chest. Of course, you always say, "Let go," as you exhale.

If you have an office job, and if it permits you, relax in this position at least twice a day. If your work requires writing, you can let one arm hang at your side, while you use your other hand. You will think better if your body is relaxed.

You do not have to twist your feet around the legs of a chair in order to add a column of figures or to write a poem. Sit relaxed at mealtimes, and notice the effect of your relaxation upon those about you. When you go to a moving picture, relax. You do not have to watch the picture with your arms, your legs, and your back. If you feel your muscular tensions at the picture, let go of them. Remember that you paid your admission in order to be amused and not to acquire a nervous breakdown.

And if you are one of those who suffer from self-consciousness at a social gathering, relax the next time you are present. Get into the proper position; talk to your arms, your legs, the muscles of your chest wall; and look decorative. You can't feel self-conscious and be relaxed simultaneously. After a while, you will relax your tensions without thinking about them, and the self-consciousness will be gone. At any social gathering, a person who can sit relaxed, calm, and apparently self-sufficient is most provocative. Normalcy is so unusual as to be interesting.

But you say that you don't want to be so vulnerable that you must play possum to control self-consciousness. You want to be relaxed while you talk. Fine. Your ambition does you credit. If you have any interest in speaking, public or otherwise, your first task is to learn to stand in a relaxed position. A nervous person alarms his audience. They feel so sorry for him that they become uncomfortable and cannot listen to what he has to say. This is specially true when the audience consists of school children and the speaker happens to be a teacher. Relaxation is the soundest of all art precepts. Reference to teachers is for emphasis, not delimitation.

Even if you never intend to say a word while standing on your feet, it is good to practice the following exercises for a few minutes every morning and night. The time for practice is while bathing or washing before breakfast and bedtime. You won't miss the few minutes; you will enjoy breakfast more; and after practicing at night, you will be better prepared for a night's restful sleep.

First stand so that your heels are about eight inches apart, with your feet at right angles to each other. This gives you the largest possible base and requires the least muscular work in maintaining balance.

Then let the jaw sag. Release the muscles of the back of the neck until your chin touches your chest. Then talk to your arms. Just say, "Let go," every time you exhale. After ten exhalations, you will feel your shoulders droop and relax. Now relax the muscles of the face. Finally relax the muscles of the chest.

Five minutes spent on this exercise morning and night will save you hours of wasted time during the day, time customarily spent on worry, useless regret, wasted emotion, wasted motion.

You can practice your relaxation even while driving a car. To operate an automobile, your mind should be clear. Your attention should be undistracted. Your muscles should be in a state of alert obedience.

Driving a car is a dangerous business. Traffic hazards are created by the very old, who will walk into the street because they do not see well, hear well, or think clearly. Hazards are created by young children, usually under thirteen years of age, who are so intent upon whatever they are doing that they will run into the street to do it, oblivious of the mathematical certainty that a car going thirty miles an hour must go twenty-two feet in half a second. Hazards are created by the husband who steps on the accelerator when he thinks of his wife's extravagance. Hazards are created by nervous drivers who are in constant rebellion against the fact that you are allowed to share the street with them. And hazards are created by the man or woman who has had a few drinks. Against these and other dangers there is one other, your own nervous tensions.

You can make driving far less dangerous, and indeed pleasurable, by learning to relax in the driver's seat.

First of all, sit well back in the seat before touching the starter. Make sure that your back touches the back cushion. Put both feet flat on the floor. Let your legs relax. This is not only good in itself; it puts you in the right frame of mind for relaxed driving. When you have done this, and there is no rush to get started, start your motor.

If your car has the conventional gearshift, you must use one foot to disengage and engage the clutch. When not shifting gears, keep your left foot on the floor, not on the clutch pedal. This will save wear and tear upon the clutch lining and your nerves. Let your left leg relax. You are not using it in driving. It isn't helping the situation, so give it a rest.

Hold the wheel lightly. I had a patient whose arms used to ache whenever he drove more than five miles. I once rode with him to observe what he did, and I was glad to be alive after he had driven one mile. He held the wheel with a grasp that would have pulled it loose had it been of the vintage of 1920. "Your steering wheel is guiding you to rheumatism," I told him.

When you find your arms aching from misuse, say to them, "Let go. This is fun, not work." A light touch is a sure sign of a person who knows his way around, in an automobile or anywhere else.

Let your face and eyes relax. You won't go any faster by staring at the road, and you will see far less. After you have finished your first ten weeks of practice, try letting the muscles of the face and of the eyeballs relax when you drive. Notice how much more pleasant driving becomes, how much farther toward the horizon you look, how much wider becomes the angle of vision.

A red light is not necessarily a vexation. It is red only for thirty seconds before changing, but in that thirty seconds you breathe eight times. This is the time to relax the muscles of your chest. A red light is your opportunity—thirty seconds of complete rest. So many people say that they do not have time to relax. They waste the countless, precious thirty seconds of their lives, and have nothing to show for them but vexation and rebellion against the inevitable.

The practice of relaxation at mealtimes will help your digestion. Let yourself relax before starting to eat. Start by putting both feet flat on the floor, and think how heavy your legs are. Give yourself to the chair. Your nerves will be grateful for your generosity, and your fellow diners won't complain. If dining at a restaurant, you must wait for your food anyway. Why not use this time in relaxation practice?

Some folk relax while the dentist drills. They have discovered that by so doing, they can lessen the pain or discomfort associated with dental operations.

It has been definitely established that your sensations of pain can be diminished by relaxation. Every doctor and every dentist knows that some patients are much more sensitive to pain than others. This difference in sensitivity is accounted for in part by the difference in the patient's ability to relax.

Actual experiments have confirmed the clinical hunch. College students, some of whom had been taught to relax, placed their hands in a solution of salt water, and an electric current was discharged through it when the students least expected it. Those students who had not learned to relax were the most easily shocked, while it took a much larger jolt to jar the boys and girls who were free from muscle tensions.

You can apply this scientific truth the next time you find yourself sitting in the dentist's chair. Don't cross your legs, clench up your fists, and wait with the stoical resignation of an Indian brave for certain torture. Instead, let both feet rest easily on the platform, while your arms hang passively at your sides. Think how heavy your legs feel. Talk to them, saying, "Let go. Let go more." And talk to your arms in the same way. This is putting your training in relaxation into practice. You will be amazed by the ease with which you will be able to endure the barbs and stings of outrageous dental misfortune. So will your dentist.

Your mental attitude will be different, and more helpful, too. Before starting to relax, you will say to yourself, "The dentist has this job to do, and he knows his business. It's his responsibility, not mine. My job is to co-operate by relaxing as completely as possible." This attitude in itself, as a substitute for the usual apprehension and fear, will be telegraphed to your interbrain and relayed to your body, and so will help you further to relax.

Sleeping, sitting, driving, reading, and writing are all opportunities for the practice of relaxation. It's really fun, once you get started, to see just how much tension you can eliminate, how progressive your relaxation can be.

CHAPTER SEVEN

How Relaxation Works

How does the practice of muscular relaxation help to cure nervousness? It is universally recognized that muscle tension is the most common symptom of nervousness. But why does treatment of this one symptom help to cure the disease? How does proficiency in the technique of relaxation reach the cause of the disease?

There can be no doubt regarding the fact that it does work. Self-direction in relaxation definitely helps in the treatment of nervousness. Results can be checked, and should be checked in a spirit of scientific skepticism. Since physiological relaxation cannot be harmful and actually is as beneficial as any other hygienic practice, you can try it on yourself and watch the results. You can teach others and watch results. You will see unmotivated anxieties disappear. You will see soul-sickening, unreasonable jealousies evaporate. In many cases you will see real health replace that half-dead, half-alive feeling. Don't believe a word of this, but give the idea a chance by practicing the technique of letting go, and see for yourself.

But if self-direction in relaxation can help your nerves, why worry about the way results are obtained? How relaxation works to cure the jitters may be interesting to the intellectual and the curious. But is it necessary to go into that right now? Yes, it is necessary to understand what relaxation does to the interbrain and to the areas of inhibition and stimulation within the forebrain, because the same results can be achieved, in part by other methods. Why should you limit yourself to a single line of attack, when you can more efficiently attain your objective by pushing on from every available angle? And you can attack from other angles more efficiently when you learn just how the practice of muscle relaxation favorably affects the disordered interbrain and the confused and self-hypnotized forebrain.

In the first place, your muscle tensions are an important part of your total emotional process. These tensions become habitual and persist even when there is no outward evidence of emotional behavior or feeling. Embarrassments long forgotten, childhood failures and ancient disappointments, frustrations and fears that lie buried too deep for excavation by memory's shovel, persist and continue to torture us. They persist in our habits of muscle tension.

All psycho-therapy is essentially re-education. It involves both learning and forgetting. Forget psycho-therapy for a moment and think of any skill, such as typewriting or playing golf, or playing the piano. When you begin to learn these skills, you are clumsy. You have muscular habits of adjustment which interfere with rapid, accurate typing or piano playing, or which interfere with your smooth swing of the golf club. As you practice and learn, you try to unlearn those muscular habits which interfere with what you are trying to do. Learning always involves forgetting. To make a progressively better adjustment between what you are trying to do and your techniques for doing it, you have to forget the less adaptive skill in order to acquire a more adaptive skill. Learning always involves forgetting and the fast learners are those who are more adept at forgetting whatever interferes with their progress.

There are certain popular writers who claim that we never forget anything, but none of these are professional, university-trained psychologists. The psychologist knows that there are laws of forgetting as well as laws of learning and that the two are closely inter-related.

Lucky is the man who has made a life practice of forgetting whatever is not pertinent to his needs. He never harbors grudges. He does not waste his time and energy in useless regret. Lot's wife disobeyed the divine injunction not to look back, and she turned into a pillar of salt. To be happy one must learn to look not backward but forward. To look up, rather than down. In short, effectiveness and contentment depend upon one's ability to live, learn and forget. And this is what self-direction in relaxation helps you do.

With relaxation—the opposite of muscle tension—we break up muscular habit patterns and so relegate ancient emotions into the limbo of forgotten griefs and fears. Muscular relaxation, then, is a process of learning to forget one's emotional habits and memories. Relaxation stops the emotions that prod the interbrain and the forebrain into misbehavior.

It seems paradoxical that relaxation and rest should be helpful, when we consider that the mental phase of nervousness is caused by the abnormal busyness of the red-light nerve cells. Relaxation is essentially a process of inhibiting muscle tensions. Oddly enough, by this very inhibition of emotional muscular behavior, we stop the abnormal activity of the centers of inhibition in the forebrain. Inhibition of muscle tension releases the forebrain from its inhibition. Superficially, this seems like pouring water on the head of a man who is drowning.

Paradoxical was just the word that Pavlov used in describing this reaction. You will remember that in his experiments, he conditioned the dogs to react to a bell just as they normally would react to food. Then he conditioned these same dogs to react to another bell just as they would respond to an electric shock. Then he substituted other bells of different tones daily.

When the tones confused the dogs, their emotions collided and they suffered a nervous breakdown.

While in this nervous state, the dogs displayed what Pavlov described as the paradoxical reaction. He found that if he rang the dinner bell softly, the dogs would respond with salivation and tail-wagging, as they would to food. He discovered also that if he rang the same bell loudly, they would not respond at all. The stronger the stimulation, the weaker the response. This reaction certainly seems paradoxical.

But superparadoxical was the reaction when the dogs were stimulated violently. When the dinner bell was sounded very loudly, a surprising thing happened. Then, instead of responding as they would to food, they cowered in a corner as they would to an electric shock. Strong stimulatory suggestions failed to stimulate the desired response, and even pepped up the inhibitory nerves of their forebrains, making the dogs contrary and negativistic.

People are like that. They respond negatively to strong direct suggestions. Tell a person that he must do something, "right now; do you hear me?" and you stir up resentment and antagonism. A domineering father can build up in his son resentment against all authority. A bullying foreman can slow up production by yelling for more speed. A hard-boiled top sergeant can ruin the morale and efficiency of his platoon. People are more easily led than driven. In fact, if you drive a man too hard, you will drive him in a direction opposite from the one to be desired.

Advertising men are well aware of the fact of Pavlov's paradoxical reaction, even though they may not understand the physiology of the nervous system. They know that a strong direct suggestion to buy makes prospects hoot and sneer. They know that a gentle, indirect suggestion sends people flocking to stores. Tell a man that he *must* buy a certain cigarette, and he replies, "Says you." Show him a picture of some fellow smoking that same cigarette, while a luscious model in a bathing suit gazes up appreciatively, and the prospective customer will think, "What's that guy got that I haven't got?" The answer is, of course, a certain brand of cigarette. The advertising man calls the paradoxical reaction "sales resistance," and the psychologist says, "activated centers of inhibition," but they both mean the same thing.

When Willie Periwinkle came to the table, his face scrubbed and shiny as a polished apple, he was ready to tear into a big dinner. But only until kindly Aunt Amanda started working on him. "Willie, take some spinach; it's good for you. Willie, put some gravy on your potatoes. Willie, eat your salad. Give Willie some bread and butter. Here, give it to me. I'll butter it for him. Willie, eat your string beans; don't you eat vegetables with your meat? What's the matter with you, anyway?"

Willie was pushing his plate away from him. What he thought was, "Let me alone, you big fathead." What he said was, "I'm not hungry, I guess. I don't feel good."

Headline: Hungry Boy Refuses Food. Willie Periwinkle, ravenously hungry, refused to eat even when cordially urged to do so by his kindly Aunt Amanda. "This reaction strongly resembled that of Dr. Pavlov's hungry laboratory animals, who refused all sustenance when strongly stimulated," stated Dr. Thorpe, of the Child Guidance Clinic. The doctor explained that Willie's refusal was a defense reaction, an unconscious protective mechanism, by which Willie defended himself against too many confusing suggestions. "Bosh," commented Willie's practical Aunt Amanda. "Cutting off his nose to spite his face, I call it."

Well, Aunt Amanda happens to be as right as anyone else. Refusing food when hungry *is* cutting off one's nose to spite one's face. And, in one way or another, that is just what the neurotic is doing all the time. He can't let go. He can't free himself from the hypnotizing effects of his stirred-up nerve centers of inhibition. He is a slave to a small group of little gray cells in his forebrain that prevents his entire brain from acting as a unit. He isn't strictly rational.

Tell him to relax, and he will become even more tense and muscle-bound. Tell him to seek company, and he will walk the dark streets at night, seeking solitude. Tell him to seek activity, and he will find a secluded spot on the beach or in the fields, where he can do nothing in peace—or, rather, not in peace but unmolested. Cutting off his nose to spite his face? Yes, but he can't help it. It's the same paradoxical reaction that we see in laboratory animals with experimental neuroses. A strong stimulation produces an opposite response, while only a weak stimulation can produce the desired response.

Learning to relax is a process of giving the brain a weak stimulation. The learner lies on a bed with his weight evenly distributed and his joints slightly and comfortably flexed. He does not try to relax. Trying is the opposite of relaxation. He only talks to his arms, says, "Let go," and lets nature take its course. Gradually the muscle tensions in his arms will diminish. And by gradually I don't mean in two minutes; I mean in about two weeks. The verbal stimulation of saying "Let go" is probably the weakest stimulation that can be devised. Yet even this slight stimulation is too much for some people. They cannot concentrate long enough to say "Let go." In such cases, a second person must stand by the bed and say, "Let's both of us talk to your arms. I will say, 'Let go,' aloud, and as I do so, you can think, 'Let go.' Now we are talking to your arms. Let go. Let go."

Notice that even this suggestion does not go against the direction of the inhibitions of the neurotic. The suggestion to let go follows his inclination to avoid stimulation.

There is an excellent reason for following this method. In dealing with mental conditions, as in steering a boat, there is no such thing as a rightabout-face. If you are headed north, and you want your ship to go south, you cannot pivot. You have to turn your boat a fraction of a compass point at a time. So with mental conditions. Strong stimulations must be avoided. Change from self-hypnosis to self-control can be brought about only gradually, one small step at a time.

When you have learned to relax your arms, you have taken a small but important step. You have changed the direction of your course, and you have given yourself momentum for further change in the right direction. The next step will be definitely easier and the movement will be more rapid. For you have set in motion forces within yourself that are stabilizing, that make for health of brain and body and mind.

These forces are the sensations which the muscles, tensed or relaxed, are constantly sending to the interbrain. Asleep or awake, your muscles are sending messages every second to the interbrain, that co-ordinating center of the body's activities. When your muscles are relaxed, they send out messages, "I'm relaxed. I'm relaxed. I'm relaxed." These messages travel up the spinal cord to the interbrain, where they are relayed to the forebrain. In the forebrain, these messages diminish the busyness of nerve centers of inhibition, diminish to some extent emotional self-hypnotization. To that extent the forebrain is set free from chains of destructive thought. At the same time, the interbrain sends out orders to the intestines, to the blood vessels, and to the lungs, "All is well. You can relax." Thus the lump in the throat gradually disappears, as does the mucous colitis and nervous indigestion.

Results are cumulative. They grow like a snowball rolling

down-hill. One by one, subconscious emotional complexes, which exist and have their being the way your muscles and your glands habitually behave, are dissipated and forgotten. Fewer and fewer centers of inhibition are constantly being activated. You are now free to look for a job, to make friends, to ride in trains, to meet people, to read, to go to entertainments. And as your social and economic adjustments improve, you get to think pretty well of yourself. You have reason to.

Your nervousness? Well, it's not easy to remember last week's sensations. Last Sunday's dinner is today's vague memory. That is what becomes of your nervousness. You were told to "Go home and forget it." Well, as soon as the nervousness goes, you do forget, even those sleepless nights, the shaking muscles, the unnamed and unnamable fears.

That is how self-direction in relaxation works. It works by diminishing and ending the unceasing nagging impulses that come from the hypertensive muscles of the limbs and body and viscera. It is a form of emotional re-education that stops the body from saying the wrong thing to the mind.

Now that you know how relaxation works, you will be able to apply other techniques to help you to accomplish the same purpose. Remember your fundamental purpose, which is to rid the brain of freezing inhibitions that prevent the centers of stimulation from functioning freely and happily. Remember that strong direct stimulation will produce no desired activity, and that a very strong stimulation will evoke opposite reactions.

To illustrate with a common situation, consider the child who is overly finicky with his meals, and who doesn't eat as much as he should. Serve him with very small portions, and very few of these. Do not be overanxious about his eating. Unobtrusively, place more food where it will be handy for him to help himself. Do not comment upon his eating habits.

In short, use common sense, based upon scientific knowledge, and be tactful. If you have lost your appetite, do as much for yourself.

The following case demonstrates how to apply these principles by methods other than that of progressive relaxation. It is the case of a problem child. Temper tantrums, daydreaming, nail biting, and truancy from school were a few of his manifestations of maladjustment. His father had deserted the family. The boy could not adjust to the feeling of insecurity and rejection.

After examination and a survey of his environment, occupational therapy appeared to be the most promising road to his freedom. But how to graft a constructive occupation upon a life given only to resentment and destruction?

At one time he had shown a little interest in collecting stamps. Perhaps these colored bits of paper that once had carried messages across oceans and continents might be contrived to send healthy messages to his malfunctioning interbrain and forebrain.

All strong suggestions, such as "Why don't you collect stamps?" had to be avoided. Even taking him downtown to help pick out an album would have been too strong a suggestion to elicit a favorable response. Instead, his mother got a stamp dealer's catalogue and left it in his room. On the cover she wrote, " 'X' beside any album is a vote for the best one." She examined the catalogue every day. For four days nothing happened. On the fifth day, she saw that the boy had made an X beside the picture of a certain album. She bought the album and, without saying anything, put it in his room.

Within a week, he had pasted all of his old stamps in the new album. One evening he asked his mother to order some stamps for him. They composed the letter together, and he addressed the envelope. When the new stamps came, he sorted them out, and started to trade duplicates with the boys in the neighborhood. His mother bought a globe atlas and put it on his desk without comment. It was not long before he was taking a real interest in geography, and later in the lives of explorers. Whenever he expressed some interest, his mother would get an appropriate book from the library and leave it in his room without comment. Two months after she had brought him his first book, the boy applied for his own library card.

As his interests developed, his problems diminished. The negativistic, inhibitory centers of his brain ceased to maintain dominance. His entire brain was set free to function as a unit. It was when he reached this stage of development that he learned to relax, in order to shake loose the habitual tensions produced by his father's desertion.

Self-direction in relaxation, while a valuable technique, is not the only method by which you can win your war on nerves. If we understand how it works we avail ourselves of other means to free the brain from domination by its parts. Excessive activity of the centers of inhibition acts like a shell to protect us from the unwanted stimulations of an irritating environment. These red-light cells keep us from using our environmental opportunities, and block rational organization of our minds.

Inhibition, when not dominating the rest of the brain, is a protective mechanism. As soon as we are born, we are beset with all kinds of stimulations and suggestions, many of which are not pertinent to the development of our integrity. It is quite as necessary to reject as to accept, to withdraw as to advance. Just as the skin is the shield that protects us from germs and poisons that would destroy after obtaining entrance, so habits of withdrawal and of inhibition form a kind of protective membrane for the mind. Sales resistance in the extreme may prevent us from buying what we need; but it also protects us from getting stuck with a gold brick.

We start early in life to develop our habits of inhibition. Life presents us with a series of stop and go signs, and it shouldn't take us long to recognize them. By experience we learn to refuse certain foods or drinks that disagree with us. We learn to avoid people and situations that are disagreeable. We learn to seek people and books and situations that tend to bring out in us those phases of our personalities that we most cherish. Normal habits of inhibition, those that help us to maintain the integrity of our personalities, we call self-discipline.

Learning habits of self-restraint enables us to live in peace with our neighbors and friends. Such habits make civilization and orderly co-operation possible. The institution of private property, although reinforced by the policeman, could not exist apart from a general practice of honesty. This amiable trait is self-enforced inhibition of the impulse to take what one fancies. Spectacular stories of theft make the headlines. But the existing marvel and accomplishment of our age is that most people never think of stealing. Preoccupation with war blinds us to the fact that never before in the history of the world have great areas such as the American continents been free from group aggression from within. This means that millions of people, acting as individuals or in groups, have had to learn to hold themselves back from doing as they please—have had to develop within themselves automatic inhibitory habits.

It should be clearly understood that self-restraint, self-discipline, and habits of inhibition are not in themselves abnormal. These habits of themselves do not produce nervousness. On the contrary, they help to maintain the integrity of the personality. A well-trained dog or horse is not necessarily flighty or neurotic; and the same thing goes for properly educated people.

It is only when conflict between emotional habit patterns of withdrawal and expansion—flight and approach—disturb the interbrain that we have trouble. Then a few inhibitory habit patterns take control of the entire situation, and a few nerve cells dominate the entire brain. Instead of a democracy ruled by the many, we have a dictatorship by a part of the organism. Freedom of thought is abolished by self-induced partial hypnosis. Suggestions that normally should call forth positive responses induce apathy or opposition.

Treatment, therefore, should begin with weak and indirect suggestions. We see that this works successfully in training in the habits of self-direction in relaxation. It works equally well in occupational therapy, as in the case of the boy who was brought back to normal thinking and feeling through his stamp collection.

But occupational therapy is not the only other tool in the kit of the resourceful psychiatrist. There are many roads to mental health. Any intelligent person can follow the map with complete assurance, provided that he understands why he must start up each hill in low gear.

CHAPTER EIGHT

Action Leads to Freedom

"I MUST LOSE MYSELF in action lest I wither in despair," wrote Alfred Tennyson. Many a nervous person has repeated this formula to himself. Aunt Amanda has never read *Locksley Hall*, but she offers the same general advice. "Keep your mind occupied," she says, "and you won't have time to be nervous. The trouble with you is that you have too much time to think about yourself."

Meanwhile the man who cannot concentrate on any activity, who fears to stick his nose outside of his own door, broods darkly upon this advice to lose himself in activity. His inability to make himself do anything gives him just one more cause for worry.

Some people force themselves to go on and on, until finally they break down. They realize as well as Tennyson and Aunt Amanda that there are escape and release in activity. They are vaguely aware of their own inhibitions which have caught their impulses to do things within a net. They struggle like trapped animals to break that net. Too often they fail because they do not know how to find release in their activities.

If you do not know how, you can learn how. The technique of occupational therapy is simple, but you should recognize that there *is* a technique in making activity work for you or against you. Doing things is one road to freedom, to mental and physical health. But work may be health-sapping, when done in the wrong manner. Work is a prescription that can be therapeutic or poisonous, according to the way it is compounded and applied.

Consider the case of Judy. One night during the depression Judy's father suddenly broke two hours of brooding silence to announce that he was going to be an inventor. Immediately after this pronouncement, he went to bed. That night he disappeared.

He had been out of work for more than a year and had ceased even to look for work. His growing moroseness and irritability were an additional burden to his wife and five children. Whether he had invented some contraption to effect his disappearance, his family could not know. They never saw him again. "One less mouth to feed," Judy's mother observed philosophically.

Judy was seventeen years old at the time. She was supposed to be attending high school. But with a blouse contrived from a flour sack, she felt ashamed to be seen in school, and she had been playing hooky. One week after her father's disappearance, Judy also disappeared. "One less mouth to feed at home," she thought.

She became one of that army of several hundred thousand homeless teen-age boys and girls who roamed the country. She rode in boxcars. She lived in hobo jungles and in those tattered settlements that grew funguslike on the edges of great cities. She picked berries or grapes or whatever crops were to be harvested. For two years she lived so, and day by day stored up vague resentment against everything in general and an ambition somehow to get even. How to get even? By getting rich, and showing those stuck-up kids in their silk blouses.

After two years she got a job as clerk in a store. She still cherished her resentments, her memories of humiliations and privations, and, above all, her ambition "to get there and show them."

She bucked the game of earning her own living for eleven years, and during this time she supported her mother and younger brothers and sisters. She found that the business world was tough to buck. Success did not come dramatically, and at thirty she was getting discouraged. "If I had only had a technical education," she cried. "Then I could get into advertising."

It was then that she met an elderly gentleman who began by giving her presents and who ended by practically supporting her and her entire family.

He wanted to marry her. She definitely liked the things his money bought for her, the nice clothes, the car, the pleasant surroundings. She liked to give money to her aging mother and she wanted to put her brother through college.

She was tired of fighting her own way in the business world, with inadequate training for the fight. On the other hand, she did not want to marry her benefactor, and hated herself for accepting money from him. She worried because her self-respect had fallen to earth and had shattered into rubble. At times she thought that she would just have to marry. There didn't seem to be any other way out. But the prospect of spending the rest of her days with this doting Lothario in his dotage was about as pleasant as the prospect of spending the rest of her life in a jail. This conflict piled on top of habits of muscular tension led to her nervous breakdown.

After she had learned to relax a little, she decided that she was going to have another go at being self-supporting and self-respecting. She enrolled in a business school to learn shorthand and typing. Within a week her old symptoms of nervous breakdown returned. Work was making her sick.

What had happened? In the old days we would have jumped at psychoanalytic interpretations. We would have said, "Aha! In her subconscious mind, she does not want to work. She wants to be a child again. Regression to infantile behavior. She has identified her elderly suitor with her father. Subconsciously, she wants his protection. Her symptoms of sickness are expressions of this wish to be sheltered from disagreeable realities. Once more the old Electra complex rears her malicious head."

But these are not the old days. Today the science of human behavior begins with the study of the behavior of the body. Pavlov and his dogs have given us a new key to unlock the door of mysterious symptoms. Dogs do not have Electra complexes or Oedipus complexes. Even the wisest dogs do not know their own pedigrees. But they do have nervous breakdowns. So instead of "explaining" her setback in terms of psychoanalytic theology, we examined the facts.

The facts were that she was attending school seven hours a day and practicing at home for six hours every day, and doing all this in a state of nervous and muscular tension. She was in too great a rush to get through her course of study. She was cramming down her lessons like a goose in a corncrib. She didn't know how to relax as she practiced penning the shorthand signs she was trying to learn. She didn't know how to sit relaxed at the typewriter. With her muscles tensed and straining, she was undoing all of the things she had been taught to do when she was learning to relax. She was losing herself in action, all right, and to such an extent that it took some time to teach her how to find herself again.

She was shown how to sit relaxed in front of a typewriter. She was taught to write "address" with the left hand, while the right hand was hanging relaxed at her side. Then she was taught to write "monopoly" with the right hand, while the left hand was hanging relaxed and resting. She was taught to relax while practicing her shorthand. (Nervous stenographers should practice these little tricks. They will prevent a lot of backache at four in the afternoon.) "If you acquire more muscle tensions while learning your trade," she was warned, "you will bring those habits of tension to your job, when you get one. If you learn to relax while you learn your trade, your future work will be fun, not torture."

After she had learned to relax while learning shorthand and typing, her progress became much more rapid. This was natural, as she wasn't fighting the battle of muscles and learning at the same time. The typing and the writing practice became a release, a retreat from her troubles, as well as a means to end her difficulties. It's very peaceful to tap out words on a typewriter when your body is relaxed.

Work, as such, can be good or bad for your nerves. Keeping one's mind occupied, as Aunt Amanada puts it, is poison if you do it the wrong way. But there are ways of keeping the mind occupied that can help you. The trick is to know how.

The first rule, of course, is to learn to relax. You may be able to learn during your spare time. If you do, you must carry your habits of relaxation over into your work. Some people find that they can most conveniently begin learning to relax during a vacation. A short vacation or leave of absence from work can be put to greatest advantage by using the time to acquire the simple skills of progressive relaxation. Two weeks so spent in learning how to live will be an excellent investment. Two weeks is only four per cent of a year, and if you increase your efficiency by only ten per cent you have made a good profit on the time invested.

Many people waste more energy than they use when they work. They use muscles that are not needed for the job in hand, unaware that they are tense. After learning to relax, they become conscious of tensions hitherto unfelt and, naturally, let go of them. If you do that, the quality of your work will improve. You will be able to give more thought and attention to your job when your own muscle tensions are not tripping you up and turning your thoughts inward.

Take the case of the nervous housewife. She had been a school-teacher. Her education for life had not included washing dishes, cooking meals, cleaning house, and marketing for food and clothing. For these simple skills—human nature's daily food—she had substituted an ability to keep classroom records. She didn't know how to boil an egg without breaking the shell, but she had learned that John Dewey had said that education is training for democracy.

She had enjoyed teaching school. She liked getting a check twice a month. She enjoyed gossiping with the other teachers. The safe little kingdom of the blackboard was a country for her to rule and to forget as soon as the last bell sounded and the last window was safely locked. And she gave up this nice, tight little, safe little chalk-dust life just to get married.

After the honeymoon, she found that she could not nestle down to her new life. She hated housework. She was afraid of cooking; what if things turned out wrong? She learned to run a washing machine, but it frightened her. Bitterly she resented the vacuum cleaner. At school, the janitor had always done the cleaning. Shopping for groceries bored her. It never occurred to her that democracy consists in the opening of new horizons and vistas that one may see larger worlds through the windows of our everyday tasks and duties. Education, training in democracy, was something that had passed this educator.

She could see no meaning in her work. Day after day resentment piled up upon resentment, building within her those muscular tensions that one day led to a nervous breakdown.

Occupational therapy cured her. What kind of occupation? Housework. For after she had been taught to relax, she was encouraged to take courses in cooking, and later in dietetics.

There followed courses in home economics, in interior decorating. "Housework is really fun when you're not tired all of the time," she told me. "I never would have thought that there is so much to it. Next fall I'm going to learn to upholster my own furniture."

Nearly any kind of work is fun when one relaxes, works easily and efficiently, and comes to see in one's work possibilities and opportunities for self-development. That's why learning the scientific and artistic aspects of homemaking helped the neurotic housewife.

You see women doing housework, jerkily jumping from one thing to another. What do they accomplish, except to make themselves and their families miserable? I would rather live on canned soup eaten in jolly company than dine upon the finest delicacies that had been cooked with some woman's heart's blood.

Activity that is not self-impeded helps to free you from your own self-hypnosis, unshackles the dynamic gray cells within your brain. Every time that you do anything, your muscles tell your interbrain. You may not be conscious of what your muscles are reporting, as when you chew gum mechanically or twist your face into a tense grimace or when you float in the rhythm of a dreamy dance. The chances are that what your muscles are saying is not overheard by you.

But your interbrain knows, and your interbrain is quick to act on its knowledge by sending out messages to all parts of your body and to all of your various organs to keep them in step with whatever you may be doing. When you are sailing through your housework or whatever you do in a relaxed and peaceful manner, health-giving messages go out to all parts of your body to make inner adjustment complete and satisfactory. Eventually, your forebrain is told that all is well, and so you are set free from your own self-hypnotic notions.

Now you are ready for Rule Number Two.

Go easy on yourself. Bite off only as much as you can chew easily.

We can learn how to be kind to ourselves by turning to the case of the dried-up author. He had been prolific and reasonably successful. He had started to write another novel, and his publisher thought well enough of the first draft to advance a substantial amount of money to the writer. Now, with his book half finished, the author found himself in the midst of a nervous breakdown, unable to write a word.

This paralysis of creative ability terrified him. His ability to write was his only source of income. After he had had a few lessons in relaxation, occupational therapy appeared to be the next step toward freedom. But to throw him back into his novel would have been too much. A failure would have erased much of the good already accomplished.

Acting upon advice, which you, too, can follow, he outlined his usual daily routine. This was his daily life. Up at seven, bath, shave, breakfast, radio program; then to his typewriter from nine till twelve-thirty. Not a bad program. He was told to follow his usual routine, but *not* to write upon his novel. "Instead," he was told, "sit down in front of your typewriter, and write whatever comes into your head. Don't try to edit your thoughts. Just write as fast as you can think."

He did this for a week, and then told me that he couldn't go on with this literary free-wheeling. "I'm tired of this James Joyce stuff," he said. "I've started to work on my novel again and yesterday I did an entire chapter."

The method that put the dried-up writer back into action can be used by any writer who feels that he is going stale. (And what writer doesn't, at times?) He should simply put aside his work, and revert to literary free-wheeling. This involves no effort and is a wonderful release. Those who have tried it say that it gets the writer back into the swing of creative work.

The logic behind such success is obvious. It is the old story of the paradoxical reaction. A challenge to yourself to do much is a strong stimulation. Such a challenge arouses strong opposition from the inhibitory cells within your brain. Intention to do just a little is a weak stimulation, which does not wake up opposition and so touches off positive action. "Just this once" is the weak stimulation that lets the sleeping dogs of conscience continue their slumbers. Inhibition is not aroused. The same weak stimulation can free you from your apathy, from your inability to get started upon whatever program you want to undertake.

If you have a stack of letters lying in your desk drawer awaiting answer, decide to answer one a day. That's enough for a starter, "Just this one." Set aside the same time every day, and leave yourself plenty of time, and write that one letter. I'll bet that it won't be a week before you are looking forward to your correspondence with pleasure, and answering as many letters as you have time to write.

Perhaps you used to play the piano. Start again. First sit at the keyboard and relax. Then play just one simple melody. Just one. Set aside the same time every day for this exercise, and let nature take its course. The course of nature will be to set you free from your own restraints. In a short time you will feel like playing for longer periods and attempting more difficult exercises.

Your desire for activity grows by what it feeds upon. The more you do, the more you want to do. If a man has been starving, you begin his nutrition by giving him small quantities of easily digested food. You do the same thing for your starved executive habits. The very nature of habit is to demand its own exercise. So you have nature on your side when you start to free yourself from your fears, worries, and timidities. Start up your hills in low gear, and before long you will be over the top, and coasting along on your own momentum. Challenge to action that formerly would have floored you soon will be taken in your stride with pleasurable anticipation and complete confidence.

You have nothing to lose by trying out this formula. I know that it works. Disregard the Aunt Amandas and the amateur psychiatrists who advise you to bite off more than you can chew. Remember that no one ever bets enough to suit the kibitzers. If you follow this advice, you can be confident that before long you will be showing your heels to your advisers in your new freedom and your dynamic activity.

"But what should I do?" I can hear the reader ask. "What activities do you advise?"

You should do whatever is pertinent to your nature. Ask yourself what you used to enjoy doing, and then take the first step toward doing it. Did you ever enjoy sewing? Then sew. Sew anything. Just make .`ches in cloth, but sew for a little while every day. It won't be long before you will become interested enough to take on a larger project. Did you enjoy carpentering? Then get some boards, a hammer and some nails, and go to it. Before you know it, you'll be attending a class in cabinetmaking. The more you do, the more you will want to do.

So we are ready now for Rule Number Three. *Do anything in which you are or used to be interested.* The best activities, of course, are those which can give you many different rewards at one and the same time. Money, self-esteem, appreciation from others, and physical exercise can sometimes be obtained all from one single activity. Your best stone will be the one that brings down many birds of satisfaction.

Take the case of the fearful foreman. He had come up the hard way, without much formal education. As a result of com-

bining brains, hard work, and ambition, he found himself at
the head of a large department in the factory. Working under
him were college graduates, men from the country's leading
engineering schools. The foreman began to feel that he did
not have what it takes to keep ahead of the procession. He felt
that he would have to run twice as fast to stay right where he
was. This was one of the causes of his breakdown.

The company gave him a vacation. He stayed at home and
spent his time counting his heartbeats. Then he came for help.
After preliminary treatment, he was encouraged to build a
shelf in his garage. In his condition, that was a big job. But
before long, he had put a new roof on his house, had painted
the house and garage, and had otherwise improved his property, much to his own and his wife's pleasure. Through one
activity, he had increased in wealth, in self-esteem, in wifely
appreciation, and in physical strength.

He could have been told that William Knudsen had risen
from the ranks without benefit of formal education to direct
and control the work of hundreds of college graduates. The
same could have been said of Henry Ford and Charles Schwab,
and was said. All of these optimistic thoughts were seed on
bare stone. He was not interested in William Knudsen, Henry
Ford, and Charles Schwab. He could think only about himself.
"They were different," he said.

It was only after he had dehypnotized himself, had freed his
brain from control by only a small part of its little gray cells,
that he was able to think rationally. Until that had been done,
argument, persuasion, and inspirational pep talks wasted good
breath and irritated the man to be helped.

Constructive activity does free the brain. Constructive activity breaks the network of inhibitions that prevent the entire
brain from functioning as an organ. When a man works at a
job that he can enjoy, he is able to whistle. His entire body gets
in tune with his healthful creativeness. His heart pumps with

new energy; his lungs expand with new freedom. In this sense,
work is recreation, for it builds up wasted muscles and red
blood cells out of newly released energy. It is through pur-
posive activity in which a man uses all of his strength and
energy and thought that he reaches the top of the joy of living.

Whatever importance we enjoy comes to us through our
work. All of us are little fellows. We are brittle. We are frail.
Created one by one with pain and distress, we are brought to
maturity only by painstaking effort and difficulty; and our
hold on life is feeble and brief. Not one of us amounts to very
much, except in our work. It is only when we compare the ant-
like smallness of the individual with the stupendous accumulations of human achievement that we are able to appreciate
the sublime quality of human life.

Individually unimportant, we create the Empire State
Building; the subways; airplanes that climb to the top of the
atmosphere; microscopes that peer into the structure of the
molecule and cameras that photograph matter too tiny to reflect sunlight; the *Rhapsody in Blue;* the speculations of an
Einstein that go beyond our solar system to encompass the universe. These are the products of our hands and of our minds
that make us something more than human. With the toil of
our hands and the straining of our minds, we pull ourselves
out of the teeming struggle of animal life into the realm of the
divine.

Losing ourselves in our work, we find ourselves in step with
that glorious band who have given human life dignity and
meaning. We march again with Washington. We fight for
freedom with Jefferson. We investigate the universe with
Faraday. We fashion our instruments with Edison. Our own
little private cares and worries wither into insignificant dust.
Who cares about how he feels? Not the man with a job to get
done. Who cares about rewards, appreciation, thanks? Not the
man with a job to do. Only one thing matters; put that work

through. Perhaps we may feel that we don't amount to much. But when we identify ourselves with a part of all human aspira' tion, we become the conquerors of the world. Individually poor, we become spiritually rich and, having our work, own the world.

When you have married the work that you have picked and wooed and won for your very own, you have divorced your nervousness. The two can't live together in the same house. Nervousness does not like neglect. Your devotion to something outside of yourself, something bigger than yourself, makes nervousness pout, pack baggage, and sneak out into the night. Washington, doggedly fighting on through seven long years for a cause only hazily defined, with a plan extemporized from moment to moment, and surrounded by deceit, treachery, apathy, did not have time to think about Washington. The war had to be won. That was all that he knew, all that he cared about. Washington didn't matter to Washington. The war did. Washington wasn't nervous.

By losing yourself in action, you can regain your good health. Look about you. Find something that needs doing. You can make yourself just as big as the job that you pick out for yourself. But at the start you will want to remember three little, simple rules:

1. First, learn to relax, in order to be able to carry habits of relaxation into all activities.

2. Set yourself an easy program at the start, and work up.

3. Choose such activities as will provide you with the largest number of satisfactions and pleasures.

But what about your attitude toward your work? What about organization of your time? What about exercise and amusement? All of these are important because there are many roads to freedom. The next chapter tells you how to improve your mental health through recreation and exercise.

CHAPTER NINE

Play Is Good Medicine

1

OUR HOUSEWIFE'S in the kitchen, baking pies and cakes. Her cheeks are flushed and she smiles happily as her hands speed from one task to another. Why is she so happy? Is she looking ahead with her mind's eye to fluffy light cakes, or pies oozing with juice? Not a bit of it.

She has made cake and pie before, and she knows how her cooking will turn out. Is she dreaming of her husband's pleasure at dinner? The last time they had pie he had remarked appreciatively, "Much too good for mere humans." Is she anticipating more praise? No, she is not thinking about her husband. Then why is she so gay and lighthearted? Because in the next room her phonograph is playing Gershwin's *Summertime*. Music and those magic lines about spreading your wings and taking the sky are giving her a lift.

Six months ago she was a neurotic housewife. Now, as she says, she hasn't a nerve in her body. Her sleep is restful and she wakes up singing. Her healthy nerves mean verve and gaiety and a bit of walking upon air.

Finding meaning and release in work was not enough to work this miracle. Play also played its part. She had to discover that sick, apathetic, self-inhibited people have to learn to play. While she was nervous she felt uneasy. She took no pleasure in anything. This condition is so common that doctors sum it up in one medical word, *anhedonia*, meaning inability to have fun. This state of mind contracts the spirit, makes the shoul-

137

ders sag and the eyes dull and listless. Her evil spirit of the doldrums departed only after she had opened the door for the radiant spirit of play.

The sick of heart must invite the spirit of play to lead them back to health. Those who are not sick of heart should make play an important part of their lives to increase their strength to withstand the misfortunes and disappointments that are a part of their lives. If you do not know how to enjoy life, right now is the time to learn how to do so.

Almost anything that you do can become play. Bernard Shaw, when asked what he did for amusement, replied, "Anything except sports." Healthy people get a kick out of their work. The teacher in the classroom and the golf professional and the housewife have light comedy and vaudeville and drama passing right under their eyes. They have all this if only they let themselves open their eyes to see, and their hearts to enjoy.

Work may be serious, but that is no reason for acting like a portentous stuffed shirt. You can be just as intense in your work as is a football player, and still enjoy it. True, you may be a good baker or you may have even a sublime gift to offer mankind. Be a cheerful giver, and smile gaily as you pass it on. Work done in this spirit is your pleasure and recreation.

A writer in the doldrums was itemizing his troubles. "At least you have fun when you're writing," I observed. He looked at me open-mouthed, speechless with amazement. It had never occurred to him that there could be pleasure in the exercise of his gift. Here was a man with a great deal to say. He was a natural in his ability to express himself dramatically, vividly, and beautifully. Because he had never allowed himself to take for granted his fine talents, he could not let himself enjoy his calling in the simple way a cabinetmaker enjoys his chisels, or the mason his trowel.

When he started to help himself, he consciously went to work to revalue his writing from the point of view of its play possibilities. He quit acting as if writing were drudgery to which he must reconcile himself. He deliberately restrained himself from thinking of his book in terms of what it might bring him. Instead, he broke up his work into small sections that he could finish in four hours each. These he regarded as experiments in writing, to be judged later—a bit of work that he was able to do with reasonable ease and enjoyment. Then he sat down to his typewriter with the thought, "This is going to be fun."

The first and immediate result was an improvement in his writing. His facility increased. New ideas came with greater ease and spontaneity. His imagination ceased to be muscle-bound. To phrase the same idea more accurately, he freed his brain from old habits of inhibition. But more important to his general mental health, he learned to write in a spirit of play, and to gain increasing pleasure from the happy exercise of his skill.

You can bring the spirit of play into everything that you do. Do you remember when riding in a streetcar was an adventure? It still can be play to a person with a fresh mind. It's a bore only to those who are bored with themselves. Do you remember how you felt when you first drove your new car? It's the same car, but the driver may be taking his good fortune for granted. When new brooms sweep clean, give some credit to the excitement of the sweeper. Perhaps with the same excitement old brooms could be made to do a creditable job.

Try this formula. Tomorrow morning, when you get up, ask yourself, "I wonder what new, exciting thing is going to happen to me today?" Carry that question of pleasant expectancy into everything you do. Try to see something amusing, something interesting, in every conversation, in every contact that you make. Your life will be richer and fuller. But something more important will happen to you. You will cease being contracted within yourself. You will expand spiritually. You will begin to cut loose from the network of your own inhibitions.

2

The play spirit can be carried over into everything you do, yet there still remains a difference between work and play. Work involves some external compulsion, such as is implied in the earning of one's daily bread. We must work and so we must restrain our wayward impulses in order to stay with the job. This does not mean that work is a curse. On the contrary, work that makes the brow sweat is a blessing. It fits erratic human nature as a brace fits a sapling, supporting it and keeping it from sprawling all over the place. Still, work is not the same as play.

Play is anything you do that you can drop as soon as it ceases to amuse. It is something you can take or let alone. Play activities appeal to the child in you. They are primitive in their appeal. That is the reason why play—recreational therapy, to those who like important-sounding phrases—is so important in helping the nervous to get over their troubles.

You remember that nervousness involves the spreading of inhibitions over the forebrain, producing a kind of self-hypnosis or loss of self-control. This loss affects first those behavior patterns that were latest in development. Behavior patterns acquired in childhood are the least affected. In other words, the neurotic is childish. Regression is the medical word for this condition. It means going back to childhood emotionally and mentally.

Recreational therapy meets this condition on its own ground. Play is appropriate to childhood. Play activities are

essential to a child's growth and development. The child without a playground becomes the man without a job. Play is as
necessary as food to a growing boy or girl. And because the
neurotic has regressed more or less to his childhood, he helps
himself simply and easily through his play activities. He can
learn to play even when he has no impulse or ability to work.
To the neurotic, then, self-invitation to play is a weak stimulation which does not arouse his strong resistance against doing anything.

"But I can't play," the neurotic wails. "If I could, I wouldn't
be this way."

Let him tell his story in his own words. "When I was a kid,
my father never let my brother and me play. We had to work
as soon as we came home from school. We had to deliver groceries or wait on trade. If anything went wrong, he used to beat
both of us. I tried to protect my brother and cover up for him,
because I couldn't stand to see Pop lick him. It never did no
good, because he always beat both of us anyhow. I was always
scared. I never had any fun. I've always been this way."

How would you approach this problem through recreational therapy? There is definitely a right and wrong method.
You will keep in mind your fundamental purpose of freeing
constructive impulses from the blocking and tackling of busy
inhibitions. You want the brain to function once more as an
organ, free from domination of its parts. This everlasting
mental shadowboxing has got to stop. And you will remember the ultraparadoxical reaction where a strong suggestion
to do sets up only a stronger resistance against doing.

With this in mind, you might ask, "What are the simplest
play activities of a child?" After all, you say, "The habits of
childhood are the least inhibited. They are the lower rungs
that lead to the top of the ladder." Right. So we go to the child
for wisdom. We find that he lies in the sunshine and dreams.

He uses the large muscles of his body. How can we apply this to our young man with the jitters?

You might advise the jittery young man to take sun baths. Lacking sunshine, he might get himself a heat lamp, and bask in its warm rays. Not much fun in that? Well, try it and see. You will find that you will be able to relax very well in the warm sunshine or under a heat lamp. You will find the sensation very pleasurable. You won't be doing much, but what you do will be pleasant, enjoyable, and therefore curative. Every part of your body will be sending messages to your interbrain that will tend to put that organ back into perfect working order. The messages from the interbrain to the forebrain will help to release spontaneous behavior from the cold chains of inhibition.

If the patient does this every day, he will find himself involved in accessory activities, such as getting undressed, bathing, getting dressed again. In building up an interest in life, every bit of activity helps.

3

Being massaged is another passive play activity that many people find most soothing. This is as infantile a pleasure as sun bathing, and as fundamentally human. Perhaps subhuman, because even a cat likes to be stroked. Massage is scientific fondling. My only objection to massage is the expense, but a gentle massage by an expert is well worth the money. Twenty minutes of brisk rubbing and patting, followed by five minutes of gentle stroking, is good clean fun, and fine for the nerves.

The serious-minded physiotherapist may resent our putting massage in the same class as play. He will be quick to point out that massage tones up blood vessels, improves circulation, helps rid the body of waste products, relaxes tense muscles, and stimulates the glands of the skin. All true, and more could be added. But to the patient, massage is a pleasure that quiets the "don't cells" in the brain, and gives the "do cells," a chance to be heard. Whatever else massage may be, it is definitely passive play.

Music is also a source of passive play, suitable for all comers. What kind of music? The kind you like. Don't feel that you ought to like music you do not like. There is nothing honorific about preferring Johann S. Bach to Jerome Kern, although some people act as if they thought they should be given a Congressional Medal of Honor for liking "good" music. Musical tastes are nothing to be snooty about. The important thing is to be honest with one's preferences, and to listen to the kind of music that one enjoys the most.

There is a trick in listening to music. That trick is to relax. You will see people at concerts, crouched down and tense, while you wonder whether they hope to pounce upon the melody. Others pretend to a critical faculty by fixing their eyes upon the pianist's hands or on the conductor, as if the performers were sleight-of-hand actors putting over a trick. Those who enjoy music sit back, relax, and let the music flow over and through them, passively thrilling to the harmonies and rhythms.

Music can serve you in many ways. You can relax to music. You can work to music. You can sing while you drive your car. Helen Wills Moody wrote that she sang a rhythm to herself while playing her tennis matches. It's a good idea. The idea of walking to music is not so original, but it's still good. That's why we have bands in parades. The next time you walk to the store, relax and walk to the time of the march that you like best. Whatever you do, do it to music. Sing it.

Music can be a source of active play. Singing, choral practice, and playing a musical instrument are activities that come to mind. But these are only a beginning. Some people collect phonograph records as a hobby. It's a good one. Building up a library of recorded music affords a continuous interest in new recordings and an opportunity to enjoy one's old records. Collecting phonograph records is more satisfying than collecting empty medicine bottles. You have something to show for your money, including improved health.

4

Active forms of play are myriad. The first that I would suggest as being almost universal is walking. You can walk out on your troubles. First, relax all muscles that are not used in maintaining your posture. Pull your shoulder blades together. Hold in your abdomen. Let your chest lead, as you breast into the world. Your legs will swing like pendulums from the hips. Now march. Strut, and let yourself know that you are as good as anyone else, and if the truth were known, probably better. The sun will shine, the birds will sing, and you will feel that it is all for you.

Some people play golf or hunt, just for the purpose of getting themselves into a situation where they will have to walk. That's all right, if they make joy, not drudgery, out of their game. "Lift up thine eyes unto the hills" after you tee off. You don't have to look at scenery as if there were a process server hiding behind every bush. Let your eyes relax. Let the horizon, the colors of earth and sky, come to you. They will, if only you do not shut them out with narrow preoccupation. They used to put blinders on a horse's eyes so that he couldn't see what was going on, but you don't have to narrow your vision with blinders of muscle tension.

Overanxiety in games or in work is a mental hazard. You will do better if you do not care too much. Getting into a stew before your stroke and kicking yourself around the course is the opposite of healthful exercise and good sport. In any event, you are bound to get the score that you deserve. You shouldn't want better and you can't do worse, so why worry? You are not under bond to break seventy or eighty or one hundred. Do your best, let go of your muscle tensions, and get a little good out of the game.

Skill, as well as good health, depends upon relaxation. Uncontrolled and unnecessary muscle tensions are bad form. They pull you out of position. Look at Joe Louis and his "dead pan." Or Helen Wills Moody, called "Poker Face" by the sports writers. Both were tops in fighting and in tennis, respectively. Neither use the muscles of the face while performing. Johnny Weissmuller on his recovery stroke was relaxed as an eel. He had to be, for on the pull his arm and chest muscles were as tense as a steel spring. These experts learned to relax every muscle except the ones they actually used. That is the essence of good form.

Each play activity opens its own door, and there's another world. Or better, many worlds, each new, different, and fresh. You are tired of yourself and you are looking for escape? Then take a dead heart to a new play activity. Follow the yellow-brick road. There's an Emerald City waiting for you just over the rainbow.

What to do? We have mentioned sun bathing, walking, massage, enjoyment of music. This list could be added to indefinitely. Some people draw or paint for their amusement. One old gentleman was fretting because the scope of his life was so limited. He was persuaded to learn to paint in water colors. Today, at seventy, his work is being exhibited by art dealers. He finds recognition very acceptable, but his real reward is the fun that he gets out of his hobby.

Photography is another door to a new world of light and shade, where art and science join hands in leading the artist down a road crossed by many a pleasant and interesting by-path. The possibilities that are opened by photography are limitless. For one person, they may lead to the study of the science of optics. For another, they may point to a deeper appreciation of the beauties of pictorial art. When you buy a camera, you never know how long a step you may be taking in your own self-development.

Hobbies have a way of leading your growth, and of developing capacities and abilities that you never knew you had. Some years ago, Professor Gustave Eckstein, of the University of Cincinnati, acquired a canary he had intended to give to a friend. Keeping the little singer, he decided to give him a mate for company. Out of the association of singer, mate, and scientist, there developed generations of canaries that had the flight of Dr. Eckstein's laboratory. These birds contributed so much to Dr. Eckstein's life that he wrote the fascinating book, *Canary,* which turned out to be a best seller.

A neighbor gave my boy a bantam hen. The boy had to build a coop. Saw, hammer, nails, lumber, and purpose equal carpentry. Later, when Henny-penny wanted to brood, he bought some fertile eggs. Soon he had a flock of chickens. He read poultry magazines. He learned something of bacteriology as applied to chickens. Later, he learned to caponize roosters, and came to recognize the anatomical relationships of skin, muscle, bony architecture, kidney, and lungs. He learned the fundamental principles of surgery. It all started with one little bantam hen.

Take the case of the friendless architect. He found himself in a state of mind where it was torture for him to have to meet people. As a result, his practice dwindled until it barely kept him alive. With time on his hands, he took to raising dahlias. These flowers, at least, could not make him feel uneasy. He developed some gorgeous new varieties and was persuaded to exhibit them in a flower show. His success and the acclaim given by flower lovers gave him a build-up and restored his self-confidence. His newly made friends and admirers helped to rebuild his practice. Best of all, his horticultural interests helped to free his brain from domination of those cells that turn on the red lights and say "stop."

You notice that all of these people started out in a small way, with one canary, one bantam hen, a few dahlia bulbs. So a woman who now specializes in children's portraits started out with a little box camera. Each of these small starts represented a weak challenge to activity. The responsibility involved was small. Later, more challenges to activity were added, until from small and trivial hobbies there grew important and valuable activities.

Anton van Leeuwenhoek kept a little drygoods store in Holland. Careful and cautious in his buying, he used to count the number of threads to the inch in his linens. For this, he used a magnifying glass.

Leeuwenhoek had fun looking through his magnifying glass. So much so, that he looked not only at linens, but also at the hairs on flies' legs. He gazed into a gnat's eyes, or anything else that came to hand. Magnification was his hobby and apparently useless pastime.

He wanted greater magnification than was possible with his simple lens, so he invented and made a compound microscope. With this instrument he was the first man in the history of the world to see red blood corpuscles and the tiny blood vessels that connect arteries with veins.

His influence upon his contemporary scientists was enormous. Because his published works include four volumes, there is no space in this book to tell of his world-shaking discoveries. For our purposes, the point is that these discoveries and inventions took root when a linen merchant began to play with a magnifying glass.

Probably most of our industrial and scientific works began as mere play. Thousands of years ago, some boy or girl in what is now Egypt found a couple of young wild ducks. The enterprising child raised the pets, and so became the world's first poultryman. Stemming from such small beginnings in play, we now have Long Island duck farms, agricultural county fairs, and a huge literature. And so with astronomy, bacteriology, and mathematics. All began in play, and developed into literature, science, and art. Our great universities have their roots deep in the play activities of our ancestors.

5

Men at work always draw a crowd of spectators. Just watching is a form of play that has its place in keeping your mental processes working in a wholesome way. Whether you stop to watch a complicated excavation or whether you attend the theater or a baseball game is a matter involving only your own personal preference. It is important only that you identify yourself with the fortunes of the performers, so that you get outside of yourself in play.

A good performance by others is an inspiration. To me it gives a new valuation of our human possibilities. I never see the man on the flying trapeze without thinking, "There, but for the carelessness of my glands, go I." But this thought does not get me down. I am moved to emulate the skill of the daring young man, not on the trapeze, but in some other arena where I have a chance. An expert playing pocket billiards, an all-American quarterback flipping a long forward pass, or a Heifetz playing the violin—all inspire me to seek perfection in my own efforts.

Whenever play gives you an inspiration, do something about

it. If you happen to be inspired by the team play of your ball team, do something to improve your team play in your home and office and shop. If you feel a lump in your throat at the theater or concert, buy someone a gift at some sacrifice to yourself. You should—for selfish reasons, for your own mental health. Inspiration without expression leads to cell death within your brain.

Do something about it. After reading this chapter, check over the play interest that might fit in with your life. Make a small start. If you think that dancing is the answer, arrange to take a couple of lessons every week. Then stay with it. Suck the orange dry. Get as much out of your play as you can. Seek to explore its possibilities. Follow those possibilities on and on, no matter where they may take you. Continue each activity with repeated small challenges for your further development.

When a poultryman thinks that the price of feed is going to rise, he puts in an order at present prices for future delivery. This is called a hedge against the price rise. You can hedge against misfortune by developing a variety of play interests. Every hobby that you acquire becomes another string to your bow. When things go wrong, and they will, you will always have something that you like to do, something to take your mind off your troubles. You will always have a road out. The more interests you can develop now, the safer you will be in the future. Play interests are a hedge against apathy, narrowness, and the horrible uneasy feeling that tortures those whose brains are conducting a civil war.

The whole theory of recreational therapy goes back to the idea that the body tells the mind. When your body is engaged in activities you like to do, your muscles telegraph wholesome messages to your interbrain, which in turn sends reassuring messages to your intestines and heart and glands. Then these organs work properly. The interbrain also sends messages of good cheer to the forebrain, and these messages turn off the red lights of unnecessary inhibitions, to free the cells that regulate your expansive and creative activities. Then you have that feeling of well-being that is so important in mental health.

Muscular relaxation, occupational therapy, recreational therapy—are these the only roads to mental health? Far from it. For there is another form of behavior that has much to do with the way you think and feel. That form of behavior involves your speech habits.

Do you believe that sticks and stones may break your bones, but words can never hurt you? We'll see about that in the next chapter.

CHAPTER TEN

Words Are Triggers to Action

1

ONCE UPON A TIME, there was no language. Our primitive ancestors ran about naked, grunting, chattering, bellowing like monkeys in a zoo. They had no dictionaries, no newspapers, no gossip, no words.

Then, one fine day, one of our brighter primitive men invented the first words of language and started the human race on its way to civilization and the jitters.

Before language was invented, people could not say, "I'm sorry, Jones, but you're fired." Or, "You'll find the key under the door mat. Bill is taking me to Reno." Or, "Dear Mr. Jones: The Directors have asked us to begin foreclosure proceedings." Or, "The trouble with you is . . ." Or, "Drunk again, Jones, eh? I think you need about six months in the State Hospital."

They couldn't say so because they couldn't think so, and they couldn't think so because they didn't have the words to think with. They were not on speaking terms with each other or with the world within themselves. So they had no jobs, no divorces, no keys, no Reno, no cocktail bars, no daydreams, no castles in Spain, and no insane asylums.

Then came speech. Some primitive ancestor pointed at the saber-toothed tiger crouching in the underbrush and shouted, "Boola-boola!"

He made a tremendous impression. He established his reputation as an orator, a man of letters, a soldier and statesman.

151

Little children followed his example. They learned to say "boola-boola" to mean "saber-toothed tiger." Later the word came to signify any kind of danger. The cry "boola-boola" would send the whole tribe scurrying for safety. Our primitive ancestors learned to respond to the word as they would respond to the tiger himself.

The word was passed from generation to generation, until it finally became the exclusive property of Yale University, since which time, of course, it has ceased to mean anything.

But one word leads to another, and other words have been invented to take its place, including fearsome, awful, ghastly, terrible, frightful, horrible, and the like.

In a few thousand years, many words, an articulate spoken language, had been invented. Men, women and children had learned to condition themselves and each other to respond to spoken words as, previously, their unspeaking ancestors had responded only to situations. Today, most of our behavior is verbally conditioned.

We think with words. We define our problems with words and figures. We get comfort from reading of victories of our armies and navy, or when we contemplate a satisfactory balance in our bank account. We get depressed when we read about war, atom bombs, train wrecks or when we get a dun from the milkman. The telephone, the radio, the printed page and the blueprint, the deed to our house, the government bond in the dresser drawer, and the note at the bank are all a part of our reliance upon words to organize our lives. Most of our living, including our closest relationships with family and friends, depends upon this greatest invention for communication, our language.

Let us return to "boola-boola," or, if you prefer, "saber-toothed tiger." What did it mean, originally? It meant "Scram," or "Beat it," or "Run for your life." The shouted word did more than define an animal. It defined a situation and led a retreat. It was a social tool for collective survival.

Words begin as directions for adjustment to environment. You may think of words as maps, but they are directive maps. They direct traffic as a policeman does. In primitive societies where choices are few, the directional quality of words is obvious. The primitive woman makes corn meal from verbal recipe exactly as her great-grandmother made corn meal, and in her group the death rate of innovators is high. In complex societies, where verbal directives are more elastic, choice is wider and freedom is greater. There is so much choice in modern society, so many directive maps, that some people think of words as only passive maps that you can take or let alone. They ignore the active, directive quality of words. The chains of modern language are long and they weigh so lightly that one easily overlooks the limitations and opportunities that words put upon power of choice.

If you must use a tool that you do not understand, you are apt to misuse it, whether it be a surgeon's scalpel or your vocabulary. Perhaps you are not required to use a scalpel, so you will not cut yourself or injure any hapless patient. But you must use your vocabulary, and you do use it constantly, day and night. You talk even in your sleep when you dream. Learning the what-for of language will increase your understanding of its possibilities, its limitations, and its good use for your peace of mind.

Take the case of a lovelorn maiden who attempted suicide when her lover jilted her. We can understand her sense of frustration. She had spun many a pleasant daydream of marital bliss. She had seen herself enjoying her superiority over her unmarried friends. She had pictured herself lolling in the sun, while explaining to her somewhat jealous mother, "Fred makes me keep servants. He won't allow me to do anything."

And then, bang—the shiny, rainbow-colored bubble is broken, the lady gets only the air, while soap gets in her eyes.

So she feels frustrated. She had been coasting down a broad highway where all the lights were green and every prospect was pleasant, and suddenly all the lights turned red with no prospect for a change to a go-ahead signal. Within her brain the go-ahead nerve cells continued to function, together with the cells that said, "Stop. No thoroughfare." This collision of nervous stimulations produced a spread of inhibitions that sent messages to the interbrain, producing nervous symptoms. She had the jitters, and she didn't feel well.

How did she interpret herself to herself? What words did she use? Did she say, "This disappointment has given me a feeling of frustration. It has interfered with my digestion. It has produced menstrual disorders. I must adjust to it intelligently. What does an intelligent person do when she is disappointed?" No, she did not. Instead, she said, "My life is ruined. I can never love again. Life is not worth living," and she made a dash for the iodine bottle.

After we had pumped her stomach empty and had washed it out, we prevented a recurrence of her folly by pumping a few sensible ideas into her head. We gave her sensible words to substitute for the meaningless words that had led to the iodine bottle.

Ruin means damaged beyond repair and use. It is a word that has made many people miserable. During the depression of the 1930's, many businessmen wrote notes, stating that they were "ruined," before making their last dramatic exit. They meant that they had lost some money. Once "ruin" for an unmarried woman meant that she was no longer a virgin.

Why pick such gut-griping words for such little ideas? "I'm ruined because I'm not as rich as I thought I was." Silly, isn't it? But of such misuse of words is the beginning of neuroses.

In the case of the lovelorn maiden, we asked, "What do you mean by 'I'? You have identified your entire self with the word 'ruin.' As a result, you naturally want to demolish the ruin. What is this 'I' that has been ruined?"

This is a good exercise for anyone. You can build a college course in psychology or in sociology around this question. Self-knowledge is the beginning of wisdom. Even a little superficial knowledge of the self is valuable, as this case proves.

She began to define "I" by thinking of her body. "This," she said, "is I." Was her body "ruined"? She admitted as she contemplated her sleek nylon-stockinged ankle that it still was in pretty good shape. What about her appearance? She had no damage to report. What about her economic skills? Were they a part of the "I"? Yes, they were, and her ability to take dictation in shorthand and to transcribe on a typewriter were unimpaired. Were her friends a part of herself? Yes. Had she lost them? No.

Then what part of the "I" was ruined? "Certain of my hopes," she said. She was disappointed.

"Have you ever been disappointed before?"

"Yes, of course."

"What did you do about it?" She did something different. If she had wanted a vacation in July and couldn't get off in July, she managed her vacation in August or September.

Yes, disappointment is a jolt. It doesn't do anyone any good at the time. Later, one may be able to say with Emerson, "When half-gods go, the gods arrive," but at first disillusionment in half-gods is disappointment and nervousness, no matter how you slice it. But disappointment isn't ruin. One adjusts to disappointment by doing something different.

Our disappointed maiden decided to adjust to the fact of disappointment, rather than to the word "ruin." So she did something that was constructive and hopeful. She made a list of qualities that she demanded in a man. Then she went out to find the man who could come up to her specifications. She found him, fell in love, and married him. Afterward she decided that she hadn't been in love with the first man at all, not really in love.

You have plenty of words with which to discover your world and your place in it. Any situation can be named in a dozen different ways. You locate yourself inside of that situation by the name that you give to it. Naming the situation accurately is half the battle of nerves and leads to victorious adjustment.

Napoleon's skill as a general was based upon his ability to use maps. Dr. Wendell Johnson in his valuable book, *People in Quandaries*, emphasizes the importance of stating your problem accurately and in the right words. Words are your maps.

You can save wear and tear on your nerves by doing this habitually, in little as well as in big things. You are driving an automobile, minding your business and singing a song. Some inconsiderate lout cuts in ahead of you, forcing you to pull over sharply to the curb to avoid being killed. Not a nice situation. It can upset your nervous system, at least temporarily. What it does to you depends upon your skill in classification, depends upon your use of words.

You can classify it as a personal attack. In this case, you can catch up with the other driver, force him over to the curb, and pick yourself a good fight. Or you can classify the situation as one of large civic interest, call a policeman, swear out a warrant on a misdemeanor charge, and make yourself a big reformer and a little nuisance. Or you can classify the situation as an ordinary hazard of driving in a wealthy, happy-go-lucky community where even the feeble-minded have cars and drivers' licenses.

If you do just that, you will say, "No bones broken. Lucky

for me that I was driving carefully. That guy is on his way to the operating table in the emergency ward." Then you will feel a little sorry for him, because life never deals kindly with dim-wits. And your anger and your jitters will die an easy, natural death.

Being well balanced is partly just a matter of picking the right word. There is a school of psychiatrists that makes this its principal method of treatment.

A woman looks into her wardrobe. "Not a single decent thing to wear," she wails. No, not a single decent thing. Only four house dresses, two suits, a few miscellaneous blouses and skirts, not to mention hats, shoes, a few coats and dresser drawers full of accessories, two afternoon dresses, and an evening dress.

Does she want another evening dress? Then why doesn't she say so? Why pick the word that is going to tie her intestines in a knot? Why not pick the calm word, the accurate word, the one that permits the brain and the body to function normally?

Extreme expressions carry no special force. They bore or disturb your friends and excite only yourself. But in understatement there is charm. Mercutio, stabbed in a duel, describes his wound, "not so deep as a well, nor so wide as a church door; but 'tis enough, 'twill serve." Would he have increased his chances by exaggerating the seriousness of his injury?

A woman who came for treatment three times a week used to say during every visit, "Doctor, please look at my throat. I feel that I'm coming down with something." We look. Temperature, 98.6. Pulse rate, 80. Throat, no sign of inflammation.

"Why did you think something was wrong with your throat?"

"Well, I don't want to have tuberculosis, you know."

She doesn't want to have tuberculosis. Who does? But what

does she want? She wants to live in a rest home, where she will be waited on, hand and foot. She feels that she ought to have something the matter with her to justify this parasitic existence. Then why doesn't she say so? Because if she did, she would be well. She calls her desire for parasitism "fear of tuberculosis," and sometimes she realizes that her wrong use of words is phony. This inside attack upon her pretenses makes her feel uneasy. It should. Uneasiness crowns the head that wears a lie. Honesty, integrity, calling a spade a spade, brings inner calm and peace.

Words are your map in time and place. Words define your relationships with your fellow men. Who are you? You tell your name. Where do you live? You give an address. What do you do for a living? You name an occupation. Your age? More words. Single or married or somewhere in between? Status is defined in words. The year, the month, day of week and of month? All defined verbally. You live in a world of words, which most of us take for granted as unquestioningly as a fish takes for granted his watery home.

Yet words are inventions of man and share with their maker his lack of omniscience and perfection. They represent the accumulations of thought and observations of millions of anonymous word-makers. They share with their makers both the ignorance and the wisdom of their times. Words at best are imperfect tools of communication. Like dynamite, they should be labeled, "Use with skill and caution," for they can blow up in your face. It seems like a good idea to learn more about words and how to use them in the interest of your mental health.

2

Like our lovelorn maiden, many people become despondent when actually there is no reason for despondency. Many people fear when there is no big, bad wolf to be afraid of. Some of our friends entertain jealousies that deserve only a yawn. The self-starter of their destructive emotional behavior is misunderstanding that begins with the misuse of words, the tools of their thinking. Thus, unhappy people boil themselves in hate for no good reason, and then they wonder why their neighbors, free from hatred, should be so serene and happy. They achieve nervousness, which is as unnecessary as it is disagreeable.

Misunderstanding brought on the neurosis of Pavlov's dogs. The dogs could not distinguish between bells that sounded almost alike. They did not know whether the intermediate bell stood for round steak or an electric hot-foot. This bell was the misunderstood cue that set in motion two opposite types of behavior.

But there is more to it than that. The dogs did not understand that the bells were only sounds, empty symbols. *The dogs identified the symbol with the event.* A bell is not a dinner, nor is it an electric shock. It's only a noise. But you can't tell this to the dogs. They were not sophisticated dogs and consequently could not make an intelligent allowance for mere sounds. That shouldn't happen to an intelligent person.

It does, though. Words, as Chief Justice Holmes said, are triggers to action. They are to people what Pavlov's bells were to his experimental animals. Habit patterns are set in motion at the stimulus of a word. Habitual attitudes, emotional and otherwise, may be compared with electric appliances, such as light bulbs, washing machines, electric stoves, electric ironers, radios, and vacuum cleaners. The word is like the switch that throws any one of these various appliances into use. That is, the right word. The wrong word is like the short-circuited switch that burns out the fuse or even sets the house on fire.

The wrong word sets in motion the habitual attitude which makes you do things you regret afterward.

Your wife asks, "What are you doing?"

You may define her question as, "always crowding me, butting into my affairs." If you do, you know how you'll respond. Or you may hear her question as expressive of a friendly interest.

One situation permits of at least two very different interpretations. Isn't it possible that you sometimes give the wrong word to like situations to your own detriment?

You have the energy within you, the energy to do and to feel. The right word releases this energy, directs it into productive channels. But if you use words badly, you use yourself badly. The wrong word can get you all muddled up, confused, give you paralysis of will, interbrain misbehavior, and the jitters. The right word puts you back on the right track. If Saint John had been a psychiatrist, he would have written, "In the beginning of the neurosis was the word."

Think back to the lovelorn maiden, or the irate motorist, or the woman who had absolutely nothing decent to wear. You will see how their words expressed judgments which did them harm. Words expressing judgments block further thought. If such words set off a chain of destructive bodily processes inside you and lead you to unsuccessful efforts to improve the situation, they put you in a blind alley, from which only the right word can bring rescue.

Before you can say the right word, it must be invented. The history of man is the history of language. Primitive man ran away from the tiger because he had no words to suggest other and better possibilities.

There are many ways of adjusting to dangerous animals other than running away. You can set traps. You can put out poisonous bait. You can build wire fences through which you run an electric current. All of these inventions imply language habits of progressively greater complexity—more flexible directive maps for adjustment to environment.

The language or our primitive ancestors was inadequate for survival, as measured by modern mortality tables. The average life expectancy could not have been much above twenty-five years. Today, insurance companies figure on a life expectancy of more than sixty-five years. Our ancestors' maps did not come even close to the world to which they had to adjust. Their directions were false and the judgments implied in their thinking was faulty. Their thinking was too simple for neurosis caused by worry about the future. But against that advantage, remember that in those good old days, famine and pestilence were ever present. Success in life meant getting enough to eat from one day to another. They had no word for tractor or grain elevator.

Progress can be defined as the process of making better word maps. In the language of mathematics there has been remarkable progress. We can measure the distances between the stars and chart the path of the subatomic-electron. Mathematics applied to physics and chemistry have given us our great airplanes and our newer medicines. When we learn how to think realistically about people and their behavior, wars will be as archaic as dueling. Better word maps will direct us to happiness.

We can describe four more or less distinct periods of verbal progress. Let us call them

1. The Age of Magic Word Maps
2. The Age of Theological Word Maps
3. The Age of Philosophical Word Maps
4. The Age of Scientific Word Maps

3

Magic was early science. Primitive people believed that like produces like, and whatever touches another becomes a part of it. Eat the heart of a lion and you will become lionhearted. Touch a woman before a battle and you will become feminine and weak.

Belief in magic still survives. Hitler was said to consult with astrologers before making important decisions. How many people carry lucky stones, rabbits' feet, birthstones, or even horse chestnuts to ward off disease or bring luck? They are the inheritors of the vocabulary of their primitive ancestors. They define their personal problems in the dim light of their ancestors' ignorance. So there are people who will not eat rabbit or pork, not because of any reason dictated by science or logic, but because of inherited prejudices (old maps) passed on from generation to generation. When they let magic guide their lives, they limit their opportunities for happiness and success.

James Henderson, eight years old, put on a Superman suit, jumped from a second-story window, and fortunately only sprained his ankle. Said disillusioned Jimmy, "The darned thing didn't work." If you are wrapping your mind in the suit of magic incantations, you are all set for a similar letdown. Your disillusionments and disappointments are going to smack your nervous system. Any psychiatrist can testify that he has seen hundreds of cases of mental trouble that stem from this one source of faulty thinking.

4

Religion could not be invented until after the creation of a considerable vocabulary of practical arts and of magic. Gradually, it must have dawned upon one of our smarter ancestors that he could do things voluntarily. He discovered that he was alive. In his life that must have been an exciting moment. "I'm alive," he probably shouted. "I want to make an arrowhead. I make one. You want to make an arrowhead. You make one. I'm alive. You're alive. The tree is alive. The ocean is alive. All the world is alive."

This primitive Saroyan must have made the wizards and makers of magic pretty sore. They probably called him a wild-eyed radical. "Listen," they exclaimed. "For years we have put on our green robes when the sun is just so in the heavens, and what happens? The leaves come out, the forest is green, summertime comes, and the living is easy. It's happened so from time immemorial. Now you say that the tree has a spirit, that it is alive. You want us to throw away our green robes, our magic words. The summer will never come, and all of us will starve to death."

But the man of religion must have prevailed, because the tribe was soon worshiping the trees and praying to the spirit that resides in trees to blossom forth. And sure enough, the prayers did work, or seemed to. For on May Day, they dressed up the tree in ribbons and garlands, and they danced around it, and they celebrated the day of the tree god, just as they do at Vassar; and the tree put forth leaves and fruit.

The wizard and maker of magic was down, but not out. You can still find his descendants along Sunset Boulevard in Hollywood, where they will look into a crystal ball and tell you whether to sell A. T. & T. if you cross an open palm with folding money. Astrologers will help you decide your life problems by "lucky days" if you give them a chance. Magic dies hard, while progress in thinking has a difficult delivery.

If there is a spirit that dwells within the tree, there must be another that dwells within the earth and who controls fertility. Our ancestors in search of a God found her; they named her Ceres, the goddess of cereals. A prayer to Pluto would bring on the rain, while a prayer to the sun-god, with a suitable gift for the priest who knew him intimately, would bring out the sunshine. Our ancestors had things all figured out and were sure that they knew what made things tick. What they couldn't do, the gods did for them.

Many people still think of God as a kind of Santa Claus. They think in terms of animistic religion. They believe that they can panhandle supernatural forces for special favors as easily as they can write to their Congressman for handouts from Washington. And when the rain fails to fall for the clod jumpers of the dust bowl, the preacher gets notice to look for another job.

What has all this to do with mental health? Well, figure it out for yourself. Suppose that you had been conditioned to have implicit faith in the power of prayer to accomplish miracles. And suppose that you went to bed every night and prayed that by morning your clubfoot would be normal, like the feet of other kids, and that you could learn to dance, and could go swimming without every kid in the pond looking at your deformity with morbid curiosity and aversion. And suppose that as soon as you woke up, you looked at your foot. There it was, as misshapen as it always had been. What do you think that this failure and disappointment and confusion would do to your mental health?

Does this mean that psychiatrists are against religion? Hardly. It means that you should not expect religion to do more for you than it does for anyone else. It means that for the sake of your mental health, you should not pray selfishly.

If you get comfort from prayer, continue to pray. But don't pray for a gift of a new set of automobile tires. Pray for an enlargement of your sense of decency and fair play. Pray for a good-humored and kindly attitude, so that you will be pleasant when you give an order to the waitress. Pray for the art of seeing things from the point of view of your adolescent son and daughter, so that you won't be a Herr Hitler in your own home. Pray for gentleness and appreciation of the integrity of personality, to keep you from pushing other people around. Then your prayer may do you some genuine good.

A sensitive young man is tangled up in the words, "eternal hell-fires." He has made one attempt on his life and is so depressed that his wife is frantic. He asks her, "What's the use of living when I know that I'm going to fry in eternal hell-fires?"

"Eternal" is a word. It means "forever," like the guarantee of certain fountain pens. I don't know who invented the word "eternal," but I do know that that word corresponded to nothing within the inventor's experience. I know what sixty seconds means. It represents the waiting for the second hand on my watch to go all the way around the dial. It is a short time, usually. When a patient has a thermometer in his mouth, it is a long time. Anyone can imagine a thermometer under his tongue for a long, long time, and invent a word to express this imaginary event. He might coin the word "eternal," which is not a thing, and which corresponds to nothing found in his experience or in nature.

And so with "hell-fire." More words. Add these sounds together, eternal hell-fire, and you get Pavlov's bell. A group of noises, a waste of breath, keeps my patient from sleeping nights, keeps him from working days, keeps him from enjoying the rich possibilities of his life.

His cure depends upon his seeing the emptiness of his awareness of danger. He must learn that words are not things and, often enough, do not stand for anything except some word inventor's distorted dream.

Just as a child learns by unconscious imitation to copy the muscle tensions of his elders, he learns in his daily speech the maps passed down from druid magic workers and anonymous theologians of a forgotten age. Nor is this all. For with the evolution of language, there came another group of word-makers, to give us a third set of false maps. These were the philosophers.

5

Philosophy is an attempt to understand the world by reasoning about it. To a philosopher, if a thing "stands to reason," it must be true. He takes for granted that the pattern of behavior of atoms and molecules and electrons and Patagonians must conform to his own verbal habits. So he creates a verbal world that must, if necessary, exclude inconvenient facts. I said "must," because in those dreary days when philosophers guided human destinies, force, even to murder by torture, was used to stop the mouths of the factfinders. When philosophers thought the world is flat because it stands to reason that it is flat, burning was too good for those geographers who said it is round.

Today, much of our vocabulary that deals with personal relationships is based upon philosophical daydreams. This applies especially to such concepts as goodness, virtue, truth and the like. The philosopher takes a word, such as "evil" or "justice," or some other abstraction that never has existed in nature, and investigates it as he would a thing or an animal. Havelock Ellis spends a chapter of his *Studies in the Psychology of Sex* explaining "chastity." These verbalisms, inventions of other philosophers, magic-makers, witch doctors, and devil hunters, are weighted with emotional meanings to befuddle and confuse. They upset troubled people in their attempts to adjust to the world of reality.

Take the word "chastity." The ordinary meaning is abstinence from sexual relations, except as authorized by clergy or justice of the peace. Havelock Ellis states that chastity is abstinence, except when authorized by love. Well, where does that get us? Who knows what love is? Love is a word that means something different to everyone who uses it. But whether used in the ordinary sense or in Havelock Ellis' private meaning, the word "chastity" has produced a world of human misery.

Jacqueline's mother was a prostitute. She lived in one of those backward states where public money is not wasted upon "frills" such as supervision of child welfare. When some public-spirited women tried to obtain custody of Jacqueline, they were blocked by the county supervisors. The eldest of these summed up the situation neatly. "After all, ladies, you must remember that whatever else Jacqueline's mother is, she is, after all, her mother."

This verbal solution blocked legal action, but proved to be profitable for Jacqueline's mother. For when Jacqueline reached her thirteenth birthday her mother received eighteen dollars and a carton of cigarettes, for which she sold Jacqueline to a white slaver.

Jacqueline ran away from her purchaser when she was seventeen. She moved to another state and worked her way through high school. Then she obtained a good job. She picked her friends with meticulous care and through them met a highly moral young man, whom she married.

The marriage was successful—so successful that after four years Jacqueline told her husband the truth about her childhood. Bang went the marriage, blown up by the T.N.T. of her word "chastity." Her husband went to pieces, and so did she. Two nervous breakdowns, because of a word that even Havelock Ellis could not pump meaning into.

When the Greeks killed Socrates, they may have been acting in self-defense. But they did too little and they were too late. For Socrates had infected Plato, and Plato infected Aristotle, and Aristotle infected the Western world. Devout and

studious followers of these three dead Greeks have mummi-
fied the masters by wrapping them in endless rolls of commen-
tary, which also became a part of philosophy. The mass of false
maps that the Greeks and their mummifiers have created has
led the thought of mankind into many blind alleys. Every
time I read a college textbook of philosophy, I wonder
whether in time of farm labor shortage a professional philosopher could be taught to milk a cow.

You want to find your way around in the world of reality.
To guide you, you have the dream books of magic, theology,
and philosophy. Without these, you wouldn't have all of the
answers, but you would know where your knowledge ends.
Life would become a journey of discovery, an adventure into
uncharted places. With the dream books, life becomes a gamble on a horse race fixed by tipsters who do not know what
horses are running. You follow the dream books to disappointment, disillusionment, cynicism, or to desperation.

6

We are now living in an era of new mapmakers—the age of
science. The scientific attitude is a modern contribution to
good living. It could not arise until there had been accumulated a large body of practical arts and techniques for handling the world we live in. These arts and techniques have
made further discovery possible. Finally, discovery for its own
sake has become a dominant interest of a large number of our
most gifted people, and modern science is here.

The scientific revolution did more than hasten the invention of thousands of articles whose use has completely changed
our way of life. It changed our way of thinking. It gave us not
only mechanical engineers but human engineers. It gave us
a new vocabulary, a new approach to the world in which we
live. Essentially, it gave us maps which, when followed, lead

us to the places where we want to go. "Spare the rod and spoil the child" has been supplanted by *Don't Be Afraid of Your Child,* by Hilde Bruch, M.D. Eventually, this attitude toward human problems will enable us to organize human relations so as to eliminate war. That is, if our leaders can cleanse their minds of the verbal nonsense of the dream books of the past.

Science has been defined in many ways. *Encyclopaedia Britannica* says that science is common sense controlled by method. Bertrand Russell seems to regard science as an outlook on life which includes the idea that statements of fact should be based upon observation rather than upon unsupported authority. I think of science as the art of creating concepts (fictions, if you will) which can be used for predicting what will happen under given circumstances.

Science begins with verifiable description, which in itself is a kind of prediction (if I say that a car stands in front of your house, I am predicting that you will see the car if you look out of your window). Science then summarizes its descriptions in terms of larger generalities. An officer of the traffic department counts the number of cars which pass a certain intersection during a certain time, and from his count made at various times during the year, predictions can be made about the number of traffic accidents the hospitals will have to deal with and predictions can be made regarding traffic congestion in the downtown areas. During the war, campaigns or smaller operations were planned; and as part of the planning, it was predicted that each operation would involve a definite number of casualties. This enabled the planners to provide adequate medical services to meet the expected demand.

When we say that some sciences are more exact than others, we mean that the degree of predictability is greater in the more exact sciences. Astronomy, physics and chemistry have a high degree of predictability. In biology the degree of predictability diminishes. Psychology enjoys a lesser degree of predictability. No one could have known in advance that Edison would invent the electric light bulb. But a competent psychologist could have predicted that his accomplishments would be extraordinary.

We have made remarkable strides. We can say with reasonable certainty how many persons in any large community will require psychiatric help at some time during their lives. With the help of more accurate psychology, we have discovered the nature of emotional conflict and of anxiety, and we know that anxiety can be diminished almost to the vanishing point by controlling emotion and resolving emotional conflict.

This is one of the most important discoveries of the twentieth century. It holds forth promise to untold millions of troubled people. It is important only that psychiatrists rigidly define their words so that instead of the Babel of confusion, each knows what the other means when he talks about emotion, conflict, and anxiety. Psychiatry is no longer the adolescent child in the family of science. It has gone through its theorizing stage. By becoming mature, itself, it can now help thwarted people to grow into their own mental and emotional maturity.

In this enterprise, you can help yourself to better understanding by doing your part. It takes only a bit of practice to learn to detect in your own thinking the words that confuse rather than clarify. Some people are helped by reading a book such as Stuart Chase's *Tyranny of Words*. It is easy reading and, from more than one point of view, worth while. Another good book about words is *Language in Action*, by Hayakawa. A reading of these books should enable you to vacate the world of meaningless words for the world of communication where maps correspond to reality. This is the verbal world of sanity.

Beginning now, whenever you become irritated by people or events, ask yourself whether you are reacting to the word maps of magic, theology, or philosophy. If so, you can know that meaningless maps are warping your understanding and directing your behavior. This knowledge should lead you back into the world of reality.

7

This seems very easy to do, and it is. However, there is one barrier to more accurate thinking. That barrier, against which you should be warned, is created by the fact that language has more than one use. Language has two functions. It enables you to talk to other people and it enables you to talk to yourself. People say things to themselves that they could not be persuaded to utter in company. They say things to customers, to policemen, to salesmen, and to associates that they would never say to themselves. They practice a double standard of speech: one for public and one for private consumption.

This fact is the nub and the kernel and the basis of verbal confusion that leads to your daily irritations with people and circumstances. As soon as you learn to distinguish between your public and your private speech habits—the speech of communication and the speech of daydreams—you will be on your way to getting along better with your friends and with yourself.

For you live in a world of words. You grow into it, make yourself at home, and finally cease to ask, "What does nervousness mean, Daddy?" You know the meanings, or think that you do, until you take your verbal world as much for granted as the air that you breathe.

Words are not only a symbol of experience; they are also

primary experiences. "Red" may mean the color of a book; it also recalls warmth, loyalty, revolution, and blood. That is why the revolutionary fathers adopted red as the more important stripe in our flag.

These meanings are private. When you ask your son to hand you that red book, you do not mean that warm, loyal, revolutionary, bloody book. Red is a word—a symbol of experience with red things. But when you select red in your decorations, you are expressing your private meanings. You want to have things about you that make you "see red."

In like manner, there are cold words, dirty words, ugly words, beautiful words. Amaryllis, to me, is a lovely word. To me, that is. To most people the name means nothing. Except to mention it by way of illustration, I do not use it in ordinary conversation. As a substitute, I might say "shepherdess." What word is dirty, clean, cold, beautiful, kindly, or revolting depends upon the private experience of the person using the word.

If you want to get along with your fellows, please remember that your private vocabulary is singular to yourself, and that other people's vocabularies often express meanings known only to them.

During the First World War, a sergeant shouted at a rookie, "You son of a bitch, keep your part of the barracks policed." The young man swept around his bed, brooding over the epithet and becoming angrier by the minute. Finally, he walked into the sergeant's office, and said, "Take off that shirt with the chevrons and I'll knock your teeth down your dirty throat."

The sergeant was mystified, and when the rookie explained, he burst into loud laughter. "Why, you son of a bitch," he exclaimed. "That means I like you. If I had meant anything unfriendly, I'd have called you Private Jones."

The science of the psychology of language (semantics, it is called) will do much to sweep up and burn the accumulated trash of so-called thought that obscures man's knowledge of himself. It will substitute meanings for nonsense in editorials, speeches by radio commentators, books of the social sciences. It will enable man to get along with man, by providing a language of real communication. It will replace the Tower of Babel with a structure in which mankind can dwell in mutual understanding. Generally and individually, it will substitute order for disorder, reason for unreason, peace for war.

But one thing it will not do. It will never make private meanings identical with public communication. Even semantics has its limitations. "An empty house" may mean the same thing to many people, but "an empty home" means something different to all of us. It may mean a home devoid of love. It may mean a home with tawdry furnishings. A scholar would say "a home without books." To some it may mean an empty cradle or a little bed that is not used any more.

From the world of our private meanings, there is no communication with the outside. This is the tragedy of human loneliness. Each individual lives alone in a little separate world of his own dreams, and there is no one who can share his private world. Subverbal communication? A handclasp? The tender, feathery caress? A kiss? These reveal much—much more than mere words. But nothing we can do or say will truly, fully communicate what we feel or think. No two people talk an identical language. No recipient of messages has shared the same experiences as the sender. "If only you could know how I feel." Only! Why, telling exactly how you feel is the essence of the arts of literature, painting, music, and the dance. To extend the limits of communication is to be greatly creative, and the greatest creators are the ones who feel their limitations the most keenly.

But there is some small consolation to be derived from these facts. Privacy and solitude are not to be despised. If there were such a thing as mental telepathy, some extranatural means of communication, so that we could read each other's minds directly, would you be pleased to have anyone look into the back yard of your mind?

For purposes of helping your nerves, this analysis of words —tools of thought—can be useful to you. The next time that people or things get on your nerves, stop and think: how are you interpreting the situation? In terms of voodoo magic? In terms of a tribal theology? In terms of a philosopher's word chopping? Or are you confusing your living room with your castles in Spain, your reality with your daydreams? Perhaps the actions of those who annoy you are appropriate in your home town, even if they are out of place in the land of your dreams. Ask yourself these four questions the next time your son makes you angry or worries you. Thus, you may be able to stall your emotional machinery before the engine starts and backfires.

Words are indeed triggers to action. The gun is always loaded. You are now able to identify your target before you press the trigger.

CHAPTER ELEVEN

Every Man His Own Analyst

1

A BIG SHOT in the moving-picture industry had made a bad decision. It was so bad that it was holding up an expensive production schedule and costing his studio thousands upon thousands of wasted dollars. His bad decision had been his refusal to hire a certain technical expert, the one man who knew how to design the historical sets and costumes. Worse, he had needlessly insulted this expert. Now the fat of big salaries was burning in the slow fire of long delay. And now the big shot was taking sleeping tablets.

Incompetence? Waste of stockholders' money? Perhaps. But before condemning, let us listen to the executive's story.

He had been a poor boy, the youngest of seven poor boys. Once a week was landlord day; once a week was family crisis. Every shopping expedition was a gamble. Would the pennies stretch to buy groceries for a meal? When shoes were needed, dimes, nickels, and pennies would be scraped together and carefully put into piles on the scarred golden-oak dining-room table, to be counted over and over. Finally, if there were enough coins, the family would troop forth to buy a new pair of shoes, for the oldest boy.

The next to oldest got his brother's shoes. The youngest got the shoes that had, in their earlier beauty and strength, protected six other pairs of feet. These, shapeless, cobbled, and scuffed, descended to him.

This youngest boy had many ambitions. One of these was to

wear a pair of new shoes. As a child, he had to pass a shoe store on his paper route. He would press his funny nose against the plate-glass window, with tears streaming down his cheeks. In high school, he would twist his feet under him so that no one could see his shabby shoes. He worked his way through college, tramping miles to save a nickel, delivering packages, running errands, doing anything to convert the energy of hot feet into that of cold cash.

He came to Los Angeles and cooled his run-down heels in other people's offices, until finally he got a job as a cutter. From cutter to director to producer, that was his decade of rapid progression.

When he found himself in the money, he had wooden models made of his feet. These he left with his shoemaker, who made thirty or forty pairs of shoes for him. He had a special cabinet with glass doors built in his dressing room, with each pair of shoes in its own compartment. One thousand dollars a week meant just one thing to him: new shoes.

"Why didn't you hire your technical expert?" I asked. "How come you let him get away?"

"His shoes," the executive replied. "They were run-down at the heels. You see, the first thing I look at when I size up a man is his shoes. If his shoes are shabby, he can't be any good. You can read a man's character in his shoes. It never fails. This is the first time I've ever missed."

I could visualize this producer leaning around his desk to scrutinize the shoes of those he interviewed. A few people knew of his idiosyncrasy. One worthless writer had talked himself into a contract by wearing rented English hand-made walking boots before applying for a job. "Funny thing about him," the producer said. "I had a feeling that he was a phony, but there was something about him I liked, so I tried to give him a break."

"If his shoes are shabby, he can't be any good." This was the blind spot of an otherwise brilliant man, a blind spot that had held up a picture schedule with a resultant loss of more money than he cared to think about. Call it word blindness, or call it a neurotic trend or a stupid prejudice or a conditioned reflex, the fact remains that its possessor was not aware of it as such. He was ready at any time to argue that a man's shoes are the surest index of his character and ability. His dirtiest epithet was "down at the heels." His own rise in the world was symbolized by better shoes, and now shoes were his symbol of all values.

All of us have these irrational attitudes which limit our possibilities for adaptation to our immediate problems. In some cases, it is a religious prejudice. In others cases, the complex is based upon racial differences. Or the basis may be sexual.

One woman whom I have treated had such a lack of confidence in men that she avoided marriage, set about making a career for herself in the business world, and failed because she could not make herself co-operate with any of the men with whom she had to associate. Her father had been somewhat of a weakling, upon whom the family could not depend. Men, to her, were the producer's equivalent of "down at the heels." In high places and low, such attitudes distort clear thinking. It is frightening to consider how much of the history of the world has been given its direction by the emotional complexes of those who happened to be in power.

We can skip Hitler and his hatred of Jews and pass by Alexander Hamilton with his fear of the poor, and proceed to the case of the alcoholic salesman. His complex could be summed up in the sentence, "It's manly to drink to excess."

This fellow had been brought up a little too much on the easy side of the street. His mother had provided everything for him and had supervised his every thought and activity. Too much maternal domination, not enough encouragement to buck the game for himself, had made him a bit of a baby. And he didn't like to be a baby. He wanted to be his own boss.

There was one person whom his mother could not boss. That person was the superintendent of their ranch, a hard-working, hard-riding, hard-drinking, poker-playing, ex-cow-boy. He was a man, and everyone in the county knew it. My patient knew it, even when he was a little boy. But the superintendent's drinking had impressed the boyish mind dramatically, because it was the one activity of the superintendent that his mother obviously could not control. So whisky came to be my patient's symbol for manliness and independence.

Now, when his mother interfered with his plans and forced upon him her gratuitous advice, he couldn't assert his independence by telling her to mind her own business. That would hurt her feelings, and he had been trained never to do that. There was but one way for him to free himself from mamma's domination, one escape from childish dependence into manhood. That escape was alcohol.

When he was under the influence of whisky, he was able to identify himself with the superintendent of the ranch whom his mother had not been able to dominate. Whisky meant freedom from the apron strings.

Bringing this unconscious complex into the light of conscious recognition went a long way toward his cure. "You drink to give yourself the feeling of freedom from domination," he was told, "but actually your drinking enables your mother to boss you even more completely. When you're drunk, you really need a keeper. Can't you seek freedom by some other means, some means that really produces worth-while results?"

2

Complexes, such as phobias and morbid fears and obsessions, are sometimes called neurotic trends. Really, they are conditioned reflexes dressed in a new terminology. Habit patterns of behavior of the entire body become established by some recurring situation. In Pavlov's dogs, cowering, dryness of the mouth, and cessation of the flow of gastric juices became established by shocking them with an electric current. Pavlov could have called these habits a "fear complex," or a neurotic trend.

Habit patterns exist below the level of consciousness. We are not aware of them. It's just the way that we are set to behave. In other words, most emotional habits are unverbalized, but they control nearly all of our conscious life.

Unverbalized habits are dynamic. They demand expression. Sometimes these habit patterns keep one from hiring the best man, or lead another into alcoholism, or otherwise prevent people from acting in their own best interests.

Habits of which there is no awareness can be a heavy drag. To prevent such habit patterns from directing you into behavior that produces maladjustment and disappointment and neurosis, you can bring them into consciousness. You can verbalize them and so bring them under control. For doing this, definite methods have been worked out. But first, let us look at complexes or neurotic trends more closely.

The late Dr. Karen Horney in her book, *Self-Analysis*, describes ten neurotic trends, with an additional fifty-seven varieties of these ten, making a total of sixty-seven neurotic trends, which to her stand out as describable entities. Her approach to the problem of neurosis indicates a spectacular advance in psychoanalytic theory away from the philosophical and toward the scientific and experimental approach. Some of these neurotic trends include:

1. The morbid need for affection
2. The morbid need for power and domination
3. The morbid need for personal admiration
4. The morbid dread of criticism
5. The morbid fear of failure

These neurotic trends and others, she says, may determine a person's character by forcing him to develop those attitudes, feelings, and ideas that are consistent with his neurotic trends. A man's mental image of himself is determined by his neurotic trends. As in the case of the motion-picture producer, his judgment of others was warped by such harmful habits. His enterprise and his relationships with the rest of the world were limited by the demands of his neurotic nature. They shut him in from the world and shut him out from opportunity. And finally, when his neurotic trends came in to conflict with each other, a real neurosis developed.

Dr. Horney's books are worth studying. They include *The Neurotic Personality of Our Time, New Ways in Psychoanalysis,* and *Self-Analysis.* They should give a new and progressive direction to the psychoanalytic movement, bringing it into closer contact with the sciences of physiology, psychology, and sociology.

Dr. Horney states that she is positive that her list is neither complete nor clear-cut. And with good reason, for each personal problem is unique and in a class by itself. As treatment, therefore, one should learn how to recognize his own special neurotic trends and learn how to rid himself of them.

The best way to change your own subconscious habit patterns is to change your mode of life. Your habit patterns have their existence in the way that you behave. Subconscious habits are like any other habits. Doing anything that is inconsistent with these habits is the switch that shunts the undesired habits over to a sidetrack, where they rest and rust in disuse. Always remember: it takes a good activity to block a bad one.

In previous chapters, you have been told of methods of changing your way of life. You have been told how to relax. Relaxation is a method of breaking up subconscious habit patterns, so that the emotions associated with muscle tensions simply dry up from disuse. You have been told how to work, how to play, how to think. All of these methods are ways of changing your mode of life, your habits of living and feeling. These methods work because there is no clear-cut and sharp line separating the subconscious or unverbalized habit patterns from those of which we are conscious. You might say that these and other methods of psychiatry are methods of re-education. I suppose that one could define psychiatry as the science that studies and re-educates conscious and subconscious behavior patterns in the interest of better living.

3

Psychoanalysis is another method by which you can eliminate behavior patterns that work against your own conscious purposes. Psychoanalysis is a method of enabling you to understand yourself. It is a form of treatment that helps you discover your unverbalized habit patterns, or (as the analyst would say) your neurotic trends, in order to bring them under your conscious control. You can't be expected to do much about your neurotic trends when you do not know that they exist. Psychoanalysis brings them into the sharp focus of your consciousness, where you can see them and do something about them.

Can you psychoanalyze yourself? I think so. Charming Lady Bountiful did it when her nerves were beginning to get her down. She complained about insomnia, palpitation of the heart, and wondered whether glandular treatments wouldn't help. She had been taking "shots" but, judging by results, they had been shots in the dark.

Among other things, we agreed to try self-analysis. She began her self-analysis by writing on paper all that she did during a typical day. Her day proved to be a hectic round of errands, mostly senseless, that she was running for other people. For example, "Drove Mrs. Smith to the hairdresser," and "Took the two Jones children to the swimming club." I picked out these two items.

"Couldn't Mrs. Smith have taken a streetcar or a taxicab?"

"Yes, I suppose that she could. Only, I called her up, and when she said that she had to have a hair-do, I offered to drive her to the beauty shop. I couldn't back out, could I?"

"What did your husband think of your free taxi service?"

"He just jumped all over me. He doesn't realize that you have to do things for other people if you want them to like you.

"He yelled at me so that I couldn't get to sleep."

"So, actually, you were generous to Mrs. Smith at your husband's expense. That's what it really adds up to, don't you think?"

"Well, I spent my time."

I decided to talk about that later. "What about the Jones children? When I was a boy and wanted to go swimming, I had to make it on my bicycle, or else I took a streetcar, or walked."

"But I had promised the children. Should I break a promise to them?"

"Here, again," I pointed out, "you were generous with your husband's car and tires and gas. And here again, you deprived .hose children of their opportunity to solve their own problems. Now go on doing as you have been doing, but keep track on paper of your daily round of activities. And after a week, study over what you have done. Name your doings in words that you would apply to someone whom you don't like. In short, look at yourself as you would at some other woman."

In a week she came in with her report.

It included many trivial errands that she had run for people in whom she had no interest. It included hours of shopping for gifts to give to people to whom she was under no obligation. And this is the point of it all—from her favors and gifts she was deriving not the least bit of satisfaction or sense of accomplishment.

"How would you characterize these activities in another?" I asked.

"Busybody. Minding other people's business. Trying to buy friendship and appreciation. Spending my husband's money, and kidding myself into thinking that I'm useful." She began to cry. "And I'm so unhappy. Nothing that I do makes me happy."

"Then ask yourself why you do those things."

Within a week she had the answer. She had written, "I run around doing things for other people to keep from thinking what a failure I have been."

"Why do you consider yourself a failure? Don't tell me. Think about it and write the answer."

She wrote, "Doctor, I always wanted to be a writer. I never dared, because I was afraid of failure. I can't stand the thought of failure. I'd rather be dead than start anything and fail and have people laugh at me. I suppose that you will call this another of your neurotic trends, and say 'Why?' I know why. My father and mother were perfectionists. Nothing that I did was ever good enough to suit them. I always had to get perfect marks in school, always had to excel at games, had to make the

best sorority. I was afraid to go to college for fear of disappoint-
ing them. And I got into the habit of avoiding anything, even
though I wanted to do it, for fear that I might fail. So I never
became a writer, and I'm thoroughly dissatisfied with my life.
I've wasted all of my opportunities. So I run errands for people because it keeps me from thinking about myself. I despise
the people who sponge on me. I hate to do things for people.
But it's better than worrying myself to death."

You will see in this progression of self-analysis how one
neurotic trend after another was uncovered. First, the neurotic need to "help" others, which was revealed as resulting in
activities that prevented others from leading their own lives
and solving their own little problems. Then came the exploita-
tion of her husband and others, using them to furnish the
means of her apparent generosity. It's easy to be generous with
someone's else's money. She uncovered her neurotic need for
activity, which she recognized as empty of accomplishment
and satisfaction. Finally came the discovery of her neurotic
and paralyzing fear of failure.

She adjusted to discovery of her neurotic trends by getting
a job as a reporter on a newspaper. Her husband was de-
lighted. "At last you're doing something worth while," he said.
Perhaps she will never be any great shakes as a writer, although one can never tell, but she is happy. "I never do anything for anyone that he can do somehow for himself," she
told me, "and even then, all I'll do is put opportunity in his
way. And now, if I'm going to help another person, it's with
my money and not my husband's."

You can uncover your neurotic trends by going through the
same procedure. First, make a schedule of the things that you
do every day. You will discover that some activities are almost
compulsive in character. Something within you makes you
follow them. Put a check mark against these Pied Piper activ-

ities; they will bear investigation. Some of them may be useful, and play an important part in your life's plan. They are good for you, resultful, and they give you a feeling of healthy accomplishment. They are not neurotic trends. But there are other activities which make you feel like kicking yourself for having done them. They result in nothing but misunderstandings, quarrels, disappointments. They make you unhappy. They disturb the normal relationships of your friends, your family, and yourself. These activities are leading you to destruction. They are motivated by neurotic trends. Double check them.

What drives you into these activities? Why do you do them? Don't answer this question by explaining the immediate situation involving each one. That will only confuse you and throw you off the scent. Remember that you are looking for neurotic trends, not for excuses for behaving in your own worst interests. For example, do you constantly quarrel with your children? Is this getting you nowhere fast? Is this a habit that you would like to break? Then don't list all of the reasons for every quarrel. Ask yourself what neurotic trend makes you quarrelsome.

In one case, a patient quarreled constantly with his wife. An analysis of his behavior at the factory where he worked showed that he habitually dodged responsibility. Having to support a wife prevented his quitting his job. He lessened his job worry by quarreling with the wife. Fear of responsibility was the neurotic trend that kept him from having a happy home life with the woman he loved. That same fear kept him from getting ahead on the job that he could have enjoyed. After he discovered his neurotic trend and found out how he had acquired it, he reacted to it by facing responsibility—to the advantage both of his work and his love life.

Your list of neurotic trends might include some of **these:**

"I have a compulsion to show off."

"I feel that I have to make some attack on every person whom I meet."

"I use illness as a means of getting my own way."

"I fear responsibilities that really are not too great for my abilities."

"I have an abnormal need for sympathy, which makes me tell everyone my troubles."

"I have a neurotic tendency to exploit other people."

"I have a neurotic compulsion to make everything perfect, which prevents me from making anything."

This list could be extended indefinitely. It is intended only to give you an idea of what is meant by a neurotic trend: a name for a group of unconscious habits or attitudes which prevent you from being yourself.

No one likes to tell on himself. That is the difficulty you will run up against in your attempt to name your own neurotic trends. Everyone has some vague sort of idea of his personality which he confuses with the front that he puts on consciously to dazzle his contemporaries. The idea of one's own self is very precious. Any object, person, idea, skill, or group that one can modify with the pronoun "my" is likely to be every man's idea of the best object, person, idea, skill, or group. About themselves, humans are like the three monkeys who are determined to see no evil, hear no evil, speak no evil. And this is what you have to fight when you start to discover your own neurotic trends.

Freud called this tendency *repression*. Any fact or experience that tends to reflect less than a flattering picture of the self is pushed out of consciousness. Repression is the very human tendency of a man to kid himself, or (to put the matter in scientific terms) to inhibit any impression that puts the ego in a shady light. And it is this tendency that you must fight if you are to understand your unhelpful or destructive habit patterns.

There is a way to fight this tendency to see oneself through rose-colored glasses. You can become objective about yourself. This is the way to do it. You have listed your activities and sorted out those that are not productive of satisfactory results. For the moment, don't bother with your motives for starting these activities. Judge the activities only by results. By their fruits you can identify the trees. Now ask yourself how you would interpret this behavior if it were the behavior of some other person. Do as Lady Bountiful did. In her case, you would have brushed aside explanations as excuses, rationalizations. You would have shrewdly put your finger right on her neurotic trends. Do as much for yourself.

Take the case of the loving wife. She wouldn't let her husband see his old friends because they kept him up too late. She would call up his office to tell the boss that her husband could not come to work because he had a slight cold. She wouldn't let him read more than half an hour because she didn't want him to ruin his eyesight. Add up these and forty more items, and you come to one conclusion: the loving wife was trying to ruin her husband's life. And why that conclusion? Because in spite of all of her loving protestations, her behavior led only in that direction. In spite of all that she might say, in spite of all her endearing statements of wifely concern, she acted as if she wanted to accomplish a diabolical result.

As if. Remember those four letters, those two words, the next time you go motive hunting. If your behavior is *as if* you wanted to fail in marriage, or in business, or in school, *as if* you wanted to hurt someone, *as if* you had to be the prima donna, *as if* you had to put on a false front, you don't have to look any further for your neurotic trend. Evaluate your motives in terms of *as if*, and you'll have the right answer.

Once a woman observed, "It looks as if I *wanted* to be a chronic invalid, doesn't it?" She wanted me to say, "No." I said, "You do, or you wouldn't act like one." The truth helped her. Treating her as a chronic invalid would have prolonged her disability. Interpreting her behavior by its results, that is, as if the results were intentional, enabled me to discover her deepest interests and desires.

4

After you have made the exciting discovery of your neurotic trends (and let him who is free from them cast the first aspersion), your next step toward freedom is to ask, "How did I acquire these emotional habits? How did I get this fear of failure or this morbid need to lean upon someone else?" The answer is to be found in your childhood conditioning. Go over the story of your life. Write an autobiography in twenty or thirty pages, not a pretentious one, but something a little more in detail than what you would write in an application for a job. But don't put your best foot forward. Don't be afraid to tell on yourself. Get at the facts of your early conditioning that established the habit patterns that you regard as neurotic.

In one girl, a childhood fear of being thought homely made her ashamed to meet people. She trembled and shook when she had to go out-of-doors. One man, an alcoholic, felt totally inadequate, because of a childish impression that his genital organs were not as large as he thought they ought to be. He felt adequate only when drunk. Adler has stressed the fact that neurotic trends often begin in a feeling of organ inferiority. The need to find some compensating achievement becomes a neurotic obsession. Whatever the cause, you will find that your conditioning took place in your childhood, giving you habit patterns, most of which are valuable, but some of which may be interfering with your adult success.

Your last step, of course, is to react to your neurotic habit patterns in a positive way. You simply refuse to react in your adult situation in a manner appropriate to childhood fantasy. In the case of the homely girl, for example, she said, "So I'm homely. I'll make up for it by becoming very efficient and likable." This wasn't enough, though. She had plastic surgery done on her face, which changed her personality more than it did her nose. That was better than hiding at home. So a boy whom his friends called "flap-ears" had a minor operation that prevented his developing neurotic trends. But this digresses. Do as Lady Bountiful did after she discovered her neurotic trends. Get into work and activity that brings results in terms of real satisfaction.

You must do something about it. Mere awareness of neurotic trends is not enough. It was once thought that if a person were "analyzed," the analysis would effect the cure. The theory was assumed that mere awareness of the cause of nervousness would end the nervousness. The theory failed to take into account that conditioned reflexes are habits that exist in the body unknown to their owner, but habits, nevertheless. Becoming aware of any habit pattern may be one step toward breaking that habit, but it is not the final step. The habit is broken only by doing things that are inconsistent with the neurotic habit pattern.

This is illustrated by the treatment of such nervous habits as tics, or muscular twitchings, or stammering. First the patient is made conscious of his habit by practicing his muscular spasms voluntarily. He does consciously what he wants to avoid doing unconsciously. Then he is taught to relax the muscles that twitch. He soon becomes aware of his muscles when they twitch involuntarily, and then he consciously lets go of his muscle tensions. He has learned to control them by bringing their behavior into the spotlight of his awareness.

You go through this same process when you psychoanalyze yourself. You know that your neurotic trends are conditioned reflexes—complicated habit patterns. You know that these habit patterns are so automatic that you are not likely to know of their existence, unless you deliberately seek to discover them. Finally, you know that discovery of neurotic trends should lead to action. Have your neurotic trends compelled you to do certain things? It's good to know that. Now do exactly the opposite.

5

When you psychoanalyze yourself, you will be helped by knowing a little more about this method. For purposes of self-analysis, it can be explained very simply.

Psychoanalysis owes its virility to two distinct contributions to medicine. The first is Freud's discovery of the subconscious. He demonstrated that our unverbalized habit patterns, of which we are mostly unaware, point the direction and give the momentum of our conscious behavior. Up to his time, consciousness and power of conscious choice were enormously overemphasized, while the power of the subconscious was hardly considered. His critics point out only the fallacies of his philosophical system, which he erected to explain the nature of the subconscious. They miss the big contribution. If there had been no Freud, we might not know that there is a subconscious to be explained in scientific terms.

Psychoanalysis' second contribution to medicine is the method of free association. This is a method you can use to discover your subconscious trends. You say whatever comes to your mind, letting one word suggest another. You do not inhibit your thought. You do not edit your phrases. You tell on yourself. This is a method of overcoming your own repressions. Instead of presenting a flattering picture of yourself, you say the things that you honestly think, letting your fond and flattering images of yourself fall where they may.

You can use this method in self-analysis. My patients call it automatic writing. They sit with paper and pencil for half an hour a day and write whatever comes to mind. Some of them are surprised at what they find out about themselves. One young man who had been ever so prim and proper that scarcely a bad word could cross his lips started to write whatever might come into his mind. At first he wrote about harmless little worries, but more and more he got to the root of his troubles. Such a stream of filthy language poured forth that one wondered where he had acquired the vocabulary. The upshot of it all was that he discovered he had a neurotic interest in sex, an interest made neurotic by his repression of all thoughts and activities dealing with sex. When he got next to himself, he said, "I have a definitely neurotic urge for sexual experience. How does one acquire a healthy or normal feeling about sex?"

Freud thought that sexual repression was at the root of all neurotic behavior. At the time that he wrote, taboos surrounding sexual behavior did produce many neurotic behavior patterns. In Hitler's Germany, where sex was free and easy, but where freedom of speech was hammered down by secret police, neurotics had fear complexes revolving around the expression of one's opinion. One school of psychoanalysis states that organ inferiority is at the basis of all neurotic behavior. This school, identified with the name of Adler, states that the love of being important is the root of all nervousness.

Modern medicine, however, avoids all philosophical "schools" of thought, theories into which all facts have to fit. Modern medicine springs from the laboratories of all of the sciences. Only facts count. And the facts are that neurotic trends or emotional habit patterns can be organized around any interest by improper conditioning. Each case is individual, with its own individual background. Furthermore, the way the mind works cannot be separated from the way the body works. Your mental attitudes and your physical posture have a definite connection. You know that there is a relationship between diet and healthy-mindedness. Improper or unhealthy behavior involves not only the brain but every organ of the body, and first of all, your motor habits, which are your attitudes.

Self-analysis is one method by which you can discover what it is that you do that prevents you from enjoying your own highest level of physical and mental health. It should enable you to readjust your activities, limit the number and bitterness of your frustrations, and so establish habits of response to life which will give you greater joy in living. Let us summarize what you can do in the way of self-analysis:

1. For several days, write exactly what you do from the time you awaken to the time you go to bed.

2. Pick out those activities which result in unhappiness, maladjustment, and dissatisfaction with yourself.

3. Group similar activities according to their motivation, which you will call *neurotic trends*.

4. Ask yourself how you happened to develop your neurotic habit patterns. Writing a short autobiography will help you. Writing whatever comes into your mind (free association) for half an hour a day will be revealing.

5. Adjust to your new insight by consciously directing your activities into channels that will produce results exactly opposite from those produced by following your neurotic trends.

Adjusting to your new insight has a technique of its own, especially when it involves one's vocation. We'll go into that in a later chapter. Meanwhile, this subject of self-analysis is sufficiently important to warrant a little more attention to the origin of neurotic trends. We'll go into that right now.

CHAPTER TWELVE

The First Ten Years Are the Hardest

1

So YOU ARE GOING TO WRITE an autobiography. Before you start, let's establish just what you want to accomplish. We'll begin by exclusion of what you do not want.

You do not want to write for publication. An autobiography written for publication is either amusing or it has political significance or has some other purpose that coincides with the reader's interests. You are not concerned for the moment with amusing or edifying the world. You are writing your autobiography for only one reader: yourself.

Your interest is to discover yourself through an understanding of the meaning of your childhood. You want to get to the bottom of your neurotic trends that you acquired in your younger days. You want to isolate your attitudes and look at them with interpretive hindsight. Only so can you adjust to them intelligently or exchange them for better ones. Now you want to learn how to understand your memories of that misunderstood child that you once were. Nearly everyone knows the external facts of his childhood, but few have the key of interpretation that unlocks the door of understanding. This chapter gives you the key.

The case of Robert Q. throws some light upon the question of how people get that way. At the age of twenty, he was a pathological liar. "I don't want to lie," he said. "I know when I am lying, and I know that it is going to get me into trouble. I try to stop but I can't. What can I do about it?"

He had brought trouble on his head by impersonating an army officer. Official investigation revealed that Robert put on the uniform only to gain prestige and admiration, so he was released with a warning. The warning did not deter him from repeating the offense. This time he was not detected. But his very success frightened him. Seeking help for his abnormalcy, he reported himself to the Federal Bureau of Investigation, and asked the officers to help him overcome his compulsion to lie and show off. Confronted with a sincerely repentant criminal seeking reform, they were helpless. They gave him the same advice that prison reformers give to law-enforcement agencies: "Enlist the help of a doctor who knows about such things."

Robert's childhood had been a seesaw between an affluent life in plush and gilt hotels and a poverty-ridden life of evictions from squalid tenements. His father was either in the money, spending recklessly, or in the pawnshops, borrowing desperately. When Robert was nine years old, his father became an alcoholic. When Robert was twelve, his father deserted the family.

His mother, a trained nurse, had to go to work. Her hours were long and irregular. She tried to make a home for her son, but for the most part the boy had to shift for himself.

Robert Q. resented having no home life. He compared his lot with that of other boys. He hadn't asked to be born. His existence was his mother's responsibility, and he held her responsible for his deprivation of a father and a real home. Children are harsh judges and make few allowances. He lost all respect for his mother, and she, in turn, reacted to his hostility, first with sorrow and later with indifference.

He worked his way through high school and earned excellent grades. He was offered a scholarship to college. His teachers knew nothing about his home situation. Robert had painted for them a remarkable picture pieced together from his childhood memories of periodic luxury. His father, he told them, was a mining engineer who worked for the English government in Persia. Other details of his life that he admitted to were based upon similar fictions.

To understand Robert, and through him, yourself, you should know the part that fiction plays in life. Man is the only imaginative animal. Man is the only animal whose perceptions can be called into being by his own unspoken words. The poet Wordsworth sees a crowd, a host of golden daffodils, and writes:

> *And oft, when on my couch I lie*
> *In vacant or in pensive mood,*
> *They flash upon that inward eye*
> *Which is the bliss of solitude;*
> *And then my heart with pleasure fills,*
> *And dances with the daffodils.*

All through his school days, Robert was living in an unseen world of golden daffodils. He had built up an imaginary world and had moved into it. This was a world from which he could not be evicted. Heaven only knows how often the walls of his narrow, shabby room had melted to become tapestried halls of marble, while unseen servants and slaves waited his bidding. He brought his Land of Oz into his home town, and half of the time he could not distinguish between the avenues of emerald and Main Street.

"When you put on a uniform, you are wearing a costume that belongs only in your dream world," he was told. "The costume means one thing to you and another thing to the authorities. Your problem is to recognize your dream world for the fantasy that it is, and the world of reality as a world of opportunity. Then you can do things in the real world with sweat and effort to make your dreams come true."

Today Robert is an army officer and wears an impressive uniform, with gold collar bars and silver wings, and he revels in the admiration and respect that they command.

When we analyze the troubles of Robert Q., we find three related processes that kept him from being happy and well adjusted:

1. He failed to grow up. As he grew in body and age, he continued to live in a childish world of play.

2. His dream world blocked his perceptions of the world of reality. Imagination, we should say here, is useful. We combine images in our minds to create new perceptions. These new perceptions enable us to see new possibilities and meanings in actual situations. Imagination is creative thinking. It is only when imagery blocks and distorts the perception of actual situations that it becomes harmful. This is what happened to Robert. He could not visualize his opportunity of earning an officer's uniform. His fantasy life blocked his perception of the possibilities that lay right before his eyes.

3. So he acted upon the images that grew out of his deepest needs for happiness. Inevitably, his actions put him in trouble. His arrest and fear of arrest pushed him back from reality and deeper into his dream world. Fantasy made adjustment difficult, and difficulties made fantasy more attractive than ever.

2

What kept Robert Q. from growing up? What is this business of growing up, anyway? To answer these questions for you, we will go back to the beginning of your life, when you were a little fertilized egg, too small to be seen, too silent to be heard, and completely free from the need to do anything that was not easy and pleasurable.

Once upon a time you were just a little speck of protoplasm, a tiny single cell. You grew, split into two cells, four cells, eight cells, sixteen cells. You became so big that you could have been seen by the naked eye. You were not much different from a jellyfish. You continued your growth by your own activity. You responded to your inner growth needs with never-ending activity within the opportunities and the limitations of your environment. In the deep dark of the womb, your environment was ideal, supplying an abundance of needed food dissolved in fluid, free for the taking. Your food was predigested and you never had to quarrel with the janitor to get more heat. Adjustment for you was a cinch.

As you grew within the womb, some cells developed into bones and muscles. Some cells became tiny fingers and little pink toes. Some developed into a highly specialized gastrointestinal tract. Some became eyes and others became ears. Some cells multiplied and became your nervous system. Their needs and urges expanded, and your activities became increasingly diversified. When you were about four months old and you needed exercise, you began to move your arms and kick your legs. Later, you learned to suck and swallow, so that by the time you were born, you were quite adept. You required very little postgraduate training in the art of getting an infant's living. In adapting to your environment before you were born, you were establishing habits that proved to be mighty useful later on.

In your case, and in the case of Sally and Ann and Robert and all the rest of us, growth involves the absorption of environment. This is obvious in the case of the tiny jellylike embryo. Anyone can see in his mind's eye, just as a scientist can see through his microscope, the little soft mass of cells sucking up chemical substances from the fluid in which it swims. You can picture the cells growing, budding new cells, developing into a larger mass of life. In the same way, you can see that the environment furnished by the mother's blood becomes a part of the baby. You can visualize the baby growing and developing new urges to make new responses. It is easy to realize, once we think of it, that all living is a continuous process of rejection of what we do not need and of absorption of that in our environment which is pertinent to our needs. We make whatever we accept from our environment into a part of ourselves.

It is important for you to understand that you absorb your environment by the responses you make to it. This fact underlies the psychological basis of life. What you are is the growth resulting from millions of responses to your environment. Response is active: it is a thing that you do. It implies absorbing a part of your environment. As you stand today in your tailored suit, and, under your neat little hat, all that you have met and seen and done in the past is now a part of you.

3

Before you were born, your development was the result of responses made in an environment that was chiefly physical and chemical. But after you were pulled or pushed into what we call the civilized world, your environment suddenly became much broader, much more complex and difficult. For the first time in your life, you entered a social environment, took your place in a man-made world.

Instead of living within a bag of warm fluid, you had to adjust to layers of clothing made of cotton grown in Georgia, woven in North Carolina, sewed in New York City, and purchased by your mother in some other place. On your ears fell the sounds of radio commentators, comedians, uplifters, to say nothing of the sound and fury of the speech of your everyday associates. You came into a world of people who had their established habits which they smugly called their way of life.

The habits of your community and of your world, together with the social heritage of houses, stores, a spoken language, scientific apparatus, trains, radios, books, police courts, paved roads, and art, we call society. To the habits of people around you, to the accumulation of things made by countless millions of people, to society, you had to make millions of adjustments.

Adjustments to society direct the growth of the personality. You grow by becoming a part of the lives of those with whom you live. You share the hopes and fears, the aims and aspirations, the failures and successes, of your family and friends. You come to depend upon them and they upon you. So their lives become a part of your life, and reaching out in an endless chain of influences, all of society that you can encompass becomes a living part of your personality.

Adjustment to your social situations gives meaning to your life. Through communication, by habitually understanding how other people think and feel, you acquire the basis for your estimate of yourself. You are constantly comparing your product or abilities with those of the people around you. Do you speak as well as they do? Do you dress as well? Is your work important? Above all, what do they think of you? It is this process of social adjustment that enables you to find your place in life.

Happy is the man who lives in his social environment as easily and unconsciously adjusted as a fish in water. He feels competent. He enjoys a feeling of security. He knows that he belongs. God forbid that any upheaval should toss him out of the favorable environment that he has come to take so for granted. For then he would discover how much of his life depended upon the social esteem he had accepted as unquestionably as the air he breathes. Few people realize their dependence upon general acceptance and approval.

But whether we are aware of it or not, it is through adjustment to social situations that we get our motivations. Drive or energy may be physical, but the direction and the concentration of drive are socially conditioned. The aimlessness of a simple primitive peon and the intensity of effort of a Yankee farmer cannot be explained on the basis of difference of climate alone. The peon loses no self-respect when he lies long hours in the sun on the step of his one-room adobe hut. The Yankee farmer wouldn't let himself be found dead in such a situation. His pride, his feeling of what the neighbors would think, drives him on to wrestle with his rocky farm.

It is the need to be well thought of that makes Sammy run. He wants to get ahead. It is the interaction between your prior purposes and needs and your social pressures that make you do the way you do.

4

When you were an infant and your stomach was empty, you cried. This proved to be a good technique. At least it brought results. The infant is a dictator, and when he says in effect, "Let there be food," there is food; and the crying ceases, the infant nurses, and everyone is happy.

Not that an infant's needs are not geared to the social environment of his parents. They are, but he doesn't know it. To alarm clocks, for example. There is no time clock in a baby stomach, but after an infant has been fed every four hours for a couple of weeks, you are able to set the clock by his demand for food. His digestive apparatus has been conditioned to his feeding schedule. Not only that; all of his needs are organized into socially conditioned habits and tastes which demand specific satisfactions. An infant's habits are formed in a social environment and these imperious habits reject substitutes.

His first serious conflict with his parent's world of reality and authority comes at weaning. This psychological crisis may appear in the person of the pediatrician who says, "It's time to wean him. Give him a formula and spinach."

If you think that a readjustment in diet is not a psychological crisis, ask any diabetic what dieting did to his nerves. And the diabetic is an adult, able to reason things out. He is adaptable, presumably, and capable of a little self-discipline. Furthermore, the diet of a diabetic is seldom changed radically; only the amount, not the kind of food, is rationed.

In the army, food constitutes the chief topic of conversation. Army food is better than the diet that most of the boys have enjoyed. But it tastes different; and the mess sergeant is never the most popular man on the post. His nicknames are "belly-robber" and "slum-burner." Dietary habits die hard.

Weaning is the climax of a conflict between established habits and the diet that fits the needs of a six-month-old baby. Nursing was what the doctor ordered for a newborn seven-pound baby. At six months the baby may weigh fifteen pounds. He needs new sources of blood and muscle-building foods. But he still retains his dietary habits of early infancy. He doesn't give up his old habits easily. They are his total adjustment to life. Hence the conflict between old habits and the need for new foods.

(A digression for parents: new foods should be introduced gradually and nursing should be discontinued gradually, so that the infant can slide from one to the other easily and without psychological upset. Abrupt methods of change are cruel and leave emotional tensions that make later adjustments more difficult.)

Doctors will tell you that infants should be breast-fed. They are right, both for reasons of physiology and of psychology. The breast-fed infant is healthier. He also develops a sense of security, of belonging, of being wanted, that a bottle-fed baby will not so easily acquire. So when the baby is weaned, he loses more than his old meal ticket. He loses the restaurant and the waitress whom he was beginning to love.

Well, a child can't nurse all of his life; but weaning to a child is what cutting a branch from your rosebush is to your plant. It may make for more symmetrical development. It may lead to growth in a more desired direction. But the operation leaves a scar. If it is not done skillfully, it may leave a stump that will not heal, but rot to cause trouble later on.

Weaning is used here as the symbol of childhood conflicts between established habits and the need to acquire new habits of adjustment to match physical growth and mental development. The child's life is just one weaning after another. No sooner does he become adjusted to one set of conditions than he is asked to adjust (do it now—right away—do you hear me?) to an entirely different set of conditions.

A young man may be drafted once in a lifetime. He moans that a year or so out of his life will wreck all of his plans. A child gets drafted into this and into that, without benefit of self-understanding, nor with benefit of adult understanding. We lop off his activities, set him new tasks, taking for granted that the child will do what he is told and like it.

Much of this is necessary, if the child is to take part some day in adult activities. It happened to you and it happened to me. But don't think that this chopping off of one activity after another does not upset the child's emotional equilibrium. This is the reason patients ask me, "Is anyone really normal?"

What happens when weaning from old habits is imposed abruptly? The answer goes to the root of the problem of the psychological cause of nervousness. The answer is that the old habits do not disappear or merge with new, more adult habits. The old habits continue. At the bottom of nervousness, of emotional conflict, is failure to grow up. Nervousness is a for of arrested development. You have seen how this worked out in the case of Robert Q. You will see the process unfold in a more general way as we go on.

5

In mental testing it is asked, "What is the difference between a child and a dwarf?" The correct answer is that a child is an immature human being, while a dwarf is a small human being. Feeble-minded persons cannot make the distinction between small and immature. Neither can philosophers who theorize about children without, however, taking the pains to observe them. They talk and write as if children were small adults. This error, to be expected only of the feeble-minded, is what keeps people from understanding what life looks like when seen through the eyes of children.

To a small child, life is a series of separate, unconnected incidents, each one of which grows out of some transient inner need. The moment one need is satisfied, the child goes to another activity, probably related in no way to the one preceding. One little pang of hunger, and he drops his toys. He is extremely distractible. A two-year-old cannot remember from one minute to another. The child of four years has no idea of the meaning of today or yesterday or tomorrow. Few children under seven can tell time. Their needs are not integrated, nor are their minds and purposes. Their needs and interests are kaleidoscopic, and their lives are what motion-picture scenarists would call a newsreel of unrelated events.

Contrast this with the life of an adult. You ask, "What are you doing tonight?"

"I'm going to bed early. I was up late last night, and I have to catch up with my sleep. I'm having a heavy day tomorrow."

What the adult does in the morning is related to what he plans to do in the afternoon and the day after and the day after that. What the child does at any time is related only to his need at that moment.

A child's needs and interests are not co-ordinated because his growth and his muscular control are not integrated. His organs grow by fits and starts. He starts getting teeth when he is a few months old and has dental trouble for a couple of years. He doesn't learn to hold up his head until the muscles of his neck are big and strong enough to support the weight. It is some months later that his back is strong enough to enable him to sit. Walking follows the development of the nerves and muscles that permit the complex co-ordinations which adults take for granted. Second dentition starts about a year after the child enters school, and there is more tooth trouble for some years, while the shape of the face and jaw and the relationships of the structures within the head undergo a radical change. At twelve or fourteen, the sex organs grow, producing emotional psychological disturbances of a profound character.

This irregular and rapid growth puts a great strain upon the child. Quite apart from the fact that he is a stranger in this world who has not learned how to find his way around, he has the additional difficulty of adjusting his special interests and needs to an adult world that is organized for people whose needs and interests are relatively stable. His difficulties are increased by the obtuseness of the adults who control his world and who can boast of only the dullest perception of the child's problems.

Obtuseness, of course, is a charitable interpretation of the attitude of many parents. The unwaxed and unpolished truth is that many parents are jealous of their children, resent their presence and their needs, hate the responsibility that children bring, and even hate the children. This sounds harsh, but it is true. Many parents are childish. They have failed to grow up emotionally, and are in competition with their own children. So they hand down their nervousness to their children by failing to give them an even break. The case of Robert Q. may be extreme, but adult animosity and cruelty take many forms. They often hide behind a mask of good will and kindness.

6

A child's business is to eat, sleep, and play. At first his play consists of random, unpurposive movements and crowings and gurglings. Motor skills are learned slowly. He is six months old before he can hold a cube with his hand and fingers, and a year old when he can use his fingers and thumb in opposition. When he is seven, he should be able to tie a bow knot. His increasing control of his hands means more than mere skill. He learns to use a spoon, a fork, a pencil, and other tools, and in so doing, he learns their uses and meaning and some of their possibilities. He becomes socialized. And all of this learning is effected through play.

Speech is also a learned skill. An infant cries shortly after birth. Babbling begins in his second or third month. As his motor co-ordinations increase, and as he acquires more specific habitual adjustments to his environment, his vocabulary increases. Since his first perceptions usually include his mother and father, his first words will be "ma-ma" and "da-da." At one year, a child usually has three words at his disposal. At the age of four, he can understand 1500 words. If he is destined to become a "quiz kid," he may have twice that number of words.

When does a child start to imagine? An image is a remembered perception. Imagery cannot exist until perceptions are reasonably sharp, distinct, and associated with words that make recall possible. About fifteen per cent of the play of five-year-old children involves their imagination. But it is probable that a child learns to play with his imagination at a much earlier age.

Within the child's mind, there is constant conflict between his old habits of adjustment and the need to discard these habits in favor of new ones. Put yourself in his place. How would you like to change your dietary habits every three months? Have you ever eaten eel? No? Now you must learn to eat eel, and like it, by George. Have you a yen for kohlrabi? Now is the time to acquire a taste for it. Do you enjoy milk shakes, imbibed through a straw? Yes? No more milk shakes through a straw. You'll get straight milk and drink from a glass, the way grown folks do.

When an adult gets older, he changes his habits to conform with new needs and interests. When he gives up dancing and late parties in favor of serious reading, he may regard the change as evidence of increased wisdom. But it is probable that his arteries and his digestive machinery have something to do with his behavior.

So it is with a child. New growth creates new needs, new interests. Every new spurt of bodily growth raises the curtain on new psychological needs and hungers. There is a time when a child should be breast-fed. There is a time when he needs passive cuddling. There is a time when he should have toys to manipulate, to handle, to pick up and throw down. There is a time for running games that develop his control over his larger muscles. Later he should have rhythm plays with music. Still later he needs games of individual skill, "teasing games" in which the timid child learns to dare more and venture forth. Then in adolescence come team games where he can learn ideals of fair play and of co-operation with his group.

The learning of new habits is made easy by two rewards: pleasure and love. If a child has fun in playing games appropriate for his age, he sneers at the "kid stuff" that used to amuse him. The new habits bring in more satisfaction than the old ones, and, as we say, he grows up. Satisfactory, successful adjustment to his needs sends wholesome physical and mental development on the next stage of growth.

Growth needs must be satisfied at the time they arise. Time is of the essence. Satisfaction of these needs later on is no good. Building blocks are not an opportunity to a fourteen-year-old boy, and singing and teasing games, while excellent for ten-year-olds, will be of little value to the lad of eighteen. Children must have their specific activities for growth at the specific time these activities are needed.

It is as though we were on a train passing once, and once only, through lovely scenery. If we do not look while we are passing, if the shades are drawn, we will never have an opportunity to see it again; and no picture post cards, however gaudy, can substitute for the original experience.

The rewards of love and of social approval are absolutely essential to normal development. Everybody needs the corroboration of being wanted. A child must have the warmth of love and protection. He must be made to feel secure. In the home he must feel that he belongs. Outside of the home, he needs to feel that he is adequate and capable. He must never be allowed to doubt that at home he is wanted for the person he is. In the playground and school, he should feel that he is wanted for what he can do.

When the rewards of love and social approval are given, the child identifies himself with those about him. They become a part of his personality. His desire to win more approval becomes the motive for his continued growth.

7

People have to make their mental and physical adjustments to situations the possibilities of which they do not clearly understand. This is emphatically true in childhood. In their childhood they may have been starved for experiences that their growth needs required. They may have suffered from rejection within and outside of the home. They may have suffered from physical handicaps. They may have suffered frustration when the persons and places they loved were snatched from them.

Take the case of the spindly-legged, freckle-faced tomboy, whose parents were getting a divorce. By simple unconscious imitation she had copied the muscle tensions of her distracted parents. She had to adjust to the fact of her disintegrating home. She had to adjust to the loss of a parent. With her playmates, she had to adjust to what she considered a humiliating situation. She felt the situation was humiliating because they did. Their standards were not of her making, but they were a part of her mental and physical being.

Her adjustments were not satisfactory, or only partially so. In school she was so jumpy and distracted that her schoolwork was bad. Her teacher cajoled, implored, and finally scolded her. She felt the disgrace of failing to keep up with her classmates. Among children of her own age, she was overly aggressive. She boasted of what her father was going to buy for her, and in her boasting she did not distinguish clearly between fact and the wishful thinking of vivid daydreams. Naturally, the other children disliked her, which added to her emotional and social isolation.

Her maladjustment affected her physical growth and development. Her facial expression became pinched and hard. Her digestion was bad. Her sleep was disturbed by nightmares. Her eyes took on the look of an ugly-tempered, injured dog licking his wounds.

Fortunately, the whole situation was changed dramatically by a spontaneous reconciliation of her parents. But, unfortunately, such dramatic changes are not common. A thoughtful teacher can pick out by their looks those children whose environments are creating pressures too heavy for little, young shoulders. The teachers know that for these children there is stormy weather ahead. In the case of this girl, the habits she acquired during her period of maladjustment will be hazards that may prevent the free and spontaneous development which rightfully belongs to her.

Frustration at any level of development stops growth, sending the child back to a level of adjustment suitable only to a lower age group. This process of seeking satisfaction in more infantile activities is called regression. It means simply that when you can't do something that is appropriate to your years, you do things that are below your level of attainment.

Adults sometimes regress temporarily when under the influence of alcohol. The sedate, responsible executive of fifty attends home-coming week and becomes for the time a college boy, much to the disgust of the fraternity brothers on the campus. They look askance at his clowning, and they resolve not to make fools of themselves when they are middle-aged.

This type of temporary regression that you see so often after football games and at national conventions is not serious. It probably does the old boy good to blow off steam and forget his cares and his years. But in childhood, regression is not temporary and may be a serious block to the growing-up process.

How disillusionment can distort a child's personality is seen in the case of Willie. Willie had been a model boy, sunny and warm and friendly. Always doing things for people. When company came he was the first to put an ash tray within reach, the last to require any special attention.

Overnight, it seemed, he underwent a personality change. From being immaculate, he became slovenly and untidy. He began to eat greedily, and no food set aside in the icebox for

Father's dinner was safe from Willie's bottomless appetite. If reproached for his callous piggishness, he either sulked or became noisily quarrelsome. He no longer played baseball with his school friends, and refused to come to the telephone when they called. Then he criticized the neighborhood, where all teachers were "cranks" and "all the kids are dopes."

What had happened? His family thought that the boy was going insane.

There was maladjustment somewhere, but Willie didn't like to talk about it. It centered around his father. He avoided his father as much as possible, and when his father was home, his bad behavior was at its worst.

When I met Willie's father, I was surprised. I had formed a mental picture of a thoroughly disagreeable personality. Instead, Willie's father was a warm, friendly man, kindly and shrewd, with a genuine love and understanding of children.

"I'll tell you what caused it, Doctor," he said. "Willie was all right until he discovered that I am a professional gambler."

Once Willie had adored his father. There was the time that his father had whittled out a sailboat. "Look at the boat we made," he told visitors. He had identified himself with his dad so completely that he had unconsciously imitated all of his father's small mannerisms, even to his father's way of wrinkling his forehead. "He's his father's son, all right," people would say.

How did disillusionment change Willie's personality? He had identified himself so completely with his father that his father had become a part of him. An inextricable part. It was more than heredity. He had imitated his father's friendliness, his infectious laugh, his speech mannerisms, Suddenly the god is overthrown. The god was not outside of Willie. He was a part of the boy's own personality.

However he might rationalize the situation, the wound was in himself. Something inside of him had been killed and was rotting. Willie was ashamed—afraid to mix with his fellows, lest they, too, find out the disgraceful truth. He was ashamed, not of anything that he had done, but of what he was—his father's son, all right.

Because of his disillusionment, Willie hated his father. Yet he was bound to his father by thousands of affectionate memories. The conflict produced a state of continuous anxiety, with all of the attendant disturbances in behavior that would prevent his living a creative normal life.

All of this required explanation to the boy to free him from his neurotic behavior. He learned to identify himself with what he admired in his father and not identify himself with what displeased and distressed him. In short, he became emotionally free, and his symptoms ceased. In fact, he went so far as to feel sorry for his father's inability to earn a living in a way more socially acceptable, and he resolved that he would do better when he grew up. He had put his father where he belonged—neither on the pedestal nor on the junk heap.

It often happens that a child does not adjust to frustration with open rebellion. Some children retreat within themselves. As in the case of Robert Q., they may live within a world of fantasy and daydream. In this case, they derive satisfactions through an escape from reality. This escape, sadly enough, is sufficiently pleasant to substitute for the games and competitions that are necessary for mental and physical growth.

Childhood regressions persist into adult life. They underlie the habits that are called neurotic trends. Childish adjustments prevent an adult understanding of life situations and provide no technique for dealing with them. They give rise to the conflicts between emotional habit patterns, and these conflicts are on an organic as well as a psychological level. Nervousness is the persistence of childish habits into adult life.

So now you have the key of understanding with which to interpret your childhood. You should be able, with this new understanding, to interpret any compulsions and obsessions that prevent your enjoying your life. Self-understanding, insight, is a large step forward to happiness.

Deprivations, frustrations, and lack of opportunities for activities that were necessary for your development at each stage of growth result in regression—a turning back to a lower level of childish satisfactions. This turning back means that childish habits persist when the need for them has passed. The unwanted habits survive as unsatisfactory methods for new adjustments. These habits are neurotic trends.

Nor is this all there is to failure to grow up. Deprivation, misunderstanding, disillusionment, and nagging by adults turn the regressive child mind in on itself. The child, unable to find satisfaction in achievement, lives in a five-year-old world of fantasy where dreams all come true and where Cinderella always marries her prince. The habits of seeking satisfaction in daydreams prevent one from adventuring into the world of bumps and bruises and face-flushing victories.

So now, when you seek to track down your neurotic trends, you will help yourself by writing a little autobiography. It will not be for other people to read. It need not have background and clarity and literary style. It need not be interesting to others. You can leave out much that published autobiographies ought to include. All that you tell yourself is what you missed in childhood, all of the troubles you have had, that have led to the establishment of habits that now are holding you down. Looking at them historically will help you to change these habits for others more productive of accomplishment, joy, and freedom.

CHAPTER THIRTEEN

Treat Yourself to a Fresh Start

1

A BUSINESSMAN READ the first draft of this chapter and said, "I'd like to tell you what happened to me." His story is so typical that it belongs to the reader as a kind of preface.

"I was run-down," he said. "I was doctoring for colitis and indigestion. I was sick and irritable. My doctor said, 'Your job is your disease. Get yourself some other kind of work if you have to live in a berry crate. Quit whatever you are doing, and do something else.'

"I was in a partnership. I had been trying to escape for two years. One day I cleaned up my desk and just quit. I didn't have a job and I didn't have a dime. My friends all commented on my courage. I didn't feel brave. I felt desperate. But after I quit, I felt fine.

"Since then, I've had an uphill climb. But it hasn't been too bad. And I owe to that doctor's advice whatever business success I have, and my good health."

This story can be duplicated by the hundred. If you don't like your work, it can make you sick. The wrong job, the job that you fight, produces its special occupational diseases of nervous tension, irritability, and physical disease. It's no good for you. For your health's sake, make a change. Treat yourself to a fresh start.

Studies of industrial accidents show that the accident rate increases when employees are unhappy in their jobs. Many so-called cases of accident are really subconsciously motivated forms of self-mutilation. To illustrate: a mother quarreling with her daughter turned suddenly and broke her own leg with her muscle tension. This happened in my own orthopedic surgery days. I asked her how she felt about her temper. Mother was unregretfully complacent. "At least, Dorlene won't be gadding about now," she said. "She'll have to stay home and take care of me."

Dr. Flanders Dunbar has collected a series of cases that looked like "accidents." Analysis proved that the so-called accident was a way of adjusting to some disagreeable situation by unconscious self-mutilation. Some of these disagreeable situations were bad work adjustments.

Employers know that the man most often on sick leave is the man who hates his job. What most employers do not know is that the job may be the cause of the sickness.

There is a philosophical school that calls itself economic determinism. Broken down into plain English, this school teaches that all of our adjustments depend upon the way we make our living. There is some truth in this theory, although as stated it is a little too inclusive. A semanticist would add "in part" after the word "depend."

Certainly, your work does influence your outlook upon life. It gives you status, a place in the community, helps other people to form an opinion of you. You, in turn, are affected by what others think of you. Your work influences your adjustments to your family and your friends. How you make a living pervades all of your other social relationships. If your work adjustments are a festering abscess, all the rest of your life is poisoned by this focal infection.

Normally, a man likes his work. Work is more than a way of making money. Work is a way of life. Work is an opportunity to create. It is an opportunity to exercise one's skills and techniques, to meet problems and lick them. Work is fun.

If you are not happy in your work, something is wrong. Perhaps something is wrong with the job. It may be that the foreman or the office manager takes out his neuroticism upon his help. Perhaps something is wrong with you. One young lady who crabbed about her job suddenly found that all was roses and wine when her lover returned to her. Perhaps the job is all right, and you are all right, but it's just a case of incompatibility. In that case, a fresh start is indicated.

Why does maladjustment in work make you sick? How does maladjustment in work affect your emotions, your interbrain, your digestion? The answer is: through frustration and conflict. You want your pay check and you want to escape from the circumstances under which you earn it. You can't have both. The result is indecision, mental confusion, and a wave of inhibitions spreading over your brain.

Maladjustment in work is the Pavlov bell that means three square meals and an endless series of electric shocks, in the shape of boredom, new defeats, and discouragements by the hour. You want and you don't want, and up pops a neurosis.

2

If this happens to be your problem, the answer is a fresh start and a new job. That is what the unhappy superintendent of schools decided when his job was getting him down.

He had started to teach when he was graduated from college. His intention was to study medicine after he had saved enough money. But he saved only his intention. In twelve years he had acquired a nice family, a good job, and a nervous breakdown.

He hated his job. He hated having to walk a political chalk line to keep on the right side of the Board of Education, the side on which his bread was buttered. He hated the administrative duties of a superintendent. Yet the job was paying four thousand a year, and that's not hay when there's a wife, three youngsters, and a dog in the manger, all wanting to eat regularly.

For years he had given to his graduating high-school students pearls of vocational guidance. At last he got piggish and threw himself a pearl.

"What would you do," he would ask his students, "if you had a million dollars?" And when the student answered, he'd lean back in his swivel chair, and say, "Act as if you had a million dollars, and do it. If you want to go to South America, you can do it, if not as a first-class passenger, then as an ordinary seaman. But there is nothing you want to do that you can't do, provided you do not complicate your purposes with too many accompanying conditions."

I've often said as much to my patients. My advice to him was to take his own advice. The following September, instead of enrolling students, he enrolled in a medical college.

Some of his best friends are amateur psychiatrists. They diagnosed him every kind of fool. They didn't realize that they were talking to a man who was desperately fighting for his only life. "Four years in medical school—one year of internship," they pointed out. "Why, you'll be thirty-nine years old before you can start in your medical practice, five years from now."

"If I don't study medicine, how old will I be in five years from now?" he asked.

Well, it didn't take him five years. He spent seven years in training. Four in medical school, one year of general internship, and two years of specialization were his preparation for his life's work.

They were hard years, but they were good years. There were some days when he didn't see how he could go on. "If only I get by this month," he would say to himself.

Then there were minutes when, looking into a microscope, he would enter a new world, a fascinating world where red blood corpuscles march in single file through blood vessels 1/250 of an inch in diameter; a world where deadly germs are the aggressors, while loyal white corpuscles fight and devour to overcome disease. A world of color and drama, life and death, in a drop of water.

Today he is the leading specialist in his field in the city where he used to be school superintendent. And today, he is the president of the Board of Education.

3

If your life has led you into a detour that is taking you where you do not want to go, make a fresh start. It may be tough; tomorrow it will be tougher, because you will be that much farther away from your destination.

You are driving, let us say, from Detroit to Los Angeles, and somewhere back a piece you took a fork in the road that has led you into Memphis, Tennessee. You could stop there. You might like Memphis; it's a good town. But years later, you would say, "When I was a young punk, I once thought of going on to the coast. And here I am, in Memphis." You might use your failure as an argument to discourage some aspiring soul from following his destiny. Don't do it. If you are such a weakling that you cannot manage your own life, at least don't meddle in the lives of others.

And there is no reason why you should be a weakling. It isn't hard to make a fresh start. It's hard only to decide. Once decision has been reached, you will be amazed at the good luck that will make your path easier. Good luck always attends the man who knows where he is going.

For this there is a reason. When you reach a decision and definitely select your course of action, you will meet obstacles, foreseen and unforeseen. Each obstacle you will handle with the means available to you; and so you develop your resourcefulness and force of character.

At the same time, unforeseen opportunities and unexpected advantages will also develop. This is what we call good luck. But if you had not started out to reach a definite goal, you would never have seen or heard of or even noticed these unexpected and unpredictable good turns of fortune. By knowing where you are going, you have put yourself in a position where good luck can reach you for a pat on the back.

Read a few autobiographies or biographies of people who have made good in a big way. You will find that many of them made new starts from scratch, not once but many times.

Robert Louis Stevenson studied civil engineering, won a silver medal for a paper on lighthouse apparatus. The same year he gave up engineering and began to study law. Four years later he was admitted to practice, only to discover that he did not want to be a lawyer. There followed a severe nervous breakdown.

He literally walked out on the law. He took a pedestrian trip to France and wrote his first book. In the world of letters, he made his fame with *An Inland Voyage*. Who can say how much his earlier unsuccessful starts contributed to his later sensational success?

Stevenson is no isolated case. From George Washington to Franklin D. Roosevelt, American history is bright with the names of those pioneers who had the courage to give up what was never theirs, and to seek a new life in an uncharted wilderness.

A fresh start after things have been shattered to bits. Beginning all over to reorganize one's life a little closer to the heart's desire. This is the story of many of our conspicuous successes.

To many, this advice to redirect your own life will sound somehow subversive, radical, and dangerous. Nothing could be farther from the truth. If you want to subvert your life, to undermine it radically, live it against the direction of the flow of your real personality. If your job makes you sick, quit it. What difference does it make how good it is if it isn't good for you?

There is something to be said for prudence; but the Chamberlain who never forgets to carry an umbrella is liable to find himself signing away his life, his past, and his future in Munich.

4

I once knew a businessman who had been fighting through financial difficulties. Failure would have cost him the savings of a lifetime and would have involved loss to many of his friends and people who had trusted him. He never lost his nerve, his gay smile, his optimism.

"Every time I get a setback," he told me, "I ask myself only one question—'How much can be salvaged?' "

Your life may seem to be going haywire. It's a tangle, it's a mess, and as you look back at it, there is room for nothing but useless regret, remorse, and surrender in defeat. Yet you still have your purposes, you have your interests. There are things that you still would like to do.

Ask yourself, then, how much you can salvage out of your situation. Write down your assets—your health, such as it is; your friends; your skills; your property assets. You might be able to produce a respectable balance sheet.

Are you in jail, convicted of the murder of your wife, under sentence to be hanged? That was the fix of David Lamson. He had been a book salesman for the Stanford University Press. He had made no spectacular use of his abilities, but had managed like millions of others to get by, until his wife was killed, his property dispersed, and his own life placed in the greatest danger.

There didn't appear to be much that could be salvaged. But as he waited for his appeal to go before the Supreme Court of California, he wrote *We Who Are About to Die*. The book was a great success. Later, the Supreme Court set aside his conviction, because it was obtained upon the flimsiest of evidence. Truth prevailed, and he never was convicted; and when finally he regained his freedom, he had become a successful and famous author.

There have been others.

At the age of thirty-four, Dorothea Lynde Dix developed an open, hemorrhaging tuberculosis. Her life had never been happy. Her father had been a shiftless, irresponsible ne'er-do-well who lived by his wits—chiefly by selling theological tracts to the witless. When other girls were sewing doll's clothes, Dorothea was stitching the pages of these pamphlets. At twelve, she was desperate, and she ran away from home.

Her grandmother taught her the three "R's"—and at fourteen, Dorothea was teaching school in Worcester, Massachusetts. This attempt to earn her own living failed; but three years later, she started teaching again, working from dawn until after midnight. Her school, a boarding school, was her sole responsibility. She was teacher, housemaid, cook, and administrator. Frail and weak, she worked day and night, until at the age of thirty-four she was through. She was coughing up blood. For two years she chased the cure. Now, nearing her forties, she was a played-out, tuberculous, old-maid ex-school-marm.

How much, do you suppose, could anyone salvage from that situation? And in appraising the total situation, remember that this was in the year 1838. Abraham Lincoln had not yet been heard from. The beginning of the Civil War was twenty-two years in the future. Women could not vote. Opportunities for women in any field of endeavor were few.

Opportunity knocked at her door, timidly, in the shape of a young theological student. He came to ask Miss Dix for advice. Would she give him some pointers on how to conduct a Sunday-school class for women in the East Cambridge Jail?

"Young man, I'll teach them myself," said Dorothea Lynde Dix.

To jail she tramped the following Sunday morning. It was bitter cold, but Dorothea Dix never permitted the inalterable to interfere with her plans. In the jail were the women "prisoners," the mentally ill of the community. They had committed no crimes. They were locked up because Boston had no other place to keep them.

Shivering, Miss Dix asked, "Where is the heat?"

The jailer smiled condescendingly. "Insane folks can't feel heat or cold," he told her.

Dorothea Lynde Dix had found her work, something to do, something to salvage from her hopeless life. For two years, she traveled about Massachusetts, investigating the care afforded the mentally ill.

She found a harmless, insane boy who was being cared for by his married sister. Sister explained, "We had rather take care of him than leave him to strangers, because we are kinder." This boy had been confined in a log pen, about eight feet square. No heat in winter or shade in summer had been provided. His feet which had frozen became gangrenous. And his sister really believed that she was doing better than could be expected.

In another town, she discovered a young woman chained naked in a manger of a barn. Alone, unprotected, she was the helpless prey of vicious men and young boys, who could visit the place at will.

She investigated further. When she had enough facts, she took them to the legislature of Massachusetts. Her memorandum began:

"I come to present the strong claims of suffering humanity. I come to place before the Legislature of Massachusetts the condition of the miserable, the desolate, the outcast. I come as the advocate of helpless, forgotten, insane, and idiotic men and women . . . of beings wretched in our prisons, and more wretched in our Alms-Houses.

"I proceed, Gentlemen, briefly to call your attention to the State of Insane Persons confined within this Commonwealth in cages, closets, cellars, stalls, pens; chained naked, beaten with rods, and lashed into obedience!"

The battle was on. There is no use in going into the details. Against public apathy, against prejudice, Dorothea Dix was a one-woman war of revolution against chains for the mentally ill.

The legislature passed a bill providing for the care of the mentally ill at Worcester State Hospital. Rhode Island was her next objective. Cyrus Butler was reputedly the wealthiest man in the state, also the stingiest. Miss Dix walked into his office with indignation in heart; she left with a check for $40,000 in her purse. This is the history of Rhode Island's Butler Hospital for the mentally ill.

On to New Jersey. To Pennsylvania. To North Carolina. Wherever there were the mentally ill, all over the United States, and even to Europe and Asia, Dorothea Dix traveled, investigated, protested, won. She drafted the bill organizing St. Elizabeth's Hospital in Washington, D.C., and obtained its present beautiful location.

Twenty-two years after she started her crusade, the Civil War broke out. Miss Dix was now about sixty years old. She was appointed to the position of Chief Nurse of the Medical Department of the Army. Another first, for no one had ever held that position. It was created for her, she for it. For her services she was given all that she asked—an American flag.

She died when she was eighty-five years old, "the most useful and distinguished woman America has yet produced."

You can salvage plenty from your life. It has to be pretty bad before it can equal in utter hopelessness the two case histories of people who wouldn't stay licked.

5

How does a person manage to find his life's work?

If you don't know just what you really want to do, do anything. Anything is better than nothing. The first job that you take may not be the right job for you, but after you've tried it, you'll be on your way to finding out just what you are fitted to do. Your next job will be nearer your fit and style.

Incidentally, it is easier for a person who is working to get a better job than it is for a man out of work to get any job. Employers make the practical test of employability. They like to hire the fellow who is making good. By hitting the ball for the home town, you make yourself a chance to break into a bigger and better league.

People who are happy in their work are able to prevent storms from arising in the interbrain, even though many other parts of their lives are out of joint. While you are at work at the nearest and best work you can find, make a list of the things you have done that have given you the greatest satisfaction. It doesn't matter whether you have been paid for these activities. The chances are that, if you enjoyed them, you have not been paid. Often a person has to give away thousands of dollars' worth of services before he discovers that they have a commercial value.

This was true of E. Y. Harburg, one of the greatest lyric writers in America. He had always written light, humorous verse. He had published much of it in F. P. A.'s "Conning Tower." But he was engaged in business, and very successfully, until the crash in 1929.

While looking around corners to keep a date with prosperity, he decided to capitalize upon his hobby. He wrote a few lyrics for an Earl Carroll show; it was a hit, and he was on his way up, doing the one thing that he most loved to do.

When all the scores are in, it will be shown that many who lost almost everything in the depression salvaged from it their own lives, by being forced to do for money what formerly they did only for fun.

But it is possible for you to do scientifically what others have accomplished only by chance. You have many well-established habit patterns associated with the best functioning of your interbrain and all of the other organs in your body. Look into yourself. Discover these habit patterns. Make a list of your abilities and talents along with those things that you most enjoy doing. Then search for some activity or job or business that combines most of them.

One patient was badly adjusted in his job as stock clerk in an automobile repair shop. He liked to be out-of-doors. He wanted to be his own boss. His life was a continuous response to: "Gimme this"—"Gimme that." In a windowless room, he spent his days passing nuts and bolts and tools across a counter. He liked gardening. His thumb was green; everything that he planted lived to bloom. He was naturally a student— enjoyed studying and reading. He loved beauty, creative work.

We went over the various professions and trades. Finally we

hit upon landscape architecture. He started in as a gardener, taking care of folks' yards and gardens for a few dollars a month. Now he has his own business, his own equipment. He studies horticultural problems constantly. Someday he will have his own nursery. He no longer fights his work, and it does not hit him below the interbrain.

His father, a writer, told me that he had never seen so marked a personality change in so short a period of time, and was inclined to give me the credit. Nature deserves the credit. Give your interbrain a chance, and you are bound to be well.

6

Once you have made your decision, act the part of the person whom you have decided to become. If you are going to be an actor, or a lawyer, or a doctor, act like one, all of the time. Every attitude must reinforce your purpose.

Every activity in your life must be subordinated to your main purpose. You must get the sleep that your purposes require. This may mean that the late parties you used to enjoy are out of the picture. That's fine; David Selznick made a fortune by his ability to cut from his pictures every scene and shot that didn't contribute to the final artistic whole. He has cut some fine photography, some excellent acting, some expensive scenes, but if they didn't belong, they were only that much film on the cutting-room floor.

Some people call this mobilization of effort their will power. When a person "cuts out" some habit, such as drinking or smoking, or just wasting his time, people say he has "will power." People tell their sick relatives to use will power. Books have been written, telling people how to develop will power. Would you feel a deprivation if I told you that there is no such thing as will power?

You experience a sense of strain when you resist yielding to the cravings of some habit. No wonder; that habit is tied up with your language habits, your interbrain habits, and the habitual workings of your entire body. But what makes you resist yielding to the habit? Simply another group of habits, more strongly entrenched in the brain and in the body.

It is the conflict between habits that gives rise to the sense of strain. It takes a habit—a good habit—to break a bad habit. If you haven't some good habits, you won't even want to break a bad habit. In fact, you won't know that the bad habit exists. Many people with nervous twitchings or tensions are not aware of them. They have not learned to relax and they have no standard for comparison.

Let a man do what he really wants to do, and he will have all the "will power" that he requires. Activities that appeared attractive and seductive become boring and stupid, once they interfere with the main purposes of his life. What people call will power is simply the organization of habits around some central purpose.

Excessive use of alcohol is easy to stop the minute you have a reason for eliminating drink. Most drunkards are people who have not been able to organize their lives around a purpose that is fundamental to their natures. When a man finds himself, he loses his way to the liquor store.

There is no good in telling the dipsomaniac not to drink. He has been telling himself the same thing for years. The things you may say to him he has said to himself many times with much more force and cogency. The various aversion treatments do not reach the root of the trouble.

To cure alcoholism, to get to the root of the disease, you must treat the will to drink. You must substitute the will to live for the will to seek the temporary suicide of alcohol. You must help the alcoholic to find himself; encourage him to self-realization, build up his self-respect and self-esteem. When you have done that, you won't have to tell him not to drink. You couldn't force him to take a drink.

When you start to organize your life around a constructive purpose, you are bound to lose a few friends. Some of your old friends and acquaintances are tied up with the things you used to do but for which you now no longer have time. They helped you waste many precious hours, playing interminable games of bridge, poker, or pool. Or perhaps they filled your life with idle gossip, or long-winded discussions about the state of the universe. They helped you to escape from the necessity of living your own life.

Don't let their loss worry you. You will continue to build friendships around your own personality. This doesn't mean that you have to give your old friends the Broadway brush-off. Just don't let them tear you down.

There is a technique for avoiding this. If you have friends who upset you or confuse you, don't discuss your personal problems with them. If you ask their advice, you place yourself under obligation to take their words seriously. If you do not discuss your problems with them, you are at liberty to refuse them the liberty to make you the subject of their open forum.

If you would live largely, you should plot your own course, sail your own boat, and wave gaily to your friends who have come to the wharf to cry, *"Bon voyage!"* You are on your way, your own way.

Let us summarize what you can do for your own vocational guidance:

1. Make a list of your talents and skills.
2. Ask yourself what kind of work would give you an opportunity to exercise those talents and skills.

3. Pick that vocation within your scope which will furnish the most satisfactions.

4. Make a decision, and get started. If you need further training, that is priority number one.

5. All of your old activities and habits that do not fit in with your new purpose are out for the duration.

Let no one imagine that this starting to lead one's own life must be accompanied with the bulldog-jaw posturing of a Mussolini. Your own life is not so unpalatable that you have to hold your nose, swallow it in a quick gulp. Quite the contrary. Your life will taste good to you; you will be able to sip it slowly, to savor every last drop of it.

The minute you begin to follow your own destiny, a ton of care will drop from your shoulders. You will feel free. You will begin to know real happiness. You will ask, "Why didn't I do this ten years ago?"

You will be able to see sunshine, blue sky overhead, instead of the artificial light of an endless tunnel.

CHAPTER FOURTEEN

Are You Allergic to Some People?

1

VICKIE HAD EVERYTHING, good looks, intelligence, lots of clothes, a loving husband, and a nervous breakdown.

It was a case of mother-in-law. Before Vickie and Adelbert were married, Bertie made it clear that he couldn't leave his mother. He said that she would be lonely, that he couldn't think of her living alone in some apartment hotel. What he didn't make clear was that Mother controlled the income from his father's estate. Nor did he make it clear that for years, Mother jiggled the purse strings to make Bertie dance like a puppet.

Mother was more than a bit on the domineering side. She had a mania to control. She audited every cent that Vickie and Bert spent. Before Vickie could have a permanent wave or a package of cigarettes, Mother had to give permission. No detail of living was too small to escape her roving eye. Privacy was out of the question. Mother had a phobia for keys, and no room or dresser drawer was spared her vigilant inspection.

Vickie soon realized that she was living in a house of bondage. She could not cope with the situation. She used every trick and artifice to get some uncensored life of her own. No use going into details. It just couldn't be licked. Finally, she realized that she was faced with a dilemma. Either she had to accept an intolerable serfdom or else she had to leave Bert.

She loved Bert, and she liked his mother, who, except for her one peculiarity, was otherwise a really nice person. Vickie even felt (at times) sorry for the pathetic old lady, insatiate in her desire for futile power and unappeasable in her demand for a more secure grip upon Bertie's life. Vickie couldn't decide what to do, and in her indecision, torn between conflicting purposes, she had a nervous breakdown.

"I tremble when I open my front door," she cried. "It's like living among head-hunters."

People with whom you have to live are your greatest mental hazard. They can build you up or tear you down. They can make you angry enough to scream. You don't scream. You swallow your anger, but you can't digest it. The result is tension and a nervous stomach.

Some people are allergic to other personalities, just as some people have food allergies. One man's friend is another man's poison. Most people can eat tomatoes or strawberries; yet these same foods give others hives, big itchy bumps. Books are written on food allergies. But too little attention has been paid to social allergies—to people who don't agree with you, and who rub you the wrong way until your spirit is skinned down to raw nerves.

Treatment of Vickie's allergy to her mother-in-law was not too difficult. She took a room temporarily away from home and learned to relax. She resumed her premarriage friendships and pleasures. By way of occupational therapy, she got a job and earned her own money. Before she returned home, Bertie had gone to work to protect his masculine pride. With both working, it was easy to humor Mother in small matters, so as to let her believe that she was managing things. Vickie was really free, desensitized from the domination to which she was allergic.

Perhaps you believe that Vickie could have got around her mother-in-law by being tactful. Perhaps she should have read *How to Win Friends and Influence People,* by Dale Carnegie.

His book is a practical manual that tells how to do unto others as you would have them do unto you. His book implies that other people will respond decently if you meet them halfway.

Generally, people will respond. You are a dynamic factor in any relationship. You give direction to your relations with others by your own attitudes and behavior. But there is a limit beyond which no one can go and still maintain his integrity. Appeasement will not appease an aggressor. Among vampires and poisonous parasites, the technique of Dale Carnegie does not apply. So your problem is to discover what to do when other people get on your nerves through no fault of your own. What can you do when turning the other cheek wins only contempt and influences people to hit you again?

How can psychoallergy make you chronically nervous?

The case of the three sisters should illustrate this problem. Their mother was a fluttery chatterbox. "Where did you buy it? How much did you pay? Did you know that Grossman's were having a sale? I wonder how it will wear? Does your husband like it? Helen bought one just like it. She has such bad taste, poor girl. Not that it might not look well on you. I was just saying." And so on and so on, forever and ever.

Annie, the oldest sister, loved this chatter. It somehow comforted her, like the chirping of a canary. Mother did not make her nervous. Quite the contrary.

Bertha, the second sister, hated it. She would exclaim, "For God's sake, Mother, give your chin a rest. It bobs up and down like a ball on a rubber band. If you don't know how to keep quiet, just shut up." Bertha felt no remorse after her plain talking. "I call them the way I see them," she would explain. "If people can't take it, that's their tough luck." So Mother did not make Bertha nervous.

Cora, the third sister, also hated Mother's endless chatter. But her conscience kept her from saying or doing anything about it. She had painted on some secret wall of her mind a picture of a perfect mother-daughter relationship. This was her dream, her ideal. She loved it. She could not let reality cast an evil light upon it. So she sat and listened and clenched her fists, and kept repeating to herself, "Please, God, don't let me scream."

Her clenched jaws started to ache, and as she rubbed them, her mother asked, "When did you see a dentist last? Did he say when you were to come again? Hadn't you better . . . ?" etc., etc. After her mother left, Cora went to the medicine cabinet for a sedative to quiet her nerves.

Now let us analyze this a little. Mother aroused in Cora a feeling of hostility that she had to smother. She was pressed between the barbs of hostility and the stinging of conscience. So she swallowed her irritation, tensed up, held in all expression of her feelings, until she became as weak as a wet rayon rag. The hostility repressed by conscience produced an inner conflict that resulted in anxiety and neurosis. She condemned herself and felt inferior, utterly futile, and helpless.

So there is your psychoallergy. Some people arouse your resentment, opposition, or hostility. They may only distract you. They may deflate your ego. They may humiliate you or embarrass you. They may thwart you or disappoint you or disillusion you. They may threaten your security. Whatever they do, they get your back up. And if you have to take it and like it, and hold in your natural responses because of some other feeling or desire within you, you will suffer from nervousness in their presence.

Inner conflict, once aroused, grows like a forest fire. Cora, for example, dreaded her mother's visits. Her fear generated new hostility. She hated her mother for making her nervous. She had to restrain her desire to throw a teacup at the woman. But this was unthinkable, so she put the momentary impulse out of mind. She denied to herself that the idea had crossed her mind. The fear of what she might do in a momentary loss of self-control created even greater anxiety. Anxiety feeds hatred, and growing hatred in turn builds up more anxiety. This effect of anxiety and hatred in mutual augmentation explains the tremendous overpowering hostility that one meets in nervous people, hostility that is as out of proportion to the cause as is a match to a forest fire.

What did Cora do? Well, with a little help she came to realize that she had two mothers. One was the dream mother that she had created in childlike fantasy. The other was her real mother. Because she had not distinguished clearly between the two, reality had continually disillusioned and disappointed Cora. Reality aroused hostility and anxiety.

When Cora gained insight into the cause of her psychoallergy, she gave the correct label to the dream of the kind of mother whom she had always wanted, and accepted the reality of the woman who was her mother. Gave up her dream? Well, not entirely. For she took to writing stories—mother-and-daughter stories, and in those stories, the dream mother is now more of a real person than many another woman of flesh and blood.

Freud calls this sublimation. There is something sublime in wringing imaginative literature out of your heart's torture. That is why it is said that there cannot be great literature without great passion and suffering.

Let no one underestimate the underlying anxiety and hostility within himself. We may not be aware of these emotions, just as we are not aware of our dynamic livers and hearts, but they are in there, producing. Consider the resentment that was caused when, during the depression of the 1930's, our government gave a few dollars a month to the unemployed for whom no work could be found other than raking leaves and cleaning up cities. That their self-respect was saved by giving them something to do didn't matter. That most of the unemployed were given constructive jobs, building schoolhouses, hospitals, parks, and streets was overlooked. Some few were getting money for "boon-doggling," and the public's latent hostility was aroused. Now contrast this attitude with the universal complacent acceptance of the spending of billions for weapons of war. War will be an obsolete institution only after we have substituted mental hygiene for hostility.

Why is there so much latent subconscious hatred and anxiety within the human heart? Is man a predatory animal, a two-legged wolf in Saks Fifth Avenue sophisticated clothing? Aubrey Beardsley, the artist, thought so when he drew heads of unimaginable malignity and selfishness upon satin-clad bodies of graceful suavity. Freud was so certain of it that he invented an instinct of death to account for man's destructiveness directed both inward and outward.

The scientific answer, however, is to be found in childhood conditioning. As we demonstrated in Chapter Twelve, children develop attitudes that are based upon defense against aggressions by their elders. Children adjust to frustration and disillusionment by repressing resentment, which, often enough, they do not recognize or understand. This generates underlying anxiety and hostility, resulting in allergy to some people or to some situations in adult life. Within the human heart is the dynamite of hatred and hostility. We must be careful of our contacts, lest friction light the fuse.

2

What can you do about people who make you nervous?

Following is the A B C of a program or method for avoiding psychoallergy. But before you can follow the program, you must be ready to apply it. You must have before all else an independent adjustment to life. You must know where you are going and why. The drifter is at the mercy of every puff of wind and cross-current. The man who steers his craft by map and compass, who has direction and drive and momentum, is not distracted and confused. When you have an independent adjustment to life, with drive, direction, and momentum, you have equilibrium and balance. Then you can adjust to other people with equanimity and peace of mind.

How to attain an independent adjustment to life?

1. Learn to relax. This is covered in Chapters Five and Six.
2. Learn to play. See Chapter Eight.
3. Learn to work. See Chapter Nine.
4. Learn to think about your problems objectively, and not in violent or emotional language. See Chapter Ten.
5. Learn to understand yourself. See Chapters Eleven and Twelve.
6. Treat yourself to a fresh start. See Chapter Thirteen.

If you do these things in the order given, you will enjoy a kind of stability that other people will have difficulty in upsetting. You will have the firmness and discrimination necessary for self-protection, and the strength to avoid hectic rejection and harshness in your human relationships. Only after such self-mastery will you be ready to apply any or all of three methods for dealing with people who upset you.

These methods, the A B C of self-protection from psychoallergy, include Avoidance, Blackout, and Charity or friendly understanding.

Avoidance means escape, and escape is difficult. It sounds so easy. People think of escape in terms of brushing off a door-to-door peddler, or call to mind the composer of music who used to scoot out the back door whenever his wife's relatives came to the front door. This escape is easy, because it is simple avoidance of impertinent distraction.

Minor distractions generate only a minor feeling of frustration. A temporary boredom, a little waste of time, and it is over. Meanwhile you give yourself an approving pat on the back for your toleration and kindness to little people. And when you walk out on such distractions, you feel no twinges of conscience. You give yourself another pat on the back for resisting temptation to waste time. Minor distractions resemble psychoallergy only as the mist resembles Niagara.

Escape from psychoallergy takes courage, the kind of courage required by the surgeon who is forced by circumstances to operate upon himself. For you are allergic only to people to whom you are bound by the ties of strong emotion. Cutting those ties even to save your nervous system is hard and difficult. And that is just what you must do to protect your nervous system and preserve your peace of mind.

A young man found himself engaged to marry a woman whom he did not love. On the day set for their wedding, he was not to be found. He had walked out on the lady, but he did not have the courage to break their engagement. He could not break their engagement. Perhaps he did not want to hurt her feelings. Perhaps he did not want to think of himself as a man who would go back on his word. Perhaps he was afraid of what the community would think of a man who for no apparent reason would jilt a woman and flout a promise. These were the emotional ties that he could not cut.

He suffered a nervous breakdown. He was so depressed and suicidal that his friends had to keep close watch over him. They even took his pocketknife. After two years, the nervousness subsided when he decided to marry the woman after all.

His premarital hunch proved to be well founded. His wife was extravagant and kept him in constant debt. She took no interest in his career; in fact, she was a handicap. In her personal relations with him, she was vituperative, disagreeable, noisy. At one time, she threw a cup of coffee in his face. Yet he could not divorce her for the same reasons that prevented him from jilting her.

The name of the man—Abraham Lincoln. He had courage enough to free the slaves, but not enough to free himself.

If you are contemplating marriage or a business association or any other relationship with a person whom you know will get you down, don't do it. If in doubt, wait. Do not let stupid pride or self-regard or your pessimistic guess what others may think lead you into such self-destruction. The very best way to combat social allergy is to avoid it. Plow under the ragweed of poisonous relationships before it pollinates to fill your atmosphere with perennial irritation.

Nor should you bank too heavily upon your ability to "reform" someone or to change his or her personality through the beneficent effect of your noble efforts and example. Such optimism is too often a misplaced rationalization of the Jehovah complex. It may be the expression of a subconscious selfish desire for power and domination that you accept because it is dressed in the robes of bland altruism.

It is said that Pygmalion fashioned out of stone his perfect woman, and in reward for his high idealism the gods brought the statue to life so that they could live happily ever after. Many adolescents go through the Pygmalion stage. Boys dream of "reforming" prostitutes, and girls spin visions of reforming drunkards and gamblers. It's a pleasant fancy. The voice of experience tells youth to leave such adventures to Don Quixote and to other unrealists. When the windmill of a clashing personality hits the lance of the impractical reformer, the reformer is going to find himself sitting in the dust, wondering what knocked him down.

Prevention of psychoallergy is better than cure. A certain minister gives engaged couples a personality test, and if marked personality defects show up, he refers them to a psychiatrist for further study before he consents to perform the marriage ceremony. In this way, personality defects have been corrected before marriage.

But what can you do when you feel you cannot escape from the person who gets you down?

You should realize at the outset that you have a double problem. One part of the problem concerns the mental state of the person who stirs you up and disrupts your life. That's the part you blame. The other part concerns you. This last is the most important half of your problem. For no one can make you very nervous if you feel free to pick up and leave. You are hurt only by those persons to whom you are bound by your own needs.

Willard Q. Carthay was faced by this problem. He was a widower in his late fifties. He missed the companionship and services of his first wife. His big apartment and his unused wealth made him feel that much more lonely and depressed. Looking apprehensively at the empty years ahead didn't cheer him up. So when he met an intelligent, lively, sympathetic woman only ten years his junior, his needs told him that he was in love.

After they were married and had furnished a home, she moved in her cats. Eight of them. Mr. Carthay had not counted on this. His new wife had been an artist and had painted some very nice things. He had thought of her as bringing to his home an easel, canvases, and tubes of paint. He had secretly dreamed of proudly exhibiting her work to admiring friends. He could see himself standing with his back to the fireplace, gloating over his wife's accomplishments, and basking in every kind of warmth all at once. But no easel, no canvases, no paints materialized. She laid no fire, nor did she invite his friends. Instead, eight cats.

He hadn't figured on cats. He had wanted a home with atmosphere—not catmosphere. Their odor knocked him down. He objected. Every time he raved and put his foot down, he stepped on the tail of a howling cat. The needs of these animals took up all of his wife's time, interest, and conversational ability.

So he told her that she would have to give away or otherwise dispose of her cat friends. She refused. They were her pals. Each one had a personality, a right to enjoy life. Behind her emotional attitude was the feeling of protection that the cats gave to her. Their needs saved her from the necessity of facing her failure to paint.

Mr. Carthay became morose. He started to drink. It was all her fault, he said, all caused by her neurotic affection for cats. But was it all her fault? Failing compromise, such as building a cattery in the garden, why didn't he pick up and leave? What undeclared needs kept him from admitting that his marriage was all a mistake, the sooner ended the sooner mended?

We analyzed his needs, his half of the problem, as soon as he was relaxed enough to think rationally. Then we listed them in this order:

1. He didn't want to admit that he had made a mistake. Pride of opinion. Needed to be right, always.

2. He was afraid of what his friends might say. They might imagine that he lacked virility. He needed social approval, even from casual acquaintances.

3. He clung to his needs for someone to make a home for him, and to companion his future old age. In spite of the facts, his dream still lived optimistically. He needed comfort for old age.

We had to analyze his needs that were generating his con-flict, because he took them so for granted that he was not aware of them. Seeing them clearly, he was able to make a rational decision, and his nervousness and his drinking caused by psy-choallergy disappeared. What did he do? What would you have done?

He saw that he was suffering from a neurosis secondary to his wife's behavior. Her preoccupation with cats was dislocat-ing his life. He shrewdly observed, "The seriousness of neu-rosis might be measured by the derangement it effects in the lives of normal bystanders." Meaning that his wife was driv-ing him to drink.

He wanted to give her a chance to make the most of her fine talents. He offered to take her to any psychiatrist whom she might choose. But his offer was refused. Mrs. Carthay was afraid of being pushed into the stream of life. She preferred to sit on the bank, watching braver swimmers struggle with the current, while she petted a cat.

So, Mr. Carthay admitted that he had made a mistake in en-tering into the marriage. He braved the wagging tongues of acquaintances and obtained a divorce. Later, he married again —this time, more circumspectly and with greater success.

3

In treating your own psychoallergy, you must first ask your-self why you need the person who is making you nervous. If your needs are not valid, if your needs are childish and imma-ture, you can choose escape as your path to freedom from nervousness. In choosing avoidance from allergy, you are also eliminating neurotic dependence upon others. But first of all, discover for yourself what ties you to the person who is making you nervous. What needs does that person represent in your life?

Let us get back to Cora. After she had desensitized herself, her mother's jabbering ceased to make her tense or nervous. At times she hardly heard it. While her mother was talking, Cora was writing a story or washing dishes or knitting a sweater. Her mind was far away. When she thought of her mother it was a kindly thought of a nice little old lady, talkative and featherbrained, but, on the whole, good and well meaning.

This is Blackout—method number two. It is a method that one can use when escape is impossible.

A cultured and charming man married a woman who turned out to be a chronic alcoholic. At times the police call up, and he drives down to the station to bring her home. At times she drinks at home and lies upon the couch in alcoholic stupor.

Why doesn't he get a divorce? Because he does not want one. When he married her, he took her for better or for worse. It turned out for worse. His own opinion of himself would be lost to him if he walked out on her now.

So he philosophically gives up any hopes of having the kind of home he had planned and he makes the best of things. He has insulated himself emotionally from her behavior. When she gets drunk he puts her to bed to sleep off the liquor. Then he goes about his business, following any one of his many interests. She does not make him nervous.

He is able to do this because he has achieved adult self-sufficiency. He is not embarrassed by her because he has no need for approval that is based upon his wife's good behavior. He is not bothered by what the neighbors think. He leads his own life, and that is all that matters for him.

You can blackout the behavior of those from whom you cannot escape only if you understand your own needs, and adjust them to the facts of your situation.

A father was made neurotic by his adolescent son. The

father was a man of limited education. He had fine intelligence, and he cherished a secret ambition to become a professional man. But when he was a young fellow, he had to go to work, and obligations of one sort or another had prevented his going on with his education.

His son did not seem to be very bright. He excelled only in social dancing of the more extreme types, and he had a good memory only for the names of dance music. As a student of more formal subjects, he was a total loss. His father was exasperated. He got so that he couldn't speak a civil word to the boy. The boy responded in kind. The father was allergic to the boy—so much so that he had a nervous breakdown.

"We—the whole family—were on a picnic," he said, in describing the onset of his symptoms. "I had climbed to the top of the canyon. The family were at the bottom of the cliff. Suddenly I became weak and dizzy. I shook all over. I was afraid to move. I lay down and called for help. They came and led me down. I couldn't drive home. And I've been nervous this way ever since."

After his confidence was won, he revealed that he had felt of a huge boulder at the top of the cliff and had found that it was loosely attached to the mountainside. His son was at the foot of the cliff. A little push would have sent the rock hurtling down on the boy. The thought of pushing the rock flashed through his mind, to be immediately smothered in revulsion. Hostility—repressed—led to anxiety.

It was easy to demonstrate the reason for his hostility toward the boy. The father had a need to succeed in a profession vicariously—through his son's success. His son's lack of interest frustrated this need.

He couldn't escape from his son. Avoidance as a method of self-protection from psychoallergy was out. But when he developed insight into his own subconscious attitudes and needs, he was able to adjust to his situations with insulation. He ceased to care whether the boy became a professional man. He gave the boy a right to pick his own trade and lead his own life. The boy, as it happened, turned out to be a complete success from the Broadway angle; but that is only as it happened. Not by chance, he saved his nerves only after he had insulated himself completely from the behavior that previously had torn his nerves to pieces.

As long as you subconsciously hold selfish private designs upon the way of life of another person, you cannot ignore what he does. As soon as you yield to another the democratic right of self-determination, you can ignore with ease whatever he does.

As some pessimist once said, "Everyone has the right to go to hell in his own way." I wouldn't express the idea so, because I believe more in heaven than in hell, but the general idea is sound.

Blackout is an effective method in dealing with those minor cases of psychoallergy where a person aggressively gets on your nerves. This special method may be called passive nonco-operation. You exercise a definite kind of dampening control to keep your muscles from vibrating in tune with another's vexations and tensions.

When one of the back-seat drivers in your life gets on your nerves, you can pull down the mental curtains for an emotional blackout. You should recognize the situation for what it is, and then relax. Relax mentally as well as physically. Do not resist or argue or even answer back. Why should you infect yourself with another's nervous tensions and emotional conflicts? You do not help the other fellow and when you identify yourself with his neurotic needs, you drag yourself down. Worse: you may allow yourself to get into a state where you cannot be of effective help.

This is not a counsel of callousness. It could be considered as a way of turning the other cheek. Kindness consists in part in respecting the other fellow's point of view and his right to hold it. I see people in endless procession who worry themselves sick because of their psychoallergies. Reactionaries in politics get red in the face, and the blood vessels of their foreheads swell, as they argue about matters that only future circumstances can adjust. Radicals in politics engage in acrimonious dispute—and for what purpose? To acquire high blood pressure or stomach ulcers?

Sit back sometime, and listen to their arguments, while you ask yourself what secret private needs hide behind the curtain prompting the disputants. You will find surprisingly often that they are airing their personal problems under the unconscious pretense of giving expression to general principles. When a certain woman argues passionately that all married women should have jobs and that all children should be brought up in day nurseries, she means that if she had been economically independent and childless, she would have obtained a divorce and married the man whom she loved.

If you were a mother with a married daughter, and if you knew that only your grandchildren stood between your son-in-law and divorce, the economic-independence, day-nursery woman might make you feel nervous. Her ideas would remind you of your daughter's insecurity. If you entered into argument with her, you might upset your nervous system further. But here you are, face to face with her. What can you do?

You can remember that the world will little note nor long remember what either of you say. Keep in mind that living-room disputations don't alter the economic system but they do disturb your nervous system.

Instead of arguing, you might ask questions. Let her air all of her ideas. Little by little, she will veer from the abstract to the concrete, until at last she is telling you the story of her life. There you can meet her on the safe ground of a common humanity. Her theoretical ideals about marriage will be seen as the shadow thrown by her real suffering. She will appreciate your listening and unconsciously show her gratitude. You will feel elevated by your poise and good sense, rather than depressed by your psychoallergy.

The idea is to let go. You will notice that this is the method of the wrestler, who when forced in one direction, consciously lets go, throwing his opponent over his head with his opponent's strength. Your own passivity is your greatest protection. When you try it, you'll find that you are saving wear and tear on your nerves, your stomach, and your heart.

This passive method of blackout is recommended to prevent hostility in cases of minor aggressions. Psychologists call this method defensive excitation of motor and sensory inhibitions. The common-sense term is a thick skin and relaxed musculature. Mosquitoes can't sting elephants.

4

This brings us to our third method of preventing psychoallergy: Charity. By Charity I do not mean the giving of alms. I use the word rather in the biblical sense as it is found in I Corinthians, XIII. "Charity suffereth long and is kind; Charity envieth not; Charity vaunteth not in itself, is not puffed up . . . and now abideth Faith, Hope and Charity, these three; but the greatest of these is Charity."

Sociologists have used the word *empathy* in this sense; but for general understanding, the word Charity conveys the meaning. Charity as used here, means a friendly, sympathetic, unselfish understanding.

Consider the case of a young doctor serving in the emer-

gency rooms of a large city hospital. On a gay holiday as many
as two or three hundred people injured in accidents or fights
are on and off the examining and treatment tables. The young
doctor is human. His heart could bleed with each sufferer.
Yet he passes through such situations with no emotional damage. He has been trained to look at suffering through the eyes
of analysis and action rather than through the eyes of feeling.
This, and this alone, saves him from his emotions.

Charity means that you drop your personal feeling and
substitute comprehension and understanding. When your
child hurts himself, you naturally experience a feeling of
anxiety. One of your precious possessions has been threatened. Indeed, you have been threatened, because whatever
you own, whatever you can modify by the pronoun "my," is a
part of yourself. You resent this attack upon yourself, and
you may blame the child for making you feel bad. This is as
irrational as kicking a chair against which you have bumped
your shinbone. It's childish.

You call a doctor, who makes a quick, competent survey of
the situation, and decides what is best to be done. He feels,
not for himself, but for the child. He has no privately personal
feeling in the matter, but genuinely unselfish compassion and
understanding.

Do doctors always exhibit compassion and understanding?
I am sorry to report in the negative. When dealing with cases
of nervousness, some of them do not know what it is all about.
Their inability to understand and their lack of program for
the patient constitute an attack upon their medical personalities. So in self-defense, they criticize the patient, belittle
his troubles, and sneer at those who are able to help. Which
proves that doctors are human, too.

But doctors who specialize in the treatment of nervousness
are not irritated by their patients. They try to understand

them. Such patients arouse no hostility, no anxiety neurosis, in the psychiatrist. The patient, in defense of his subconscious trends, may attack the psychiatrist. This is called "resistance," a word used technically to mean that the patient resists the surrender of his neurotic attitudes because he fears the difficulty of making a better adjustment. Doctors who treat nervousness see this several times a day. It doesn't get them down. They understand it and don't take it personally.

And that is what you must learn to do. Someone has been arousing your hostility. You cannot escape, and you cannot black out his aggressions. In this case you can diminish your hostility and resultant anxiety by understanding the aggressor. In effect, you become a psychiatric nurse.

This is what Abraham Lincoln did. Instead of getting wrought up over his wife's behavior, he tried to understand her. Cora did this in becoming adjusted to her fluttery mother. She saw that her mother's jabbering was only the release of nervous energy, and she let it go at that. The ambitious father of the unambitious son relaxed when he learned to accept the boy for what he was. He found to his surprise that he had a pretty good boy, hard-working, fun-loving, and responsive to understanding and kindness. And, as it happened, capable of his own kind of success.

If someone arouses your hostility, ask yourself first what it is that you are defending. If you are defending a picture you've made of how the person ought to act, then question your right to your demands. Free yourself from arbitrary demands upon others.

Your next step is to understand the person who is making you nervous. Apply the lessons of Chapters Eleven and Twelve to him. Ask how he got that way. Ask what it is that he demands of life. Ask what experience or lack of opportunities have misdirected his attitudes and behavior into trends that you find disagreeable. To understand all is to forgive all, and to forgive all is escape from hostility and anxiety.

Incidentally, understanding others leads to understanding yourself. It is only through the give-and-take of understanding others that you can arrive at a correct appreciation of your own limitations and possibilities. So, in this case, the virtue of compassion is not only its own reward, but gets a valuable bonus thrown in.

Let us sum this up briefly. Psychoallergy is caused by hostility that others arouse in you, when for some reason within yourself you feel that you must repress this hostility. Hostility and its repression—the conflict between hate and love—lead to anxiety and nervousness. How this ties up through the interbrain with the behavior of your stomach and heart and muscles has been discussed in other chapters. Also previously discussed has been the effect of nervousness in spreading waves of inhibition over your forebrain, paralyzing your best creative abilities.

You treat your psychoallergy first by developing direction and momentum and purpose in your life. How to do this has been previously discussed.

Your next step is to analyze the reasons for your repression of hostility. Before you fly off the handle with retaliatory aggression, stop and think. What subconscious need of your own are you defending? Ask yourself whether it is worth the defense. After you have done this, you react to your hostility, not by repression, but by judicious choice of the methods of Avoidance, Blackout, and Charity. That these methods are not each exclusive from the others but can all be applied at different times in a single situation has also been illustrated by case histories.

Every situation is different, requires individual handling. As you apply the A B C of the treatment of psychoallergy, you will develop ingenuity and resourcefulness in your technique. Be assured of one thing, that your use of this technique will give greater freedom and power to your personal development and individual success, and will diminish the sum total of hostility and anxiety in this troubled world.

When each of us learns to understand and control his own subconscious hostilities, friction between employers and employees, friction between racial groups, friction between social classes, and friction between nations will be correspondingly dissipated.

CHAPTER FIFTEEN

Try On a New Attitude

1

IF YOU BOW AND KNEEL and grovel every time the king or the lord of the manor rides by, before too long you will come to feel that you are saluting a superior person. And if you are taught to brush aside or discriminate against people of any particular race or color, you will in time inevitably feel that you are better than they are.

Whole populations have been kept in servitude by teaching the multitude the ritual of bowing the head and bending the knee. Later comes the rationalization. When it is demonstrated beyond any doubt that the superior officer is a nincompoop and a heel, the well-trained soldier says, "I salute not the man but the uniform." Or the Chinese say, "I venerate not the person but his many years." Which is silly, but very human. We come to believe in what we do. We tend to become the way we act. We learn to feel the way we behave.

Act servile, and you'll be a slave, and what is worse, you'll like it, and you will start to invent reasons to justify your master's superiority. Act like a queen, and you will feel like one. You will believe in yourself and, acting on your belief, you will do the things that lead to success.

Your attitudes are the higher-ups, the big shots, in your mental life. They are the habits that sit in the driver's seat. They control your lesser habit patterns. When you can boss them, you are in control of your own life. You become invulnerable, and nothing can hurt you.

A golfer had built up excellent habit patterns of good form in posture and in swinging his clubs. Experience had given him good judgment in choosing the proper club and the right swing for every golf situation. When he was right, he was a top-flight player, able to hold his own with any player in the world. Yet he never won an important match.

He was able to control everything except his attitude, and his attitude cost him five strokes in eighteen holes. His attitude was a feeling of inferiority. "Who am I," he would ask, "to be competing with the great names in the golfing world?" He was able to hold in this thought on cloudy days, and then his game was good. But on those days when the sun stood high and his shadow lay small at his feet, he saw himself as a midget, and that licked him.

Everything in the way of treatment that has been discussed hitherto was indicated in this case; and in addition, he needed to acquire an attitude of self-confidence. How you can do this for yourself will be explained later on.

How did his attitude of inferiority develop? He had been a poor kid who lived on the other side of the tracks. After school, Saturdays and Sundays and during summer vacations, he had caddied in a swanky golf club. Alert, good-looking, and of sunny disposition, he won the hearts of his patrons. In turn, he worshiped them. He identified himself so completely with the rich golfers whose bags he carried that he could not think of himself except as one of them.

At night he left the marble halls and spacious ways of easy living to return to his shabby, narrow house. His brother aped the refinements of speech that he brought home. His parents looked with apprehension upon his love for good clothing. They did their best to knock that nonsense out of him. Later, when he gave up caddying and took to teaching golf instead of learning a solid trade such as plumbing, they let him know that he was headed straight for the poorhouse. Who had ever heard of making a living by playing golf?

He lived in two worlds, and in each of them he was emotionally isolated. In neither world did he have a soul with whom to share his vague aspirations. From one world, the world of the family, he tried to escape. But there was no escape, for he carried it with him wherever he went. Into the other world of the fairways there was no entrance, except the servants' entrance.

So he became a professional golfer, a teacher of golf. He did very well. His skill and form earned him the reputation of "golfer's golfer." But when he entered into competition, he could not feel that he was of the elect. He was still the ragged kid from the other side of the tracks. He couldn't feel that he belonged.

And so when the sun was high and his shadow small, he saw himself not as a big, broad-shouldered he-man, but as a little man, a midget, a being made for vulgar curiosity and disparaging laughter.

Our golfer had built up his attitudes by a process known as identification. It will be easy for you to understand this process if you think of it in terms of your own experience. You are a member of many groups. You have your family, for example, and when you were a child, you may have belonged to boy- or girl-scout groups. You belonged to a team, perhaps, and certainly belonged to a school. You had your intimate friends whose life you shared. Each of these groups or persons enlisted your loyalty. You thought of them in terms of "we" and "us." Through participation in group life, in your adjustments to members of the group, in your competitions, rivalries, and acts of co-operation, you enlarged your personality to include the larger social whole.

The unfortunate golfer belonged to two groups that he

could not introduce to each other without embarrassment. They, his family and his golfing associates, had nothing in common except hostility and amused contempt for each other. The attitudes that were appropriate for either group were conflicting, disharmonious. This disorganization of his social life was reflected in the disorganization of his private and personal life.

Anything to which you attach your interests becomes a part of your personality. Your family, your friends, your team, your city, your country, your world, and all become an extension of yourself. By adjusting to this group life, and identifying yourself with it, you build up your larger concepts of right and wrong, of purpose in life and the meaning that life holds for you. Through social living and identification, you create habitual responses in group life. Let us agree to call these general habitual responses your attitudes.

It sounds abstract at first, but it isn't really. Life consists not of abstractions, but of concrete adjustments between desires and opportunities. The golfer, when he was a schoolboy, had to earn money to buy his clothes. He got a caddying job, and the adjustment resulted in success. He took a personal interest in those for whom he caddied. They gave him tips, requested his services, and were kind to him. This successful adjustment in a leisure-class group led to attempts at repetition and success within that group.

He adopted their standards of what to wear, how to speak, and what to think. He accepted their opinions and outlook on life as his own. He became ashamed of his family, of their lowly position and uncouth manners. Yet because of numerous concrete acts of adjustment within his family, he felt a part of it, too. His sharing of their hopes and fears and defeats and victories made him theirs, and they were all a part of him; and he was ashamed of his shame of them.

Out of his diverse concrete experiences, out of his failure and successful adjustments, he built up his general attitudes. They can be summed up in a few simple sentences. "Only rich people count. Whatever they do is right. You might as well be a dog as be poor. Work is for suckers. I must become rich. Then I'll amount to something. But will I ever amount to anything? I'm no good. I'm not a gentleman, really. I'm just a phony. If anyone I care about could see my father sitting around in his undershirt, I'd be sunk. If you're not born rich, you're nobody."

These generalizations, inconsistent and at cross purposes, were his tools for understanding life. They represented his attitudes, his habits of preparedness to meet new situations. Through them, he interpreted every stray item of news, every event in his life. He acted on his distorted perceptions, and his pattern of living was controlled by his attitudes. For that is what attitudes are, habits of preparedness. They determine when and which way the frog is going to jump. And his attitudes and his consequent adjustments gave him only a feeling of inferiority and of frustration that made him cynical, morbid, and unhappy.

Your attitudes, then, are not only an organization of habits acquired in previous adjustments. They are springs of action. They decide what you pay attention to or even notice in your environment. They decide what you will ignore. They are stimulants to future adjustments. Interacting together, in your search to resolve inner conflict, in your attempt to think things through and bring order out of chaos, they are your personality. Your attitudes are you.

Some people organize their attitudes slowly and consciously. Others change their attitudes almost overnight, in a process similar to a religious conversion. Before conversion, these persons suffer from profound unhappiness and dissatisfaction with their way of life. They blame their unhappiness upon a sense of values that they perceive to be false. Suddenly they attach new meanings to their lives, new principles to live by that can bring unity to their purposes and peace from their unfulfilled cravings. Overnight, they become different persons from what they had been.

Something like this happened to our golfer. He had become friendly with a great surgeon to whom he gave lessons on Sunday mornings. He happened to ask the surgeon how he happened to become a doctor. The surgeon, usually very reticent, opened up. Perhaps he felt the golfer's need for a broader point of view.

This surgeon, born in Russia, was a boy of twelve when the First World War began. At that time his father was a wealthy farmer. The farm was overrun by soldiers. This boy had seen his father and mother killed, the flocks seized, his home burned to the ground. He escaped only by a near-miracle, and made his way by night travel through famine-stricken territory to a village where the Society of Friends was furnishing relief. He came to the United States, taught himself English, and worked his way through literary and medical college. Today, he is a teacher in a medical college, and a great name in surgery.

"And now you're in the money and you amount to something," our golfer observed enviously.

"I am not in the money," the surgeon replied. "When I saw my father's flocks stolen and our home and barns burned, I lost all desire ever to own anything. All that I want is to do in my way for others what the Friends did for me."

"Think of it," the golfer told me. "And him a foreigner. It makes a fellow think."

The golfer saw that he could contribute in his way just as the surgeon had in his. Recreation may not be the most important need of mankind, but it is a need. He persuaded his father to learn to play golf, and gave him a season ticket for the course. He replaced his feeling of inferiority with a new assurance. "You and I are both in the health business," he told the surgeon. "I keep the doctor well."

2

How irrational attitudes can distort personality was strikingly shown in the cases of two young men whom I had occasion to examine in the county jail. They were charged with murder. Each of them pleaded not guilty by reason of insanity.

The first to be examined (call him H. B.) had shot a man who had been conducting an affair with his wife. H. B. had learned about what was going on. He procured a revolver and surprised the couple. Bang, bang. Then he telephoned to the police, told what he had done, and calmly waited developments.

H. B. combined a startling surface aggressiveness with a background of gray submissiveness. You sometimes meet this type in ticket offices or behind a post-office desk. Such persons take orders from their superiors with the docility of a well-behaved dog; but let some customer suggest any deviation from routine to meet a special situation, and they pop off like a bunch of firecrackers.

I asked H. B. if he were sorry that he killed the man.

"Certainly not," he exclaimed. "He got just what was coming to him. If I had broken up another man's home (I wouldn't, of course), I'd expect him to shoot me."

"But your wife is an independent human being," I argued, "and so was the man whom you killed. They had the right to live their own lives. They deceived you—not very nice—but deception does not carry a death penalty."

"The wages of sin are death," he replied.

"But you could have left the penalty in the hands of religious or legal authorities," I persisted. "Do you think that you should take the law in your own hands?"

"If a soldier sees an enemy, he shoots him. That snake I killed was an enemy of society."

He was not considered insane, but because of the special circumstances and because his life had been an example of straight and narrow thinking and doing, he was given a rather light sentence. The law proved to be more generous, broader in mind, and more adaptable than Mr. H. B.

G. L. had shot his wife because she would not go with him to a moving-picture show. "I wanted to see this picture, and she wanted to go dancing and drinking," he said. "We did that the night before. We always go dancing and drinking. I wanted to see a picture for a change. We got to arguing, she made me mad, and I let her have it."

"How do you feel about it now?"

"I should have let her have her way. I'm sorry I shot her. I wouldn't have done it if I had thought, I just got mad, I guess."

"Did you love her?"

"Sure I loved her. I lived with her more'n any other woman, I guess. More'n a year."

G. L. had lived a disorderly life. His stepmother had been erratic. She quarreled with her neighbors and persuaded her husband to move from one town to another every two years.

G. L.'s home life had been so irregular and unhappy that he ran away from home when he was ten years old. He was arrested in Salt Lake City and held in a kind of children's prison for six weeks. From that time on, running away from home became a habit. He became familiar with hobo jungles, with the backwash of civilization that is identified with pawnshops, missions, and flophouses.

He never worked for more than a few weeks at a time. He was easily bored. No matter where he was, he felt he would be happier somewhere else. He had to be on the move.

His code of honor was more than elastic. In fact, it stretched to cover anything he wanted to do, and had no spring-back to it. On one curious point, however, he was inflexible. "I never cheated a bookie," he told me. "If I owe one two dollars, I pay him two dollars, if I have to steal it. Cheating a bookie is bad luck."

So there you have your two extremes in ways of organizing one's attitudes, the narrow inflexible and broadly disorganized. Most people fit somewhere in between and partake of the nature of both. Most people are unreasonably inflexible in some situations, vacillating and indecisively weak in others.

H. B. was not at all adaptable. He had his established attitudes, his methods of dealing with new situations. They lacked elasticity. They didn't work—resulted in disaster. He could not help it. He was like a train on a single track, could go only forward and backward, but never sidewise. So he was all wound up for trouble, because the day was inevitable when his inadequate interpretations of life would collide with a new situation.

G. L., on the other hand, had no such airtight organization of his habit patterns. He was capable of the most surprising generosity and heroism. Some of the things he did, and I believe him, make one proud to share a bit of world with him. Yet he was capable of stealing the last dime from a man who had befriended him and then burning his barn just to see the fire.

We say that a person has a weak character when his organized habit patterns, his attitudes, are inconsistent. Such a person is not dependable. He is weak. The last person who has his ear has his number. On the other hand, a strong character is the result of highly integrated, closely intermeshed, consistent attitudes. The danger of strong character is narrowness. The danger of weak character is instability.

Attitudes that are narrow and attitudes that are poorly organized are frail tools with which to meet the new and puzzling situations that life dishes up to us. Poorly organized attitudes lead to behavior poorly conceived, with insufficient prevision of results. Unbending attitudes also fail for exactly the same reason. Attitudes uncontrolled by reason bring disaster.

3

Can a person control his attitudes? Take the case of college student Merwin C. He had been brought up in a respectable middle-class environment. Dinner-table discussions were conferences between his father and mother regarding leases, rents, options, sales contracts, and the like. Idle gossip about the families of his friends dealt with who was making how much money. The stories dealing with the history of their failures and successes were to Merwin twicetold tales. He soaked up his commercial ideals and ideas as cotton sucks up dye.

At school he was unpopular. He lived in a snooty neighborhood in which the social life of the boys and girls was controlled by high-school fraternities and sororities. Either one belonged or one didn't. Exclusions meant isolation. Participation in high-school debating and athletic activities depended upon fraternity membership. The schoolteachers were members of faculty advisers of these clubs, and they shared the petty snobbery of the students and their families. And Merwin belonged to no fraternity. Socially, he was a leper. He inhabited two worlds, his home and his school, but he lived in neither world.

He reacted to this situation with the attitude that he was

Going to Show Them. He'd get Rich. He daydreamed of someday owning a big factory where he would hire some of his snooty classmates to perform menial jobs. His greatest dread was that of being poor, of going to work in overalls carrying a lunch pail and living in a wooden frame house.

This attitude was intensified by an experience during a school vacation, when he got a job in a sheet-metal factory. Here he associated with unskilled workers, came to understand their problems of supporting a family on day wages. When a fellow worker was laid off and protested with tears in his eyes, Merwin was unable to sleep for several nights.

His father sent him to college. Away from his snobbish prep school, he tried to adjust to a world of new ideas. He discovered to his amazement that Edgar Allan Poe was a more important man than George Babbitt. The heroes of Horatio Alger, he discovered, were not as important as heroes of science and art. He read about the seven deadly lies of civilization, and his ideas of what constitutes success were given a jolt. His scheme of values was turned upside down and inside out. He was completely disillusioned, thoroughly confused.

While the yellow pigment of materialistic philosophy was being bleached in the acid bath of larger values, nothing to take its place was given to him. He tried to discover a meaning in life to substitute for the dust and ashes of his values and aims. And the conflict between hostility to new ideas, the fear that this hostility created, and the hold of his old ideas gave him a nervous breakdown.

He recovered from this nervous condition only after he had experienced something like a religious conversion, during which he created a new set of values by which to live. How he did this is so interesting and so helpful that we will go into more detail about it later.

The important point for the moment is to understand that

you can intelligently change your attitudes if they are not helping you to adjust to a confusing world. Of all your habits, your attitudes are those that are most easily subject to your rational control. This is most fortunate for you, because your attitudes direct and manage all of your lesser habits. So by controlling your attitudes, you win complete control over your life.

Merwin C. accomplished this by digging down to bedrock in his thinking. What, he asked, are the conditions for leading a successful and happy life? He began his quest for happiness by making a survey of his needs.

1. Physical—need for
   a. Food
   b. Clothing
   c. Shelter
   d. Exercise
   e. Relaxation
2. Personal—need for
   a. Self-expression
   b. New experience
   c. Amusement
3. Social—need for
   a. Security
   b. Friendship
   c. Status
   d. Love

In discussing these needs, nothing further can be said about food, exercise, and relaxation. But in reference to clothing and shelter, you will notice that Merwin classified these under the head of physical. His meaning and intention are clear. He meant that he desired only enough clothing and shelter to enable him to function. He meant that he needed only a minimum of these things. Making a splurge, ostentatious display of more than enough for useful living, he ruled out. More than enough housing, like more than enough food, is a liability rather than an asset. His analysis is worthy of your consideration.

When you are clarifying your scheme of values, interpret your physical needs in terms of function. Do not be influenced by such motives as envy or need to show off. Ask yourself what you should have and what you do not need in order to produce your best work. Remember that no two people have the same needs, and that one person's adjustment is another person's poison.

Some people require for their peace of mind a home with five bedrooms and three baths. Others would find such a home a distracting and oppressive burden. An actor needs a large wardrobe. Other men might find that such an outfit requires more time and space than it is worth.

In considering your personal needs, self-expression should be given much thought. Self-expression requires activities you enjoy for their own sake. Some people find self-expression in handiwork, such as carpentry or masonry. Others prefer rendering more personal services. Some prefer working alone. Others like to work on a team. You should discover your own field for self-expression and hold out for it.

Your need for security is very individual and personal. You should be free from pressures that prevent freedom to think about your important interests. Here, again, what is security for one person is insecurity for another. Security does not mean absence of obligation to work. It does mean opportunity to do the kind of work for which you are best fitted. What kind of economic security do you need?

Your greatest security lies in your friendships. Everyone needs friends. People need your friendship. Getting friends is the easiest thing in the world. Lonely hearts won't believe this, but it is true, nevertheless. You make friends by being friendly.

Status means a recognized place in the community. It involves recognition and response. Everyone needs it. Without it one loses faith in himself. Children must have recognition and praise lest they develop a sense of inferiority. There are some tough-minded people who get satisfaction from imagined praise from imaginary persons. They are rewarded when they ask, "What would Professor Johnson say?" or "What would the Lord think of me?" But even these sturdy souls get a build-up from firsthand recognition in their own home towns, and the build-up does them good.

Last of all, everyone needs to feel that he is needed, is wanted, is loved for what he is. It is a terrible thing to be emotionally isolated. Knowing that you are needed, that someone depends upon you, will get you over many a rough spot in life.

Like Merwin, you should know what your needs are. But what can you do about them? You can do what Merwin did. Take account of them and then take them for granted. Do not concentrate upon them. Do not ask, "What is the world going to do for me?" This attitude constricts and contracts your personality. It leads to chronic discontent, envy, jealousy, and finally to disappointment and frustration.

You can begin to satisfy your needs by asking, "What can I do to be of service or of value in this world?" Merwin took account of his abilities, his skills, his talents that he could put at the service of mankind. He looked about him for something that he felt had to be done, and asked, "What can I do to help?"

There is so much to be done. The hungry ask for food. The

shelterless ask for lodging. The weak and afflicted wait for someone to bind up their wounds. The ignorant cry out for education. The lonely beg for companionship and understanding.

There are bridges to be built and transportation to be designed. There are mysterious diseases to be studied and germs to be fought. There are fields to be planted and new foods and fibers and plastics to be developed. There are dramas to be written and music to be composed. What can you do to be of help?

4

You can sum up your attitude in these words—*self-expression in social service*. When Merwin did this, and only until he did this, did he find peace. This attitude organized his life. It not only led to success. It was success.

What becomes of greed for wealth, for power, for domination, for fame? What becomes of your need to pretend that you are smarter or richer or younger or better than you really are? These needs simply evaporate. You need nothing except a chance to be of service. In your service you have your satisfactions, and so you become invulnerable to the changing winds of fortune.

A person with the attitude of seeking only to serve cannot be nervous. He has nothing to lose. No aggression can arouse a hostility that he must repress. Losing himself, he finds himself. Servant of all mankind, he knows no master.

Nor can the troubled state of the world ruffle his nerves. Radio commentators cannot upset him. He is insulated from the state of other works of man, and is unaffrighted by what goes on about him. He takes a keen interest—certainly, but it is not personal. He does not ask how events will affect him. He asks only how he can be of help; and if there is something he can do, he does it. If there is nothing he can do, he pours all of his powers into the work that he has chosen.

Nor is he a prig or a stuffed shirt, full of the sense of his own righteousness. He walks humbly with his God. No matter how much power flows into his task, he realizes that it is very tiny compared to what waits to be done. He realizes that he is not the indispensable man, and so he sometimes takes his fun where he finds it and thanks God for his good luck.

A normal man or woman feels at home even in this jumbled and confused and disorderly world. He is like an architect who, amidst the piles of lumber, the groaning of the cement mixer, the pounding of hammers, the confusion of each trade intent on its job, still has before him the blueprint and has in his mind a picture of the home, complete even to its landscaping and interior decoration.

How are you going to find order and peace and calm in a world where apparently there are only disorder and war and confusion?

Man finds himself on this earth to discover only that his days are numbered and too few. He finds that he is capable of enjoying a few pleasures, and capable of feeling an almost unlimited amount of suffering. Man finds that life is hard to create, easy to destroy. Many are the tragedies that are a part of human existence for which there are no anodynes, no prescriptions for cure or for relief. He finds that he is beset by innumerable enemies and catastrophes, from invisible germs to floods, tidal waves, and earthquakes. He finds that merely to sustain life he has to wage an endless war against an indifferent nature, that gives weeds every break as against cultivated plants, and that sends dust storms, drought, and overabundance of rain without any regard for the continuation of human life.

He finds, further, that ignorance, folly, and greed set man

against man for no good reason. In a world where every force is at war with mankind, traitors lead a civil war of man against himself.

It is in such a world that you must find certainty. It is in such a world that you must not allow yourself to become confused. It is in such a world that you must keep your faith.

If you cannot have faith in a blind nature, or in the intelligence and good will of your fellows, what can you put your trust in?

You can put your trust in our need of one another. You can put your faith in your own life, in your own integrity. In this turmoil and confusion you can resolve to be yourself. You can give yourself wholly, freely, and sincerely to the work *that you have chosen as your own.* When you have found self-expression in service to mankind, you have lost your misery. You have replaced confusion with certitude.

Each man brings to the altar a different sacrifice. There is the legend of a juggler who was so poor that he had nothing—not even a penny to offer to the Madonna. All he could do was to juggle—do tricks that he had done in the market place to amuse the children. So he went to church, and alone before the image of his Lady he juggled. And when the astounded and horrified priesthood came upon this blasphemous scene, the statue of the Mother of Sorrows had lowered her arms in benediction over the poor little juggler.

Discover the work that expresses you in service to mankind, and give your life to it. Never mind your living. People will reward you with enough material things. This is your time for worry. See to it that you are not crushed by rewards. It is more important to make a life than it is to make a living.

No, your work should be done because it is your work. Work without hope for any return in love, in praise, or in understanding. Love, praise, understanding, these are all extras. They will come all right. See to it that they do not overwhelm you. But your real satisfaction will lie in your enjoyment of your own integrity and your own invulnerability. As long as you have your work, nothing can harm you.

And you will begin to see your life in proper perspective. Many things that once appeared to be important will now be recognized as really trivial. You will recover your sense of humor, your feeling of joy and gaiety. You will be able to look calmly at events where wars are lost and wars are won; where tyrannies arise and where dictators are overthrown.

Meanwhile, life goes on. The eternal truth that goodness springs out of the very nature of human nature remains a torch in the hand of the Statue of Liberty. And you, working in your own special way, will find your life by giving it to keep that light forever burning brighter.

CHAPTER SIXTEEN

Tranquility Without Tranquilizers

TRANQUILIZING DRUGS of themselves do not produce tranquility.

Some fortunate people who have benefited greatly from the use of these drugs may at first feel inclined to disagree; but, if they read attentively what follows, they will realize that they, themselves, have contributed greatly to their own cures. Tranquilizers may have eased them over the rough spots and helped them generally—no one would dispute this—but, in themselves, tranquilizers are not the last word in the treatment of mental disorders.

Tranquility—true peace of mind—comes only from liking one's self, other people, and the world in which one lives. More than this: for those of active temperament with a need for accomplishing something, tranquility comes from effectively organizing their thinking, time, and energy, so that they can look back at the work of their hands and call it good. Those religiously and philosophically minded will find tranquility by discovering a meaning in life that seems more important than their small, private concerns. When Nathan Hale said, "I only regret that I have but one life to lose for my country," his tranquility did not come from the drugstore, but from his dedication to an ideal. The same can be said for Joan of Arc on the final day of her martyrdom.

Dr. Alfred Adler once described the tranquil personality as having a psychological balance wheel, the spokes of which he called Work, Play, Love, and Worship. Freudians criticized this concept as being too superficial, but if one thinks of the hub of the wheel as self-control through self-knowledge, their objection might be met. (As Freud put it, "That which was id and superego shall be ego," which was his way of saying that self-control comes through self-knowledge.) At any rate, my point is that tranquility is not something that comes in a bottle. It is built into a person who creates his own tranquility. A balance between work, play, love, and worship is a good practical goal, especially when accompanied by self-knowledge, self-control, and wholehearted self-acceptance.

For an understanding of tranquility, there is still another way of thinking that will appeal both to parents and modern psychotherapists. Tranquility comes from personality growth through the assimilation of new experience.

We grow physically by digesting and assimilating what we eat. In a somewhat analogous way, we grow intellectually, socially, and spiritually by assimilating what we experience, but with this difference—mental growth may continue well into very old age.

Now, when a child (or for that matter, an adult) experiences something he cannot understand or accept, something he cannot incorporate into his already established system of thinking and feeling, it sticks in his craw, so to speak. He cannot digest this new experience and cannot assimilate it. (We call this a traumatic experience, that is, a damaging experience.) It is damaging because of the way one reacts to it. One can behave as if it never happened (repression). One can react by retreating from all new experience, which prevents new intellectual and social growth. One may react with habits of hostility to men or to women or to anyone in authority.

There is no limit to the number or variety of maladaptive habit patterns that one can learn in order to tolerate an unassimilated traumatic experience, but one thing remains constant: until the traumatic experience is reinterpreted and assimilated, the result is nervous tension, and there never was a liquid, pill, or capsule that could enable one to reevaluate and assimilate his traumatic experiences. Only psychotherapy, self-administered or given with outside help, can do this trick.

Does this mean that tranquilizing drugs are worthless? Hardly. As we shall see, they play a highly useful role in the treatment of mental disorders.

For one thing, tranquilizers make life tolerable for the victims of nervous tension. More importantly, they smooth the path he must follow in order to cure himself. Tranquilizers are to mental disorders what crutches are to orthopedic diseases; and let only him who has never had a badly damaged ankle sneer at crutches.

Alcohol was the first tranquilizer to make life tolerable for our prehistoric ancestors, whose lives were made miserable by mosquitoes, malaria, wood ticks, and predatory, even cannibalistic, relatives. Ample evidence has been discovered to prove that long before man invented reading and writing, some enterprising soul found a strange brew, probably in a hollow log or abandoned pottery jar of fruit juice. He let curiosity get the better of prudence, dipped in his cup, and drank. Once this venturesome gastronaut was whirling in orbit, he communicated his discovery to his friends, and the cocktail hour was on its way to acceptance as a part of gracious living.

Of course our primitive ancestors couldn't know what turned fruit juice or barley and water into wine or beer. They had no microscopes to magnify the tiny, wild-yeast plants that float in the air and settle into apple cider and the like to change an innocuous drink into a potent tipple. But primitive men were practical fellows who might have said that they didn't know much about science but they knew what they liked, and they liked beer and wine and the tranquilizing effect of alcohol; so eventually they became pretty good brewers of beer and vintners of wine and ardent imbibers of both.

Alcohol in any drink acts as a tranquilizer by making people stupid. It dulls the mind by poisoning the brain. People used to think it was a stimulant but science has proved just the reverse: it's a depressant. Taken in large amounts, it can serve as an anesthetic, and has. When I was an intern, I had to sew up the lacerated alcoholics brought into the emergency ward by police or ambulance drivers. More often than not, the patients slept peacefully during the operation. I have seen people who were bone-tired take a few drinks and drop off to sleep, something they could not have done without partially anesthetizing their aching, quivering muscles. Alcohol anesthetized them out of awareness of their feelings, and they slept the sleep of the drugged. Of course, any other depressant and analgesic would have succeeded equally well. And been cheaper too.

Almost always, I counsel my patients not to use alcoholic beverages as a sedative, and I'll tell you why. People build up a tolerance for alcohol, so that it takes more and more of it to obtain a sedative effect. It is also habit-forming, that is, one can acquire a craving for alcohol. Add these two facts together, and the answer is chronic alcoholism—a disease in itself—which prevents its victims from conquering the nervous tensions that led them to their dependence on the bottle. And that isn't all I have to say against alcohol as a sedative. The aftereffects of alcohol—gastritis, hang-over, feelings of

TRANQUILITY WITHOUT TRANQUILIZERS

guilt and depression—hardly make alcohol a desirable drug for the tense and nervous.

I have one practical rule: if you think you need alcohol to give you a lift, don't touch it—it's poison for you. It won't just let you down—it will drop you without benefit of parachute.

I've spoken so much about alcohol as a physiological and psychological depressant partly because it is so widely used and abused, and partly because whatever is said about alcohol can be applied to many other tranquilizing drugs. Consider, for instance, the next most commonly used tranquilizer —the barbiturates. They, too, are depressants when used in small quantities, and hypnotics (they put you to sleep) when used in larger amounts.

Medically, barbiturates are far superior to alcohol. Dosage is more easily controlled. Also, they are less apt to be habit-forming. It is true that some tolerance can be built up, but the fact is that there are not nearly as many barbiturate addicts as there are alcoholics (over five million in the United States). Although both of them may leave their users with a hang-over, the side effects of the barbiturates, such as an upset stomach, are not likely to be as severe as the side effects of alcohol.

There are many different kinds of barbituric acid compounds. Some work rapidly and are quickly excreted from the body. One such drug is sodium pentothal, the so-called "truth serum," which when injected directly into a vein induces rapid sedation. This drug is often used as an anesthetic for such surgery as can be completed in a short time. Other barbiturates produce sedation that lingers on for forty-eight hours, while a third group, used as sleep-inducing medication, is usually excreted from the body in about eight hours.

Because administration is so convenient and results so predictable, doctors do not hesitate to prescribe the proper barbiturates in selected cases. Some dentists prescribe barbiturates before they work on their patients. They find that a little sedation helps smooth over an otherwise unpleasant situation. Properly used by doctors and patients, barbiturates are relatively harmless. Properly used, I said. Barbiturates, however, are no substitute for the built-in relaxation that results in true tranquility.

Barbiturates cannot directly reduce nervous tension. They do dull the mind, even to the degree of inducing sleep, but the underlying emotional conflicts continue to keep muscles tense and bodily reactions hyperactive. At best, these drugs are useful before, during, and after surgery. They can also be usefully employed in small, infrequent doses to alleviate the miseries of neurosis. But as a continuing medication, taken regularly, they are worse than useless. They are harmful.

For patients suffering from peptic ulcer, high blood pressure, or other medical conditions in which emotional conflict complicates the situation, your doctor has better drugs.

The so-called phenothiazines fall into this category. They have definitely established their usefulness, and best of all, they are not especially dangerous. They seem to work as dampeners of the overexcited autonomic nervous system, but indirectly they produce a remarkable sedative and even hypnotic effect. It's truly amazing to see how an overexcited patient can fall into a quiet sleep minutes after one of these drugs has been injected into a muscle.

Treatment with phenothiazine is often extended over a period of months, under close medical supervision, of course. When given to patients who are willing and able to co-operate with a competent psychiatrist, results have been excellent.

The best tranquilizer for use in nervous tension is Meprobamate. This drug works on the voluntary muscles of the body, causing them to relax. It does not appear to be especially habit-forming, although some cases of undue dependence on the drug have been reported in medical literature. Serious side effects are few and apparently not as important as those experienced with other tranquilizers.

In addition to these four—alcohol, barbiturates, phenothiazines, and Meprobamate—the market is flooded with other preparations for which the manufacturers make extravagant claims. Disappointment with these preparations has cast a pall of cautious skepticism upon my hitherto trusting nature. Because no tranquilizing drug is without its drawbacks, I keep hoping that tomorrow will bring a better one for my patients. I'm still waiting.

Tranquilizing drugs do help some people, especially in times of physiological or emotional crisis. They dull the senses, induce sleep, and make living tolerable for those whose nerves feel so frayed that mere existence is like a waking nightmare. They give the sufferer time to collect himself.

All tranquilizers are depressants and hypnotics, that is, they make you dopey. A successful, neurotic writer gave me his bottle of Meprobamate, saying, "I'd rather be jumpy and creative than dopey and frustrated." Without drugs he proceeded to build his tranquility and increase his creativity.

To sum it all up: alcohol, the most commonly used tranquilizer, is the least valuable and the most dangerous. Various barbiturates and phenothiazines have a limited value and are safe only when their effects can be controlled by a watchful physician. Meprobamate is safer, but it too can be abused by those who expect it to cure their nervous tensions.

If you need the help of a tranquilizer, your doctor can prescribe one for you. But remember that tranquility comes only with a new outlook on life—one that gives meaning to Man's striving for better things. Only he who relates his purposes in life to the Eternal will find meaning in what he does here and now.

Learning to relax at will (with or without benefit of tranquilizers) builds tranquility and serenity into your body and mind. Control of the mind begins with control of the body. With this newly recovered tranquility you can then organize your time and energy so effectively that you will be able to pursue your objective zestfully. Your outlook will broaden. Your activities and interests will be less constricted. Narrowness and rigidity will be replaced by a good-natured flexibility. You'll discover not only how to look gently on your fellow man but how to be gentle with yourself. And best of all you will have the peace of mind that comes to those who know that every life that has been well lived has earned its own transcendent importance.

About the Author

David Harold Fink received his B.A. and M.A. from the University of Michigan and later graduated as a Doctor of Medicine from the Detroit College of Medicine and Surgery. He served in the First World War, taught sociology at the University of Michigan, and did social work for several years. For eight years he served on the full-time staff of Veterans' Administration Hospitals, where he examined and treated thousands of veterans suffering from nervous disabilities. At present he is a practicing neuropsychiatrist in California.